Modern European History

A Garland Series of Outstanding Dissertations

General Editor
William H. McNeill
University of Chicago

Associate Editors

Eastern Europe
Charles Jelavich
Indiana University

Great Britain
Peter Stansky
Stanford University

France
David H. Pinkney
University of Washington

Russia
Barbara Jelavich
Indiana University

Germany
Enno E. Kraehe
University of Virginia

MODERN EUROPEAN HISTORY

The Establishment of the Bulgarian Ministry of Public Instruction and its Role in the Development of Modern Bulgaria, 1878–1885

Roy E. Heath

Garland Publishing, Inc.
New York and London 1987

Copyright © 1987 Roy E. Heath
All rights reserved

Library of Congress Cataloging-in-Publication Data

Heath, Roy E., 1950–
    The establishment of the Bulgarian Ministry of Public Instruction and its role in the development of modern Bulgaria, 1878–1885.

    (Modern European history)
    Thesis (Ph.D.)—University of Wisconsin—Madison, 1979.
    Bibliography: p.
    1. Education and state—Bulgaria—History—19th century. 2. Bulgaria. Ministerstvo na narodnata prosveta—History—19th century. 3. Bulgaria—Politics and government—1878–1944. I. Title. II. Series.
LC93.B9H43   1987   379.497'7   87-7403
ISBN 0-8240-8025-4 (alk. paper)

All volumes in this series are printed on acid-free, 250-year-life paper.

Printed in the United States of America

THE ESTABLISHMENT OF THE BULGARIAN MINISTRY OF PUBLIC
INSTRUCTION AND ITS ROLE IN THE DEVELOPMENT
OF MODERN BULGARIA, 1878-1885

BY

ROY E. HEATH

A thesis submitted in partial fulfillment of the
requirements for the degree of

DOCTOR OF PHILOSOPHY
(History)

at the

UNIVERSITY OF WISCONSIN - MADISON

1979

PREFACE

My interest in the problem of how the newly independent countries of the Balkans set up systems of government administration led me to plan a dissertation which would be a definitive study of the Bulgarian bureaucratic system from 1878 to 1900. I explored this idea with several people well-versed in Balkan affairs who unanimously cautioned that such an undertaking would likely require very considerable amounts of research and besides was too broad for a dissertation. In the course of narrowing the original focus and purpose, I was privileged to have the advice and counsel of my major professor, Michael B. Petrovich (University of Wisconsin-Madison), Professor Philip Shashko (University of Wisconsin-Milwaukee), Professor Emeritus James F. Clarke (University of Pittsburgh), and Professor Thomas J. Meininger (York University-Toronto). From their cumulative suggestions, I decided to undertake a study focused on a particular ministry of great importance to the people and having the greatest contact with them-- the Ministry of Public Instruction. The choice proved to be extremely practical and fortunate.

The study of the Ministry of Public Instruction in the newly established state of Bulgaria presents a valuable opportunity to examine important issues and problems in government administration and education in a developing nation of the nineteenth century. A country newly released from five centuries of foreign rule and faced with the difficult tasks of development, progress, and modernization, Bulgaria constitutes an excellent case study for the Balkan peninsula. The Bulgarian experience is especially conducive to such a study first, because of the particular importance which educational affairs had in the movement for national independence and second, because of the particular emphasis given to this problem in the first decades of the state's existence.

The purpose of this dissertation is to show that no matter how developed school affairs were in the period before 1878, the Ministry of Public Instruction found it necessary to begin from the ground up to fashion a system of education and that a systematization of school affairs was considered a necessary precondition if the country was to progress towards modernization. The focus of this dissertation at all times will be on the institution and its workings. However, as any institution is comprised of people, I have attempted to use, as much as possible, the records and memoirs of the people who comprised the institution, in addition to bureaucratic records. Unfortunately, few of these individuals have left records, and many of the memoirs that do exist spend little or no time on educational affairs. Instead they focus on the political problems wracking the new state. On the other hand, those that do exist were written by very important individuals and offer interesting insights.

This study does not pretend to be all inclusive. Rather it focuses on the Ministry of Public Instruction in the Principality from 1878 to 1885. In March, 1878, according to the terms of the San Stefano Treaty between Russia and Turkey, an extremely large Bulgarian state was established. In July, 1878, that treaty was superseded by the Treaty of Berlin, which divided the huge state into three basic regions: the Principality of Bulgaria; an autonomous province of Eastern Rumelia with a Christian ruler responsible directly to the sultan; and the Macedonian and Thracian region which was returned to the Ottoman Empire. This dissertation then deals only with the Principality. I chose the time period 1878-1885 because in 1885 Eastern Rumelia was reunited with the Principality, which occasioned a reorganization of educational affairs. Also, this dissertation deals with the most important problems encountered by the Ministry of Public Instruction in the arrangement of school affairs. To include the Ministry's activities in matters such as the National Library or the Academy of Sciences would be too unwieldy. Besides, excellent histories of these two institutions already exist and have been used in this dissertation. These will be listed in the bibliography at the end of this thesis.

This dissertation is divided into two parts. The Drinov period preceded the actual constitutional period and receives a special treatment in Chapter Two. The rest of the dissertation deals with the functioning of the Ministry of Public Instruction after the promulgation of the Turnovo Constitution.

There is no lack of histories on Bulgarian education, but odd gaps still exist. There is no study, for example, of how local communities involved themselves in school affairs; and while there is an excellent study on education in Eastern Rumelia for 1878-1885, no such work exists for the Principality in this period. Also, I know of no other work that details the functioning of a single governmental institution in Bulgaria, outside of Cyril Black's still classic work, <u>The Establishment of Constitutional Government in Bulgaria</u>, (Princeton: 1943). Incidentally it was this work by Black which helped inspire this dissertation.

This dissertation is based as much as possible on archival sources and published primary sources. I had the rare fortune of using two particular archives not usually available to Western scholars. These were the Central State Historical Archives and the Church-Historical Archives. I also used the following archives in Sofia: Bulgarian Historical Archives; City Provincial Archives of Sofia, Samokov, and Gabrovo; the Archival Institute of the Academy of Sciences; and the Archives of the Institute of History of the Academy of Sciences. Other research facilities used include the National Library "Cyril and Methodius," the Academy of Sciences Library, the Memorial Library of the University of Wisconsin-Madison, and the Hillman Library of the University of Pittsburgh.

The research for this study was made possible by two grants. One was from the International Research and Exchanges Board in New York. The other was from the Department of Health, Education, and Welfare, Office of

Education, Fulbright-Hays Doctoral Dissertation Program. Without this funding, my stay in Bulgaria and hence this dissertation would not have been possible.

Substantial portions of the second chapter of this dissertation have appeared in my article "Marin Drinov and the Formation of the Department of Public Instruction in Bulgaria, 1878-1879," in <u>Balkanistika: A Journal of Southeast European Studies</u>, vol. 5 (1979). That material is used here with the written permission of the editors of that journal.

Several technical problems inevitably arise in works dealing with the Balkans and other parts of Eastern Europe. Most of the correspondence and documents used in this work use the Old Style or Julian Calendar, which was twelve days behind our present (Gregorian) calendar in the nineteenth century. Whenever a date is written with the abbreviation N.S. after it, that signifies a date in the modern calendar

The style sheet used in this dissertation is that of Kate L. Turabian, <u>A Manual for Writers of Term Papers, Theses, and Dissertations</u>, 3rd edition, revised, (Chicago: 1967). However, Turabian is of limited use to the Slavic scholar when it comes to archives and certain records such as parliamentary citations. For the latter, I have devised a shortened citation (based on the manner in which Bulgarians cite them). This is explained in the first footnote using those records (Chapter Three, footnote 48). For archival works, I use the citation system suggested for Russian archives (which is closest to the Bulgarian system) by Patricia Kennedy Grimstead, <u>Archives and Manuscript Repositories in the USSR</u>: Moscow and Leningrad (Princeton: 1972). Thus, F. represents <u>Fond</u>, etc. See the List of Abbreviations for details.

In the course of research and writing, I have been assisted by many individuals in this country and in Bulgaria. I must express here my deepest appreciation to the members of the Institute of History at the Academy of Sciences who went out of their way to help me secure access to archives. These include Elena Dilovska, Tsvetana Todorova, Aleksandŭr Velichkov, Voian Bodzhinov, and others. In this country, I have also received invaluable assistance from the professors named in the opening paragraph. I should like to single out, however, my major professor, Michael B. Petrovich, whose practical suggestions and unerring critique saved me much time and embarrassment of error. Of course, any errors or omissions that remain are my own. I would like to express my appreciation to all the members of my graduate seminar at the University of Wisconsin-Madison who read carefully my first drafts and offered many valuable suggestions for improvements. Finally, I must thank my wife Barbara not only for typing so many drafts, but for her excellent advice as editor of first instance.

Having selected a dissertation topic in Bulgarian history has introduced me to a group of fellow Bulgarists distinguished by their warmth, generosity, and concern for their younger colleagues. It has been a joy to know them both professionally and socially, and to all of them, I dedicate this work.

                                        Roy E. Heath
                                        Madison, Wisconsin
                                        May, 1979

TABLE OF CONTENTS

PREFACE..ii

LIST OF ABBREVIATIONS......................................xi

CHAPTER ONE: THE HERITAGE: TO FREEDOM THROUGH EDUCATION..............................1

CHAPTER TWO: MARIN DRINOV AND THE FORMATION OF THE DEPARTMENT OF PUBLIC INSTRUCTION DURING THE RUSSIAN OCCUPATION 1877-1879....................................28

CHAPTER THREE: FIRST CONCERNS OF THE NEW MINISTRY...105

CHAPTER FOUR: PROBLEMS OF PRIORITY IN EDUCATIONAL POLICY.................................193

CHAPTER FIVE: POLITICS AND THE MINISTRY............238

CHAPTER SIX: THE MINISTRY AND THE PEOPLE: THE ROLE OF THE INSPECTORATE.............273

CHAPTER SEVEN: THE MINISTRY OF PUBLIC INSTRUCTION AND THE BULGARIAN ORTHODOX CHURCH....301

CHAPTER EIGHT: CHARTING A COURSE OF ACTION: SUCCESS AND FAILURE IN FORMING EDUCATIONAL POLICY....................343

CONCLUSION..425

SOURCES CONSULTED...436

ABBREVIATIONS

ABAN	*Arkhiven institut pri Bŭlgarskata akademiia na naukite* (Archival Institute of the Bulgarian Academy of Sciences)
a.e.	*arkhivna edinitsa* (archival unit)
AIIBAN	*Arkhiv na institut za istoriia pri Bŭlgarskata akademiia na naukite* (Archives of the Institute of History of the Bulgarian Academy of Sciences)
BIA	*Bŭlgarski istoricheski arkhiv* (Bulgarian Historical Archives)
F	*Fond* (individual archival collection)
ODA	*Okrŭzhen dŭrzhaven arkhiv* (Provincial State Archives)
ONS	*Obiknoveno Narodno Sŭbranie* (the Regular National Assembly)
SGODA	*Sofiiski gradski okrŭzhen dŭrzhaven arkhiv* (City and Provincial State Archives for the Sofia Region)
SSTsIO	*Tsentralen tsŭrkoven istoriko-arkheologicheski musei pri Sveti Sinod: Tsŭrkovno-istoricheski otdel* (Archives of the Central Church Historical-Archeological Museum of the Holy Synod: the Church-Historical Division)
TsDIA	*Tsentralen Dŭrzhaven Istoricheski Arkhiv* (The Central State Historical Archives)
op.	*opis* (archival inventory)

(All of the above archives were used in Sofia, Bulgaria.)

CHAPTER ONE

THE HERITAGE: "TO FREEDOM THROUGH EDUCATION"

One of the most important phases in modern European history was the cultural awakening of the nations of Eastern Europe that had been subjected for centuries to the domination of one or more powerful neighbors. This awakening occurred from Finland in the north to Greece in the south at various times but always with certain common themes. A key role was always played by the rediscovery of long-forgotten customs or traditions. Most important of all, perhaps, was the dusting off and revitalization of a native language, the use of which until then was usually relegated to illiterate peasants. In every country, one or another symbol became a rallying point for national re-emergence. During Bulgaria's "Renascence," the watchword was education. Generations of Bulgarian historians--professional as well as amateur--have consistently argued that the key to Bulgaria's awakening as a nation was education.[1]

---

[1] The most eloquent treatment of the role of the schools in Bulgaria's national Renascence is Ivan Mutafchiev, "Dukh i zaveti na vuzrazhdaneto," *Otets Paisii*, VII (October, 1934), 198-200. Other good elucidations of this question are in N. Ivan Vankov and

This was no idle or ill-conceived claim. Although the final cataclysm that released the Bulgarian people from subject status to the Ottoman Empire was steeped in blood, the foundation of the Bulgarian struggle for freedom was truly education. When the troops of Alexander II ventured into the Bulgarian provinces, their generals were surprised to discover so many schools existing in what was believed to be a poor, underdeveloped region. The surprise of the Russian officers was shared by many other foreign observers in the second half of the nineteenth century. What they had no way of knowing was that the existence of so many schools was the result of a popular association of the words "freedom" and "education." From the very beginning of Bulgaria's struggle for cultural and national rebirth, education was the constant weapon urged on the people by the leaders of the Renascence. In fact, if

---

Petur Minev, Razvoi na uchebnoto delo i uchilishtnoto zakonodatelstvo v Bŭlgariia (Sofia: 1906), pp. 3-27; Naiden G. Chakŭrov, Uchilishtno zakonodatelstvo (Sofia: 1950), pp. 20-25; Khrŭstiu Krachunov, Iz Bŭlgarska kulturna istoriia (Sofia: 1935), pp. 9-12. Bulgarians were not alone in connecting their schools with their political liberation. The Czech historian Josef Konstantin Jireček, for example, believed the entire history of the Bulgarian Renascence to be simultaneously the history of the Bulgarian schools as well; see his Glavno izlozhenie do Negovo Visochestvo Kniaza vŭrkhu polozhenieto na uchebnoto delo v Kniazhestvo Bŭlgariia (Sofia: 1882), p. 5.

any slogan could be said to have characterized the whole Bulgarian Renascence, it would be the phrase "to freedom through education."[2] Schools became political weapons, offering a potential means of deliverance. Teachers became political leaders, revolutionaries, and also military advisors.

No other explanation seems possible for the existence in 1878 of so many schools, spread so widely across the Turkish province in which Bulgaria lay. This is not to say that the schools that did exist were even worthy of the name; many were not. But a foundation existed upon which the newly independent country could build a modern system of education--the existence of which would be a key to the successful development of the country. Paissi, a monk of Bulgarian origin at Hilendar Monastery, issued his famous clarion call to Bulgarians to study their language and proud history in 1762.[3] When he did so, Bulgarian education was in a pitiable state. The only schools in existence were the "cell" schools (kiliia), so called because they usually

---

[2] The Bulgarian historian Khrŭstiu Krachunov was the first to use this phrase as the best explanation for the role of the schools in the political struggles of the people; see Iz Bŭlgarska, p. 28.

[3] Paissi Khilendarski, Slaviano-Bŭlgarska istoriia, ed. by Petŭr Dinekov (Sofia: 1972), pp. 35-44.

consisted of a handful of boys studying religious subjects taught by a monk in his cell.[4] Sometimes monks (the *taxidiotes*) who regularly travelled to nearby villages for food and alms would establish cell schools in those villages. The schools located in the villages also used the name cell school.[5] In the town of Kilifarevo in the eighteenth century, for example, there were three cell schools opened by three monks of the nearby Holy Mother of God Monastery.[6] The educational level of these cell schools was primitive at best, utilizing rote memorization. Eventually, some of these schools were conducted by lay teachers, and, in a few cases, girls were admitted.[7] Always, however, the orientation of the subjects was religious. The incalculable importance of the cell schools did not lie in

---

[4] These schools were also known as Church schools; Vankov, Razvoi, p. 11.

[5] Ibid., p. 13; Veliko Iordanov, L'Instruction publique en Bulgarie (Sofia: 1926), pp. 11-12.

[6] Iordan Georgiev, "Selo Kelifarevo i manastirŭt mu Sv. Bogoroditsa," Periodichesko spisanie na Bŭlgarsko knizhovno druzhestvo, LXVII, 5-6 (1906), 433.

[7] Chakurov, Uchilishtno zakonodatelstvo, p. 25; Khristo N. Gandev, Faktori na Bŭlgarskoto Vŭzrazhdane (Sofia: 1943), pp. 37-46.

their numbers which were certainly small.[8] Their importance was their sheer existence in the face of impossible odds and in the example they provided of independent organization and, perhaps, of even the power of education.

Such activity by Bulgarian monks encountered opposition not so much from Ottoman authorities as from Greek religious officials. As Orthodox Christians, the Bulgarians came under the jurisdiction of the Patriarch of Constantinople. The Patriarchate was firmly controlled by the Greeks who exercised great influence in many of the affairs of the Ottoman government. The influence of Hellenism proved very powerful on the other peoples of the Rum millet and was to play, in fact, a significant role in Bulgaria's national revival.

In the second half of the eighteenth century, Greeks rose to ever greater heights of influence within the Ottoman Empire. The key to their power was largely their control over the maritime affairs of the Turkish Empire. But while Greeks controlled the navy and commercial matters at the highest levels, many of the subject peoples, including the Bulgarians, also played

---

[8] Chakŭrov, Uchilishtno zakondatelstvo, p. 25; Gandev, Faktori, pp. 37-46; Iordanov, L'Instruction, pp. 11-12.

significant roles. This forced Bulgarians to learn Greek--a crucially important language of commerce for much of Europe at the time. Bulgarians were also educated in Greek schools.[9] Thus, when the Greeks experimented with a new form of education in the 1800s, it was to have profound consequences for the Bulgarian Renascence and, by extension, for the Bulgarian schools.

The experiment engaged in by the Greek merchants centered around the establishment of special secular schools to teach subjects relevant to the commercial world.[10] Schools along these lines opened at this time in Iași, Korfu, and Smyrna. This in itself was a radical break with prevailing educational philosophies. But they also adopted a system from Europe that came to be known as the Bell-Lancaster or, simply, the Lancastrian method. (This was also known as mutual

---

[9] Bulgarians could attend schools in several locations: Greece, Greek colonies throughout Europe and the Mediterranean area, or in the Bulgarian part of the Turkish empire. Greeks had set up schools throughout the Bulgarian regions after assuming total control of Bulgarian Church affairs in 1767. As Bulgarian commerce increased in the late eighteenth century, more Bulgarians learned the language of commerce (i.e. Greek) in such schools. Vankov, Razvoi, p. 59; D. Tsonkov, Razvitie na osnovnoto obrazovanie v Bŭlgariia ot 1878 do 1928 (Sofia: 1928), p. 9; Petŭr Noikov, Pogled vŭrkhu razvitieto na bŭlgarskoto obrazovanie do Paisiia (Sofia: 1925), pp. 48-51.

[10] Vankov, Razvoi, pp. 33-59; Noikov, Pogled do Paisiia, pp. 53-56; Tsonkov, Razvitie, p. 10.

instruction.) According to this system, the brightest students would be taught a lesson, and, in turn, they would teach a larger group of fellow students on the same level or in the lower classes. This allowed a very large number of pupils to be accommodated by only a handful of teachers.[11] Combined with the introduction of secular subjects such as geometry, geography, and history into the schools, this system caused a revolution in education among the Greek merchants.

Greeks, of course, were not the only ones to enroll in these new types of schools. Bulgarians and other foreigners also received the new training. The Bulgarians were sufficiently impressed to begin establishing schools that also taught subjects more akin to the needs of the commercial world or to introduce such subjects into schools already in existence. This

---

[11] Tsonkov, Razvitie, p. 9. The Bell-Lancaster method was developed by a Scottish clergyman Andrew Bell (1753-1832) who wished to overcome the problem of teacher shortages by using brighter students as teaching assistants. He described his theory in a pamphlet entitled A Theory of Education (Glasgow: 1797). But his ideas had little success until expanded and redefined by the English educator Joseph Lancaster (1778-1838) who issued his Improvements on Education as It Respects the Industrious Classes of the Community (1803). His ideas on education for the common people enjoyed a brief vogue on the continent and in England and America. Its real successes came in the Balkans. The history of this entire episode in Eastern European education has yet to be written.

occurred, at first, in schools supported by Bulgarian merchant colonies in the Romanian Principalities and in the Odessa region.[12] The Lancastrian system, however, was not necessarily a counterpart of this new fascination with secular subjects.

The real importance of the Bulgarian experience with secular and mutual education was its eventual impact in the homeland. The introduction of secular subjects and the mutual instruction method, either alone or in combination, was a remarkably rapid process. When this development was coupled with a reform movement inside the Ottoman Empire, the results for Bulgarian education were explosive.

The exact manner in which secularism came into schools in Bulgaria has never been satisfactorily determined. Almost certainly it was through a combination of many factors. First, the cell schools had gradually allowed many lay teachers to assume teaching duties, and some of these were Greeks who had studied in the secular schools. Moreover, exclusively Greek, Church-oriented schools had existed in Bulgaria ever since the Greeks had gained control of all religious

---

[12] Vankov, *Razvoi*, p. 26.

affairs in the Rum millet.[13] Naturally, they did not remain unaffected by the secularization process occuring in other parts of the Greek-controlled world. Thus, mutual education and secular education existed in Bulgaria before Bulgarians themselves began to introduce it in their own schools. None of these developments was very welcome among the powerful Greek conservative faction known as the Phanariots, who carefully guarded the interests of Greeks in the affairs of the Empire. Church officials especially looked askance at the secularization process and the nationalistic revival that inevitably followed. They rightly feared an independent Greece would cause a loss of power for those Greeks living in Istanbul itself.[14] Bulgarians also would have to deal with this powerful opposition when attempting to set up their own schools.

Traditionally, the opening of a mens gymnasium in

---

[13] Petŭr Noikov, Vŭzrazhdane na Bŭlgarski narod. Tsŭrkovno natsionalni borbi i postizheniia (Sofia: 1930, reprinted and reissued in 1971, pp. 41-46; Zina Markova, Bŭlgarsko tsŭrkovno-nationalno dvizhenie do Krimskata voina (Sofia: 1976), pp. 11-44; Vankov, Razvoi, pp. 16-26; Tsonkov, Razvitie, pp. 9-12.

[14] The Greeks who lived in the Phanar (literally, lighthouse) district of Istanbul wielded immense power through their ability to secure appointments as governors of areas in the Rum millet.

1835 in the city of Gabrovo has always been considered as the beginning of the modern Bulgarian school, based on secular learning and mutual instruction. However mutual instruction and secular instruction had been introduced before that date. The Greek schools were one such example. Bulgarians themselves had toyed earlier with such ideas, though, through the efforts of such individuals as Raino Popovich in Kotel, and Khristaki Pavlovich and Emanuil Vaskidovich in Svishtov.[15] Raino Popovich introduced the method into his school in Kotel and transferred it to Karlovo in 1826 when he moved there. However, Popovich taught in Greek, as did also Khristaki Pavlovich; and while Vaskidovich called his school "Slaveno-bŭlgarsko," Greek was the primary language of instruction.[16] Thus, the founding of the Gabrovo school took on immense importance for Bulgarians.

That school was established through the concerted efforts of two wealthy merchants living in Romania, Vasil Aprilov and Nikolai Palauzov, the one a Bulgarian,

---

[15] These are only a few of the important names in Renascence school affairs; others included Petŭr Beron and Konstantin Fotinov. A good discussion of the personalities involved in Bulgarian education in that period is Eniu Nikolov and Tsvetan Minkov, <u>Stroiteli na novobŭlgarskoto obrazovanie</u> (Sofia: 1935); Vankov, <u>Razvoi</u>, pp. 16-17; Iordanov, <u>L'Instruction</u>, pp. 4-14.

[16] Vankov, <u>Razvoi</u>, p. 26.

the other a Russian citizen. Bulgarian merchants had opened and supported schools in other areas, but never in the homeland itself.

Aprilov was impressed enough by what he had seen of the Bell-Lancaster method to believe that it could have immense applicability for his countrymen. Aprilov was spurred to action also by the fact that while in Constantinople in 1831, he had come to believe that the Ottoman Empire was about to launch a great reform program. This was a result of growing pressure on the sultan both from the Great Powers and from reform-minded individuals within the Empire itself.[17] Aprilov and Palauzov decided to write to Bulgarian civilian officials in Aprilov's home city of Gabrovo with an offer to set up a modern, fully-furnished Bulgarian school, teaching secular subjects through the mutual instruction method.[18] The offer was accepted, and Neofit Rilski was invited to supervise the new school.[19] Aprilov's major goal in establishing the Gabrovo school was to

---

[17] Vankov, Razvoi, p. 33; Vasil E. Aprilov (letter to Gabrovo community, August 16, 1833), Sŭbrani sŭchineniia, ed. by Mikhail Arnaudov (Sofia: 1940), p. 361.

[18] Aprilov, Sŭchineniia, p. 362.

[19] Vankov, Razvoi, p. 34; M. M. Gechev, "Neofit Rilski--pŭrvi novobŭlgarski uchitel," Narodna prosveta, XII, 1 (1956), 46-53.

further another dream of his: to establish a higher educational institution for Bulgarians. He realized that this was impossible without adequate numbers of trained teachers and well-prepared students. These, he hoped, the Gabrovo school would provide.[20]

The Gabrovo experiment not only helped achieve that goal, but also set off a chain reaction in Bulgarian education by serving as a model for other such schools which sprang up quickly after 1835.

The Gabrovo school differed from previously existing Bulgarian schools in one other important aspect, perhaps the most important one of all as far as this is concerned. It was controlled entirely by officials of the Bulgarian civil community. That is to say, it was not opened and operated by Bulgarian monks or Greek clergy, but by local officials whose powers the Ottoman government officially recognized. Thus, in effect, it was the first "communal" school.[21]

The importance of the communal organ in fostering

---

[20] Aprilov, letter to Gabrovo community in 1837, Sŭchineniia, p. 372.

[21] These schools were also called "narodni" or "popular" schools in recognition of the support of the people themselves. In later periods, "popular" became the more frequently used appellation. See Iordanov, L'Instruction, p. 17.

the advancement of the Bulgarian school network existing before 1878 has not been sufficiently appreciated by Bulgarian historians until very recently.[22] When the Turkish forces secured their victories over the Balkan peoples in the fifteenth and sixteenth centuries, they did not completely eliminate local self-rule. In fact, quite a large amount of local self-government remained, as each town or village was organized into communities with designated leaders. Greeks assumed power in many of these communities, but not entirely, sometimes exercising control through the local bishop (of Greek origin, of course).[23] But with the coming of the Tanzimat period, the powers of the communal officials increased significantly. This was especially true after the second major decree of the Tanzimat period, the Hatti-Hümayun of 1856, which granted even greater

---

[22] Khristo Khristov, the author of a superb study of the Bulgarian communities, claims that his is the first study which investigates their role in school affairs as well. His claim is thoroughly justified and well-supported by his work. But much remains to be done on the rise of school boards and their function, as well as on the early history of teachers councils. The relevant section of Khristov's work is Bŭlgarskite obshtini prez vŭzrazhdaneto (Sofia: 1973), pp. 71-126.

[23] Ibid., pp. 44-66; also Stefan Bobchev, La Lutte du peuple bulgare pour une église nationale independente (Sofia: 1938), pp. 1-2.

amounts of self-government to Bulgarians and other subjects of the Empire. It also guaranteed, in theory at least, the right to build and to maintain schools.[24] The reforms of this period taken together had an immediate impact on Bulgarian school affairs by helping to foster the development of local organs of self-government which in turn began to take part in the arrangement of local school affairs. It was in this period more than any other that the school board had its origins, coinciding with the accelerated expansion of secular, mutual, community-supported schools.

Not all of the secular schools which began to blossom after 1835 were cut along the same pattern as that in Gabrovo, however. Many did not even employ the Bell-Lancaster method of instruction. The schools springing up all over the Bulgarian part of the Balkans had many names, a source of potential confusion to foreign observers and later historians of education. Furthermore, these new schools, under whatever name they were known, existed alongside of the traditional cell schools which did not suddenly die out at the appearance of the secular schools. In fact, the cell schools did not really disappear for quite some time,

---

[24] Noikov, *Pogled do Paisiia*, p. 26.

around the 1870s.[25] The secular schools consisted of two basic types. Those which used the mutual method of instruction were called class (klasni) schools. These schools taught higher subjects on a yearly basis and were also known as chief, high, great, or big schools.[26] The other type of school was the class or form (klasove) school which did not employ the rote learning of the Bell-Lancaster method and in which students were ranked along traditional patterns found in other parts of Europe.[27]

Both types of schools were usually communally supported after 1856 and accepted students from all social classes and, to a lesser extent, of both sexes. However, most girls receiving educations at this time

---

[25] Vankov, Razvoi, p. 56.

[26] The Bulgarian names for the mutual schools were: vzaimno (mutual), pŭrvonachalno (primary), obshtesveno (communal), narodno (popular or public), osnovno (basic). The names in Bulgarian for the non-mutual schools (usually attended after the mutual school) were: klasno (class), glavno (chief or major), visoko (high), gorno (high), or sometimes gimnazialno (gymnasial). See Noikov, Pogled do Paisii, pp. 20-22; Tsonkov, Razvitie, p. 11; Chakŭrov, Uchilishtno zakonodatelstvo, pp. 23-25; Vankov, Razvoi, pp. 11, 29, 53, 62-63; Ekaterina Zlatoustova, "Devicheskoto obrazovanie v Bŭlgariia predi osvobozhedenieto," Uchilishten pregled, XXIX, 9 (1930), 1415.

[27] Vankov, Razvoi, pp. 62-63.

went to special schools established for them. Such girls schools were opened in Stara Zagora (1857) and Gabrovo (1862) and in Ruse and Shumen in the 1840s and 1850s.[28] The subjects taught were similar to those in the boys schools, but also included courses in needlework and housekeeping. Girls' education always lagged behind that of boys but not only for cultural and financial reasons. Parents concerned with education often preferred to enroll their daughters at the boys schools, if possible, rather than to send them to a separate institution of inferior quality.[29]

The exact numbers and locations of these schools, whether for boys or girls, has never been determined satisfactorily. The safest assumption is that by 1878 almost a thousand inhabited places (cities and villages) had some kind of school.[30] Some sources indicate that

---

[28] Chakŭrov, Uchilishtno zakonodatelstvo, p. 25; Vankov, Razvoi, p. 53; Zlatoustova, "Devicheskoto," pp. 1407-1417.

[29] Vankov, Razvoi, p. 55; Krachunov, Iz Bŭlgarskata, p. 18.

[30] Statistics on schools are quite unreliable as the various historians who mention figures at all never explain how they arrived at their accounting. The lowest estimate (based on towns and significant villages) is that of Tsonkov who cites more than 1,500 populated places as having schools, Razvitie, p. 11. See also Vankov, Razvoi, p. 35; Iordanov, L'Instruction, p. 16.

while around 200 schools (cell and secular) existed in 1835, the number had risen to about 1,600 on the eve of the revolution that gave the country its independence.[31]

As the number of schools grew, and the communities assumed greater control over school affairs (by mandate of the Ottoman government), school boards came into existence to govern school affairs.[32] Fierce political battles often occurred between established and wealthy conservatives (chorbadzhi) who sat on the school boards and the teachers and guilds who favored more progressive measures.[33] The chorbadzhi were often closely aligned with dominant Greek and Turkish authorities. The

---

[31]Tsonkov, Razvitie, p. 11.

[32]Khristov, Bŭlgarskite obshtini, p. 118; Vankov, Razvoi, pp. 27-28; Noikov, Pogled vŭrkhu razvitieto na bŭlgarskoto obrazovanie ot Paisiia do kraia na XIX vek (Sofia: 1926), p. 19; V. N. Zlatarski and P. Dimitrov, Iubileina kniga na Veliko-Tŭrnovskata narodna mŭzhka gimnaziia "Sv. Kiril" (Tŭrnovo: 1933), p. 111; Vice Consul Sir John Elijah Blunt, "Report on the Educational Movement among the Bulgarians in the Vilayet of Adrianople," AIIBAN, F. 4 (British Diplomatic Records), op. 20, ae. 190, pp. 804-805. Philippopolis is modern day Plovdiv, while Adrianople was also known as Odrin (Bulgarian) and Edirne (Turkish).

[33]The best record of this was made by Raicho Karolev, a man who taught in Gabrovo and eventually became Minister of Public Instruction, see Raicho Karolev, Istoriia na Gabrovskoto uchilishte (Sofia: 1926). Another good treatment of this strife, in general, is Gandev, Faktori, pp. 168-175 et passim.

battles between teachers and chorbadzhi signalled a beginning of the teachers' role in the struggle for greater independence from Turkish and Greek control. Much of this struggle aimed not at complete political independence, but at autonomy from the Greeks. Eventually, the struggle focused on the establishment of a separate Bulgarian Church--the so-called Exarchate question.[34] This struggle was of great importance for Bulgarian educational affairs because of the close ties that existed between schools, both secular and cell, and the churches. With the loosening of restrictions on church building during the Tanzimat, Bulgarian notables took more interest in their churches, as well as in the schools, and many churches were either built anew or restored. In turn, the churches allowed schools to use their facilities, especially courtyards, for communal school affairs.[35] Also, teachers played an active role

---

[34] This is another question in Bulgarian history which has been the focus of innumerable studies. A classic and still valuable work is Nikov, Vŭzrazhdane; a good modern study is Markova, Tsŭrkovno dvizhenie. For a discussion of the diplomatic issues surrounding this movement, see Thomas A. Meininger, Ignatiev and the Establishment of the Bulgarian Exarchate (Madison, Wisconsin: 1970).

[35] Liuben Beshkov, Petŭr Todorov, Rada Vurtuninska, et al. Edin vek klasno uchilishte v Dobrich (Sofia: 1972), p. 13; Dobre Ganchev, Spomeni, 1864-1887 (Sofia: 1939), p. 2.

in the struggle for an autocephalous Church.

Bulgarians who had studied abroad were to play a significant role in the struggle for the Exarchate, especially since ever greater numbers now ventured abroad thanks to the activities not only of Bulgarian merchants but also the Russian Panslavic benevolent societies. These Russian societies, especially the Moscow Slavic Benevolent Society, began to bring young Slavs (mostly from fellow Orthodox countries) to Russia for good educations. The plan was to tie these countries closer to Russia in the hopes of eventually uniting all Slavs.[36] But Russia was not the only country to which Bulgarians went to study. Bulgarian merchants such as those in Odessa and in Romania established schools or endowment funds to support Bulgarian youth abroad.[37] Also, the American missionary school in Istanbul, Robert College, began to train Bulgarian students.[38] Most of these Bulgarians returned to their

---

[36] A. Nikitin, *Slavianskie komitety v Rossie v 1858-1876 godakh* (Moscow: 1960), pp. 66, 103-108, 137, 162 *et passim*.

[37] Khristov, *Bŭlgarski obshtinite*, p. 115; Andrei Tsviatkov, "Marin Drinov--lichnost i delo," *Uchilishten pregled*, XLV, 3-4 (1946), 174-175.

[38] Robert College was founded in Istanbul by the American philanthropist Christopher Robert in 1863. The

native country as teachers or priests, the only occupations really available to them. The Russian-educated, especially, were infused with the goal of throwing off Turkish and Greek rule. The first challenge then was the Church struggle, which was resolved in 1870 when a special firman established the Bulgarian Exarchate.

The establishment of a special Exarchate brought new vigor into all Bulgarian cultural affairs and also brought the possibility of establishing order out of the chaotic situation of Bulgarian schools.

Until this time, Ottoman authorities had had no definite policies in regard to the schools appearing among Bulgarian cities and villages. Other than giving the communities of Bulgarians the right to establish schools and even in certain cases to collect taxes for them, the Turks resisted efforts to subsume such schools under official government administration or protection.[39]

---

purpose of the school was to furnish a sound Christian education to the different nationalities of the Ottoman Empire, and instruction was conducted in twelve languages, including Armenian, Greek, Bulgarian, Hebrew, Turkish, Farsi, English, French, and Italian. Almost half of the students were usually Bulgarian. See George Washburn, Fifty Years in Constantinople and Recollections of Robert College (Boston: 1909), especially pp. 1-14.

[39] Blunt, "Report on the Educational Movement," AIIBAN, F. 4 (British Diplomatic Records), op. 20, ae. 190, pp. 794, 836.

The establishment of Bulgarian schools, independent of Greek control, was not perceived as a threat to Turkish interests. However, this benevolent attitude changed when the Church began to intercede in school affairs in the 1870s.

Active Church intercession began as a response to a growing realization among prominent Bulgarian educators that the mere existence of a school did not guarantee anything substantial was actually being accomplished. Observers inside and outside of Bulgaria who bothered to look at the situation with a critical eye were aware that many of the schools were hardly worthy of the name and that only a small number of schools had the proper teachers and resources to offer any kind of worthwhile education. Furthermore, there was often little or no communication or unity among schools even within a single city. Each existed independent of the other and employed uncountable numbers of different standards and arrangements. Powerful figures among the Bulgarian intelligentsia such as Liuben Karavelov, Nesho Bonchev, and Marin Drinov subjected the schools to detailed criticisms and concluded that the vast majority of the schools were very poorly situated and that most teachers were not adequately prepared. In many of the supposedly better schools, children learned entirely by rote and, in fact, were learning nothing.[40]

In order to discuss this situation, as well as to unite efforts to improve it, teachers in some locales such as Stara Zagora in 1868, came together in a special congress. A few other congresses were held in Plovdiv in 1870 and in Prilep, Gabrovo, and Tulcha in 1871.[41] Nothing significant, however, resulted. Such was not the case when Church officials in Shumen convoked a teachers congress in 1873. The firman or decree establishing the Exarchate recognized the Church's central role in the cultural affairs of the nation.[42]

---

[40] Two of the strongest and most thorough critiques were those of Nesho Bonchev and the revolutionary Khristo Botev, but they were not the only ones crying out for reform. See Nesho Bonchev, "Za uchilishtata," Periodichesko spisanie na Bŭlgarskoto knizhovno druzhestvo (Brăila), I, 3 (1871), 3-16 and I, 4 (1871), 26-51; Khristo Botev, editorial in Nezavisimost, March 30, 1874; pp. 189-190. Also, Noikov, Pogled do Paisii, pp. 30-31; Ivan Stamenov, "Ideiata za trudovo vŭzpitanie i obuchenie sled Osvobozhdenieto," Narodna prosveta, XIV, 7 (1958), 88-98; Naiden Chakŭrov, "Liuben Karavelov --viden predstavitel na nashata revoliutsionna pedagogicheska misŭl," Narodna prosveta, XV, 3 (1959), 80-81.

[41] Nikolai Zhechev, "Uchitelskiiat sŭbor v Shumen prez 1873 g.," Narodna prosveta, XVIII, 2 (1962), 77; Iordan Nikolov, "Poiava i razvitie na uchitelsko profs'-iuzno dvizhenie," Narodna prosveta, XV, 7 (1959), 51; Georgi pop Vasilev, Ucheben sŭvet i ucheben komitet (Sofia: 1925), p. 17.

[42] Chakŭrov, Uchilishtnoto zakonodatelstvo, p. 30; Bobchev, La Lutte du peuple bulgare, pp. 14-15.

With this in mind, the bishop of Varna-Preslav, Simon convoked a congress to discuss, among other things: a unification of programs, courses, texts, and academic year; improvement of physical conditions; improvement of teachers' work conditions; and a more orderly arrangement of financial matters. The teachers congress did, in fact, discuss all of these things and formulated useful recommendations. One such recommendation was the establishment of a central inspectorate.[43]

These activities did not escape the notice of either the Turkish authorities or Bulgarian revolutionaries. The latter were wary of such interest by the Church in school affairs. They feared that the Church officials might subvert the secular nature of the schools and turn them into factories for religious fanatics. The revolutionaries also were suspicious of the Church's uncomfortably close ties to the Turkish government, fearing that once the Church completed its work of unification, the Turks would step in and use the school for their own ends.[44]

---

[43] Chakŭrov, Uchilishtnoto zakonodatelstvo, p. 29; Noikov, Pogled do Paisii, p. 38; Ivan A. Georgov, "Nekolko dumi za nashite uchitelski sŭbori predi osvobozhdenieto," Uchilishten pregled, VI, 4 (1901), 302-305.

[44] Botev, editorial in Nezavisimost, March 30, 1874, p. 189; Zhechev, "Uchitelskiiat sŭbor," p. 81.

Such was not to be the case because the Turks had their own suspicions about such activities. The return of so many Russian- (and other foreign-) educated Bulgarians as teachers had already alarmed the Turkish officials. The banding together of so many potentially subversive elements at the Shumen Congress was apparently too much, and further congresses were forbidden.[45]

The action of the Turkish government was not without warrant, for indeed a revolutionary movement was growing, and teachers were prime figures in the movement. The schools, however, were not the only sources of trouble, allowing as they did, for example, military drills thinly disguised as gymnastics.[46] Teachers had also figured in the founding of reading rooms (chitalishta), a combination of library and discussion group which played a social and political role as well as an educational one.[47]

---

[45] Georgov, "Nekolko dumi," pp. 302-305; Aleksandŭr N. Berovski (pseudonym of Aleksandŭr N. Zhekov), Pŭrviiat rektor i pŭrvata bogoslovska shkola v Bulgariia (Sofia: 1939), pp. 41-49; Ivan Umlenski, ed. Pŭrva gimnaziia, "Neofit Rilski," Kiustendil Iubileen sbornik (Kiustendil: 1959), p. 9.

[46] Khristo Negentsov and Ivan Vanev, Obrazovanieto v Iztochna Rumeliia, 1879-1885 (Sofia: 1959), pp. 15-16.

[47] Krachunov, Iz Bŭlgarskata, p. 23; Noikov, Pogled do Paisii, p. 27; Karolev, Istoriia, p. 255. The classic work on the chitalishta, although now somewhat dated is

Bulgarian school affairs, on the eve of that country's struggle for independence, had reached a stage of development which was to surprise foreigners when the critical events of 1877-1879 forced their attention to that country. Januarius A. MacGahan, the American reporter whose news articles helped fan the flames of war, confessed that before his tour of the country in 1876, he thought of the Bulgarians in the same terms as he did American Indians--poor and illiterate savages. Instead, he learned to his surprise that "almost all Bulgarian villages had a school maintained in a conspicuous position by voluntary contributions, free for both rich and poor."[48] The literacy rate, he noted, was no smaller than that of England or France. MacGahan's observations were shared by other foreign visitors such as Laveleye, Kanitz, and others.[49]

The British, thanks to their excellent and perceptive consulate system, had known for quite some time

---

Stiliian Chilingirov, Bŭlgarski chitalishta predi osvobozhdenieto; prinos kŭm istoriiata na bŭlgarskoto vŭzrazhdane (Sofia: 1930), especially, pp. 117-135.

[48] Januarius A. MacGahan, The Turkish Atrocities in Bulgaria. Letters of the Special Commissioner of the Daily News (London: 1876), pp. 24-25.

[49] Krachunov, Iz Bŭlgarskata, pp. 18-25.

how developed the Bulgarian schools were. Consuls such as Sir John Elijah Blunt in Philippopolis (Plovdiv) were sending to Whitehall long detailed reports on the state of school affairs. In one dispatch, Blunt noted that Bulgarian schools were multiplying rapidly. As an example, he cited the fact that in 1870 in the region of Philippopolis, there were: one gymnasium (male), six central schools, one preparatory school, 281 elementary schools, and 24 girls schools for a total of 337. This represented 108 more schools than were listed in his last survey, five years previous.[50]

What most foreigners did not fully comprehend, however, was that some Bulgarians at least were not impressed by such figures and knew that most of these schools were not fulfilling their basic tasks. At least one foreigner, the same Blunt, suspected that things could be better. After his long and thorough examination of school affairs in the Philippopolis region, he concluded that the Turkish government had made a mistake in not associating itself more favorably with the school movement among the Bulgarians. He correctly predicted that the proud spirits raised among Bulgarians by the appearance of so many schools would raise the

---

[50] Blunt, "Report on the Educational Movement," AIIBAN, F. 4 (British Diplomatic Records), op. 20, ae. 190, p. 836.

aspirations of the people educated in them to dangerous levels. He also correctly concluded:

> As it is, the groundwork of a national system of education has been gradually prepared by the people themselves, but what in my humble opinion is now indispensible in order to improve it in a way which may confirm and increase the benefits which have already been derived from it is uniformity in the course of instruction, and above all, government control and support.[51]

Bulgarians would receive such a guiding authority in 1878, but not before a war that devastated much of the hard work that had taken place in the past 70 years.

---

[51] Ibid., p. 833.

CHAPTER TWO

MARIN DRINOV AND THE FORMATION OF
THE DEPARTMENT OF PUBLIC INSTRUCTION
DURING THE RUSSIAN OCCUPATION 1877-1879

The slow but steady progress that had marked Bulgarian education from 1835-1876 was brought to an abrupt halt by the April Uprising of 1876 and the course of events which followed. The courageous but foolhardy attempt by a handful of Bulgarian revolutionaries to stir up a general rising against Ottoman rule in April, 1876, succeeded only in generating a brutal Turkish repression. This event, when added to the tense situation in the Balkans already created by the Bosnia-Hercegovina crisis, helped touch off another war between Turkey and Russia which lasted from 1877 to 1878.

The war was fought largely on territory comprising modern Bulgaria, and the carnage and destruction dealt a severe blow to all aspects of the developing educational structure. Most tangibly and immediately damaged were the school buildings, which were used as hospitals by both sides wherever they still existed. The teaching cadre was severely diminished not only by the enlistment of teachers as soldiers and guerrillas but also by the need for clerks, secretaries, and translators when Russian soldiers began their occupation. In the struggle for national liberation, there was little time to think of schools and of school affairs.

Nevertheless, not long after Russian troops entered Bulgaria in 1877, action was taken to ameliorate the situation. The representative of Imperial Russian authority, Prince Vladimir Aleksandrovich Cherkasskii (1824-1878), took the first step towards restoring order by issuing the Statutes for the Civil Administration in Bulgaria on August 8, 1877. This instruction, as the title indicates, established guidelines for the setting up of a civil administration system largely following already existing Turkish models.[1] The Statutes' only reference to schools, however, was that the newly established provincial councils should be responsible for the re-opening and financial support

---

[1] In many cases, pre-existing administrative divisions were simply given Russian names. Thus, a *sanjak* became a *guberniia*, a *kaza* became an *okrug*, etc. See Muratov, ed., *Dokumenti za deinost'ta na Rusite po uredbata na grazhdanskoto upravlenie v Bŭlgariia ot 1877-1879 god.*, *Materiali za istoriia na Bŭlgariia* (Sofia: 1905), I, p. 117. (Hereafter cited as Muratov, *Dokumenti*.)

of the schools.[2] The Russian authorities were too busy with administrative and military affairs on the national level to be able to concern themselves with such matters.[3]

As the Russian Army proceeded to liberate Bulgaria, it designated officials to set up new administrative systems in the cities and villages. The Russian officials charged with these tasks were able to tap the services of many well-educated native Bulgarians. Recognizing the need to include Bulgarians on his staff, Prince Cherkasskii had written to the Bulgarian community in Bucharest and to his Panslav associate Ivan Aksakov in Russia, asking them to supply credentials

---

[2] "Utverzhdennyi Velikim Kniazem Glavnokomandiushchim 8-go avgusta 1877 g. proekt vremmenykh pravil ob upravitel'nykh sovetakh v okrugakh i gorodakh Bolgarii," document no. 11 in Russia, General Staff, Sbornik materialov po grazhdanskomu upravleniiu i okupatsii v Bolgarii v 1877-78-79 g.g., ed. by N. R. Ovsianyi (St. Petersburg: 1903), I, p. 52. (Hereafter cited as Ovsianyi, Sbornik materialov.)

[3] Arkhiven Institut na Bŭlgarskata Akademiia na naukite (AIBAN), Fond 62K (Mikhail Sarafov), opis 1, arkhivna edinitsa 8. Hereafter, the abbreviations F. for Fond, op. for opis or inventory number, and ae. for arkhivna edinitsa or storage unit will be used to facilitate the efforts of scholars wishing to locate this material.

on Bulgarians who had been educated in Russia and who were qualified to serve on his staff.[4]

From the list supplied by Aksakov especially, Cherkasskii selected as aides such notable figures as Naiden Gerov (1823-1900), Todor Burmov (1834-1906), and Marin Drinov (1838-1906). Naiden Gerov, born in Koprivshtitsa, had received a primary education in his native town but finished the gymnasium and lycée at Odessa in 1845. Sometime afterwards he became a Russian citizen and returned to Bulgaria, first as a teacher and then as a Russian Vice-Consul in Plovdiv (1857). Gerov was destined to compile and publish the first comprehensive dictionary of the Bulgarian language (1894-1905). Todor Burmov was a native of the village of Nova Makhala and like Gerov, finished his higher education in Russia, or more precisely in the Ukraine at the Kiev Theological Academy in 1857. He returned to Bulgaria soon afterwards to teach at the Gabrovo gymnasium and other local schools. He had also established and edited journals and newspapers

---

[4]Letter of N. Nikolaev to Todor Ikonomov, May 22, 1877, document 65, in Sergei A. Nikitin, et al., eds., Osvobozhdenie Bolgarii ot Turetskogo iga (Moscow: 1964), III, p. 95; and in the same volume, the letter of Ivan Aksakov to Prince V. A. Cherkasskii, June 13, 1877, document 92, III, p. 118.

such as Sŭvetnik. Burmov would become, one year later, the country's first Prime Minister.[5]

Aksakov pointed out in his reply to Cherkasskii that there was no need to supply information on Marin Drinov since the Khar'kov professor was already personally acquainted with Cherkasskii. Aksakov was doubtless referring to the fact that Drinov, soon to be appointed Director of the Department of Public Instruction in the Russian Provisional Government, had been associated rather closely with Panslavist circles in Russia, as was Cherkasskii himself.[6] Drinov so impressed Cherkasskii with his administrative abilities that even before Russian troops entered Sofia in December, 1877, Cherkasskii wrote to Commanding General Grand Duke Nicholas for permission to name Drinov as Vice-Governor of Sofia to assist Petr Nikolaevich Alabin (1824-1896), who was to be governor. Cherkasskii, in his letter, described Drinov as one of the most completely educated Bulgarians on his staff, fully loyal

---

[5] T. Panchev, Naiden Gerov (Sofia: 1926), pp. 1-20; Marko Balabanov, "Todor S. Burmov," Letopis na Bŭlgarsko knizhovno druzhestvo, VII (1906), 84-119.

[6] Sergei A. Nikitin, Slavianskie komitety v Rossi v 1858-1876 godakh (Moscow: 1960), pp. 66, 103-108, 137, 162, 170, et passim.

to the interests of Russia, and indispensible for work of any political character in the central administration.[7]

Thus Drinov became an active member of the Russian provisional administration. He used his influence in this capacity to rejuvenate the Bulgarian press and to lay the groundwork for the establishment of a Bulgarian central public library. In this work he was aided immensely by the cultured governor of Sofia, General Alabin.

However, Drinov was not to remain in the position of Vice-Governor for long because of the new state of affairs occasioned by the signing of the Preliminary Peace Treaty (San Stefano) between Russia and Turkey on March 3, 1878 (N.S.). That treaty set up a large Bulgarian state and gave Russia the right to appoint an Imperial Commissioner. This Imperial Commissioner had the duty of introducing, in two years' time a full civil governmental structure in Bulgaria. At the end of those two years, Russia would turn over administration of the country to a native government.[8]

---

[7] Russia, General Staff, Sbornik ofitsial'nykh razporiazhenii i dokumentov po bolgarskomu kraiu (Odessa: 1878), VII, pp. 6-7.

[8] See Article VII of the San Stefano Treaty, document 28 in Ovsianyi, Sbornik materialov, p. 158.

Because of the death of Prince Cherkasskii on the very day the San Stefano Treaty was signed, the newly created position of Imperial Commissioner was entrusted to Prince Aleksandr Mikhailovich Dondukov-Korsakov (1820-1893), a graduate of the University of St. Petersburg and former governor of Kiev, Volhynia, and Podolia. Soon after his appointment, Dondukov-Korsakov received a lengthy set of instructions from St. Petersburg which laid down the basic lines of government until such time as Bulgaria elected its own national assembly and prince.

The major task charged to the Commissioner by these instructions, in fact, was to set up a system of government that would ensure a smooth transfer of power when Russia's mandate in Bulgaria expired. That mandate was supposed to last two years but was changed to nine months when a new treaty replaced the San Stefano accord. The Great Powers (especially Britain) had become alarmed at the size of the Bulgarian state and at the long period of time Russia planned to occupy the liberated area. Thus, a conference in Berlin in July, 1878, imposed a new treaty on Turkey and Russia. The Bulgaria of San Stefano was divided into three parts. Thrace and Macedonia returned to direct Turkish rule. The southern part of the previous territory became a semi-autonomous province ruled directly by the sultan. The remaining part became an autonomous principality with a Christian government.[9] Russian authority was limited to the Principality of Bulgaria. The instructions, then, to Dondukov-Korsakov included a command to set up an Administrative Council to manage affairs and to formulate projects and regulations.[10] This Council was to be attached to the Commissariat and to consist of seven departments: (1) War; (2) Finance; (3) Internal Affairs; (4) Justice; (5) Post, Telegraph, and Public Works; (6) Central Chancery; and (7) Public Instruction and Religious Affairs. One member of the Administrative Council headed each of these departments, and the Commissioner had full authority to appoint and dismiss the directors.[11]

Finally, the instructions to Dondukov-Korsakov described, although only in general terms, the duties of each department. The duties of the Department of

---

[9]Charles Samwehr and Jules Hopf, eds., *Nouveau Recueil général des traités et autres actes relatifs aux rapports de droit international*, 2nd ed. (Göttingen: 1879), III, pp. 449-466.

[10]Russia, State Chancery, "Obshchaia instruktsiia kniaziu Dondukovu-Korsakovu," April 10, 1878, in Muratov, *Dokumenti*, I, p. 80.

[11]*Ibid*., pp. 80-81.

Public Instruction were described as follows: "The Department of Public Instruction, notwithstanding measures taken towards the restoration and opening of already existing schools, is to concern itself with the formulation of statutes for these schools, both primary as well as secondary."[12]

To carry out the duties assigned by these instructions, Dondukov-Korsakov turned to the man Cherkasskii had described as the most completely educated Bulgarian --Marin Drinov. Drinov was still serving as Vice-Governor of Sofia when he received a telegram on May 24, 1878, from his superior, Governor Alabin, ordering him to proceed at once to his new position in Plovdiv (Philippopolis).[13] The Department of Public Instruction was thus placed in the hands of a native Bulgarian who was a citizen of Russia, while the other departments went to native Russians.[14]

Drinov's appointment began what really must be

---

[12] *Ibid.*, p. 84.

[13] Bŭlgarski istoricheski arkhiv (BIA), F. 111 (Marin Drinov), op. 1, ae. 24. Plovdiv (ancient Philippopolis) became the capital of Eastern Rumelia after the Treaty of Berlin, while Sofia became the capital of the Bulgarian Principality.

[14] Nikitin, ed., *Osvobozhdenie Bolgarii*, III, p. 10.

called the "establishment" or, perhaps more suitably, the "formative" period of the Ministry of Public Instruction. The Department or <u>Otdelenie</u> of Public Instruction was a prototype of the later Ministry but unlike it in several significant ways. First, it was a temporary arrangement because it was part of a Russian administration set up only provisionally until such time as a state system could be created for Bulgaria. Second, it was not a true ministry in the sense of the word which implies a form of government responsible to a king, to a parliament, or, most importantly, to a constitution. Although many of Drinov's proposals were discussed within the Administrative Council of the Russian Provisional Government, Drinov did not have to explain or to argue his programs and policies on the floor of a parliament as did later ministers of education. That does not, of course, discount the importance of the Department and its work. Indeed, Drinov is almost universally referred to by his biographers as the "father of Bulgarian education," because in his approximately one-year tenure of office, he set down the basic lines, physical and philosophical, of the educational system.[15]

---

[15]For an excellent guide to the important works on

The man responsible for this important contribution to Bulgarian education was born into a poor family of artisans in Panagiurishte in 1838. He received his education in the local schools, along with his good friend Nesho Bonchev (1839-1878). Both eventually became teachers in those same schools, but not for very long. Because of their services to the community, the two youths attracted the attention of local officials, who arranged for the boys to continue their education in Russia. This was made possible by the cooperation of Bulgarian merchant colonies in Istanbul, Vienna, Bucharest, and elsewhere and the Russian Panslavist organizations--especially the Moscow Slavic Benevolent Society.[16] Before setting off to Russia, Drinov was furnished with a set of credentials by local officials, which attested to his excellent academic record, his worthy service to the community, and to his honorable and exemplary behavior.[17]

Drinov see the article by Virzhiniia Paskaleva, "Prinos kum biografiiata na Marin Drinov," in Aleksandŭr K. Burmov, Dimitŭr Angelov, et al., eds., *Izsledvaniia v chest na Marin Drinov* (Sofia: 1960), pp. 1-50.

[16]Nikitin, *Slavianskie Komitety*, pp. 93-110.

[17]BIA, F. 111 (Marin Drinov), op. 1, ae. 1.

Drinov began his studies at the Kiev Theological Seminary in 1858 but finished his education at the History-Philology faculty of Moscow University in 1865, after which he accepted a position as tutor to the aristocratic Golitsyn family. This position enabled him to travel and to use European archives, which in turn were used to carry out research leading to a master's degree in 1873 and to a doctorate in 1875. He received an appointment to teach history at Kharkov University in 1873, a position he kept until the end of his days.[18]

Bulgaria's first formal director of public instruction was a man well-versed in both Russian and Bulgarian affairs. Fluent in Russian and Bulgarian, he was instrumental in acquainting Russian society with Bulgarian problems through public lectures and newspaper articles.[19]

---

[18] Andrei Tsviatkov, "Marin Drinov--lichnost i delo," Uchilishten pregled, XLV, 304 (1946), 175-176; Naiden Chakŭrov, "Marin Drinov i razvitieto na bŭlgarskoto obrazovanie," Uchilishtna praktika, VIII, 3 (1956), 162. Drinov's first scholarly work was "Pogled vrŭkh proiskhozhdan'eto na bŭlgarski narod i nachaloto na bŭlgarska istoriia," published in 1869, see Marin Drinov, Sŭchineniia, ed. by V. N. Zlatarski (Sofia: 1915), I, pp. 1-69.

[19] An excellent example of this is his article, "Bolgariia nakanune eia pogroma," delivered as a public lecture at Kharkov University in November, 1876, and published in the St. Petersburg journal Slavianskii sbornik, II (1877), 23-45; Drinov, Sŭchineniia, III, pp. 23-55.

Many of these activities occurred under the auspices of the Slavic Benevolent Societies with which Drinov was associated. Besides this valuable experience in Russia, however, Drinov also brought with him to his new job some very definite ideas about what Bulgarian education needed and did not need.

Drinov was aware that although hardly any village was without some kind of school, this did not mean that such schools were of significant value. In a hard-hitting yet poignant letter to Bulgarian intellectuals in 1868, he pointed out that Bulgarian schools, despite the efforts of some teachers to improve them, remained primary schools, providing only the basics of reading and writing and not giving much of an education to Bulgarian youth.[20] Furthermore, he had also spoken out on the need for a central organization to correlate the various educational activities. In 1869, he wrote an article urging the establishment of a Bulgarian Literary Society to serve such a function. He described the problem thus:

> Deprived of a ministry of public instruction, of a spiritual leadership, of a chief board of

---

[20] Marin Drinov, "Pismo do Bŭlgarskata inteligentsiia," Sŭchineniia, III, pp. 13-16. First published in Narodnost' (Bucharest), III, 4 (1868).

trustees, of any kind of authority which would strive for its public enlightment and education, the Bulgarian people will not be able to have an organized direction which would facilitate the path of its intellectual development.[21]

Drinov also came to office with very clearly defined views on what the Bulgarian people did not need for its intellectual development. For one, they did not need to waste any more time on the all-consuming struggle to achieve a Bulgarian autocephalous Church, he wrote in 1871, because a separate Bulgarian Exarchate had finally been established in 1870. He urged instead that the "School Question" immediately should become the second great question to which the Bulgarian people should devote all their energy and attention.[22]

Drinov also spoke out against what he considered to be the self serving meddling of foreign religious sects in the education of Bulgarian youth. His antipathy towards Catholics was surpassed only by his ill-will towards Protestants and towards Greek Representatives of the Eastern Orthodox religion. The educational

---

[21] Marin Drinov, "Bŭlgarsko literaturno druzhestvo," Sŭchineniia, III, p. 17. First appeared in Dunavska zora (Brăila), II, 35 (1869).

[22] Marin Drinov, letter to the Bulgarian Literary Society in Brăila, March 23, 1871, BIA, F. 111 (Marin Drinov), op. 1, ae. 2. This Society was established in Brăila, Romania, in 1869 with Drinov as president.

activities of these sects were inimical to the existence of a Bulgarian national self-identity, he claimed, and no Bulgarian had anything to gain from the educational efforts of such people. He even went so far as to dismiss all their learning as old wives' tales.[23]

Despite his rejection of foreign interference in Bulgarian education, Drinov brought with him a cosmopolitan knowledge of foreign educational systems, especially the Russian. He was also, however, much impressed by the pedagogical thinking of a native Bulgarian, his old school friend Nesho Bonchev. Bonchev had written a long, cogent analysis and critique of Bulgarian education with a concise list of suggestions for its improvement.[24] It was Drinov, in fact, who was responsible for sending the article (entitled "On the Schools") to the Bulgarian Literary Society, along with a cover letter strongly urging its publication and endorsing

---

[23] Marin Drinov, "Strashni li sa za narodnost ni fanariotite i iezuitite?," Sŭchineniia, III, pp. 3-9. First published in Vremiia (Istanbul), II, 12 (1866) and II, 14 (1866).

[24] Nesho Bonchev, "Za uchilishtata," Periodichesko spisanie na Bŭlgarsko Knizhovno Druzhestvo, I, 3 (1871), 3-16 and I, 4 (1871), 26-51.

the views presented in the article.[25] Bonchev's basic thesis was that existing Bulgarian schools meted out a useless education and that what his compatriots needed most was a system which would quickly (in 3-4 years) give a child a basic education. In addition, the establishment of several well-ordered secondary schools was of top priority for the future of the nation's education.[26]

Bonchev's suggested program was a relatively limited, but practical, one. And Drinov did well to endorse it because a more elaborate program was out of the question considering the situation that greeted him as he assumed authority. The problems confronting him ranged from severe destruction of school property to critical shortages of teachers, textbooks, and talented

---

[25] Marin Drinov, letter to the Bulgarian Literary Society, March 23, 1871, BIA, F. 111 (Marin Drinov), op. 1, ae. 2. Some of Drinov's biographers are in disagreement over whether or not Drinov was influenced by his friend. Krŭstiu Krachunov maintains that Drinov never gave any evidence whatsoever that he endorsed Bonchev's ideas, see K. Krachunov, Marin Drinov (1838-1906) Zhivot i deinost' (Sofia: 1938), p. 52; N. Gorinov, however, claims Drinov followed a path suggested by Bonchev in his work, see "Nesho Bonchev kato uchilishten deets i negovite vŭzgledi za obrazovanieto," Uchitelska Misŭl, XIV (1933), 519. Neither author cites this letter which seems to be irrefutable evidence.

[26] Bonchev, "Za uchilishtata," p. 7.

people to help formulate solutions. The Imperial
Commissar, Dondukov-Korsakov, succinctly evaluated the
situation in his first report to General Eduard
Ivanovich Totleben of the War Office in St. Petersburg:

> The Bulgarian public schools previously existing were reduced to absolute decay by the last war and by the ravages of the Turks that preceded it; many schools were destroyed, while a large part of the ones that survived were turned into civilian and military hospitals or had to be closed for lack of material means or teachers, the majority of whom entered service on the state register.[27]

The first concerns of the new Director of Public
Instruction were thus relatively simple to define, but
were difficult to alleviate. In fact, Drinov and the
Provisional Government had a task before them much
larger than simply re-opening the schools and stocking
them with teachers and texts. Education had an entirely
new purpose in a free and independent country. Now that
Bulgaria, after five centuries of Ottoman rule was to be
the master of its own affairs, it needed a pool of well-
educated and well-trained individuals to assume the
reins of power after the Russian Provisional Government's mandate ended. After 500 years as the ward of a
large and sprawling Oriental empire, this newest Balkan

---

[27]Aleksandr Mikhailovich Dondukov-Korsakov, "Otchet," July 16, 1878, in Muratov, *Dokumenti*, p. 117.

nation was thrust unprepared into the last quarter of the nineteenth century. Furthermore, although Bulgarian schools had, since earlier in the same century, aimed at preparing educated citizens and even leaders, these same schools were unequal to the task of preparing civil servants with the specialized and higher education needed to run the affairs of a sovereign state.

Both Drinov and Dondukov-Korsakov realized the need for a new guiding principle and major emphasis. The meeting of the Administrative Council of July 7, 1878, and Dondukov-Korsakov's subsequent report to General Totleben serve as an outline of what was to come and indeed can even be used as a measure to evaluate the activity of the Department durings its term of office. These reports noted the widespread existence of schools before the war, so widespread that hardly any village lacked a school built and maintained by the local inhabitants.[28] On the basis of this past performance, Drinov decided to leave the support and construction of schools entirely to the people and to limit the role of the central government to the purely "moral" side of affairs. He delineated three basic activities

---

[28] Ibid., p. 118. No mention was made of the often sorry conditions prevailing in these schools.

for the Department of Public Instruction. First, it would encourage the public to open new schools. Second, it would establish well-defined curricula in the secondary or so-called chief or _glaven_ schools. These schools were a carryover from the Renascence era when their name major or chief (_glaven_) was more in line with their true status. The word _glaven_ at that time had the connotation of "most advanced," "best," and "highest," and these schools were, for a while at least, the most advanced in the country.[29] The chief schools were secondary schools only in the sense that they followed the primary schools, which usually lasted three to four years. They also offered the more advanced subjects (history, geography, sciences) while the primary schools provided only the basics of reading, writing, and arithmetic. The name "chief" remained in use even after the establishment of the Gabrovo gymnasium and other higher schools. The chief schools were more expensive to operate and therefore tended to exist only in larger cities or towns.[30]

---

[29] Naiden Gerov, _Rechnik na Blugarskyi iazŭk_ (Plovdiv: 1895-1900), I, p. 217. Gerov defines _glaven_ (plural, _glavni_) as "that which is the first, the best, the greatest, the most advanced."

[30] Chakŭrov, _Uchilishtno zakonodatelstvo_, pp. 23-25; Vankov, _Razvoi_, pp. 11, 29, 53, 62-63; Tsonkov, _Razvitie_, p. 11.

Drinov's proposal to establish well-defined curricula for these chief schools was extremely important because the absence of organized education plans was a prime cause of the inadequacy of existing educational institutions. In fact, this same question received much attention at a teachers' congress convoked by church authorities in Shumen in 1870.[31] (The proposals that had resulted, however, were only applicable to the diocese (eparkhiia) of Shumen and not to the entire country.) Finally, the Department would attempt to ensure that only worthy individuals were appointed as teachers and that these teachers would be protected from the abuse and arbitrary treatment which they had suffered at the hands of influential but often ignorant members of the communes in Turkish times.[32]

Drinov's efforts to carry out these tasks were facilitated by the availability of a limited number of talented and gifted individuals. Especially noteworthy

---

[31] Zhechev, "Uchitelskiiat subor v Shumen," pp. 77-89.

[32] Dondukov-Korsakov, "Otchet," in Muratov, Dokumenti, p. 118; AIBAN, F. 62k (Mikhail Sarafov), op. 1, ae. 8. An excellent account of chorbadzhi-teacher relations may be found in Karolev, Istoriiata na Gabrovoskata uchilishte, pp. 89-130.

in this respect were the efforts of four men who shared
many common features: Ivan Giuzelev (1844-1916), Raicho
(or Racho) Karolev (1846-1928), Petŭr Genchev (1843-
1905), and Iosif Kovachev (1839-1898). All four had
played and were to continue to play important roles in
Bulgarian education. All of them were native born
Bulgarians but had received at least part of their education in Russia. Genchev, Karolev, and Kovachev were
graduates of the Kievan Theological Academy, while
Giuzelev had completed his higher education in Odessa.
All of them, after the completion of their studies, returned to their native land and taught in the local
schools. Genchev, Karolev, and Giuzelev returned to
Gabrovo in 1871 and were instrumental in improving educational affairs in that city. These three men became
identified with the mladi or "Young" faction in local
politics. This faction, as opposed to the stari or
"Old" faction, was reform-minded and progressive. They
also instituted or tried to institute changes not only
in the affairs of the gymnasium but also in affairs of
the local primary schools. These factors caused difficulties with the local notables (chorbadzhi) who also
controlled, by and large, the purse strings of the
school boards. Furthermore, the Turks viewed them as
Russian agents, and upon the outbreak of revolutionary

activities in 1876, Genchev, Karolev, and Giuzelev found themselves arrested and sentenced to death. They were spared only after the intervention of the Odessa Bulgarian community and Russian diplomats, primarily Count Ignatiev.[33]

Iosif Kovachev, on the other hand, had returned to his birthplace of Macedonia to teach in schools there. Besides teaching, however, Kovachev was also noted for the introduction into Bulgaria of new pedagogical methods, as well as for writing some of the first Bulgarian-language textbooks for use in the schools. His most valuable contribution concerned the introduction of the so-called *zvuchna* or phonic method of teaching the alphabet (in which the individual letters are learned in and of themselves rather than being associated with a word such as *az*, *buka*, etc.) In fact,

---

[33]The information in this paragraph came from the following sources: N. Nachov, "Raicho M. Karolev," *Letopis na Bŭlgarsko knizhovno druzhestvo*, XI (1927-1928), 67-73; Emanuil Ivanov, "Ivan N. Giuzelev," *Letopis na Bŭlgarsko knizhovno druzhestvo*, XII (1915-1917), 156-160; n.a., "Petŭr Genchev," *Letopis na Bŭlgarsko knizhovno druzhestvo*, VI (1905), 92-102; P. Zarev, ed. *Sto godini Bŭlgarska akademiia na naukite, 1869-1969* (Sofia: 1969), I, pp. 140, 175, 314, 328; Karolev, *Istoriiata na Gabrovskoto uchilishte*, pp. 229-231. Sofia, University of Sofia, *Almanakh na Sofiiskiia universitet sv. Kliment Okhridski* (Sofia: 1940), pp. 298-299.

this method was the subject of one of his textbooks, The Bulgarian Primer in the Phonic Method, published in Vienna in 1875.[34]

Kovachev was not the only one of this group of four who had published textbooks, however. Ivan Giuzelev had also published a Short Elementary Geometry (Prague: 1873), as well as a Manual of Physics (Prague: 1874).[35]

All four of these individuals, like Drinov, found themselves in the service of the Russian Army during the war of 1877-1878. Eventually, by request of Drinov, all of these dedicated men entered into the service of the Department of Public Instruction. With their help thus assured, Drinov set a goal of opening the war-shattered schools in September and began compiling the statutes and programs necessary to achieve that end.

The goal of opening the schools in September, 1878, was rather optimistic considering that the country had hardly begun to recover from the war. Nevertheless, Drinov enlisted the aid of Dondukov-Korsakov who gave orders in July to evacuate the sick and wounded

---

[34]Zarev, Sto godini, p. 328.

[35]Ibid., p. 175.

from all school buildings and who allowed school authorities to take measures to disinfect them in anticipation of a September opening.[36] Finally, the most important decree to come from this entire period was published on August 29, 1878, The Temporary Statute for the Public Schools. This Statute served as an enabling act by which the Department proposed to carry out its duties. Its effect, however, was felt far beyond the period of Russian occupation, and it created some severe problems for the Ministers of Public Instruction who followed Drinov.

It was in the Temporary Statute that Drinov gave legal force to his belief in the desirability of popular sovereignty in educational affairs--one of the most important aspects of the legacy of Drinov's period. He explained it thus:

> It is generally recognized that public instruction progresses most where the populace itself takes direct part in the material support of the public schools. This is why the /present/ administration not only sees no need to change the present method for supporting public schools in Bulgaria, but even legalizes this method by giving the populace the right to levy a tax for the use of the schools.[37]

---

[36] Dondukov-Korsakov, "Otchet," in Muratov, Dokumenti, I, p. 118.

[37] Marin Drinov, "Zapiska za deiatelnost'ta na privremennoto Russko upravlenie v Bŭlgariia," in

This thought was expressed, although more formally, in Section II, article 26 of the Temporary Statute which also noted that the Department of Public Instruction would aid the communes only in unusual circumstances and then only temporarily. No indication, however, was given of what might constitute such an unusual circumstance.[38]

In the Statute, Drinov listed the four chief sources which the communities would use to support their schools financially. These sources were: (1) income from school real estate, (2) a portion of church income, (3) voluntary contributions, and, if necessary, (4) a permanent or temporary tax on all members of the community. This listing was the extent of the discussion of school financing in the Temporary Statute. Drinov gave no details, explanations, or indications that other sources could or should be explored.[39] This indicated

---

Sŭchineniia, III, pp. 155-156. First published in Bulgaria, Narodno Sŭbranie, Protokolite na Uchreditelno Bŭlgarsko Narodno Sŭbranie (Sofia: 1879).

[38] Bulgaria, Department of Public Instruction, "Privremenen ustav za Narodnite Uchilishta," Uchilishten sbornik koito sŭderzha uchebnoto delo v Kniazhestvo Bŭlgariia ot vreme na okupatsiia do kraia na 1882 godina (Sofia: 1883), p. 8. (Hereafter cited as Uchilishten sbornik.)

[39] Ibid., pp. 8-10.

a weak understanding by Drinov's administration not only of past practices but also of the realities facing the communities after the war of 1877-1878.

All four means cited by Drinov had been used effectively in the past. Church support had come from either a portion of the collection at services or in outright lending of buildings for classroom use. The voluntary contributions referred to by Drinov were either solicited by school boards or bequeathed by benefactors such as Vasil Aprilov in Gabrovo. Some communities, especially in the commercially advanced parts of eastern Bulgaria, had special buildings, meadows, or pastures, the proceeds from which went for the support of the community schools. Sometimes a community would levy a special tax on all adult members of the community whose children attended the school or schools. However, the sources of support listed by Drinov were far from inclusive and made no mention whatsoever of the serious difficulties facing those communities which tried to use even the four sources Drinov suggested.[40]

---

[40] These observations are based on a detailed examination of communal school financing methods from a variety of sources. Since the whole question had to be dealt with anew by later Ministers, a complete discussion of the problem will be found in Chapter Three of this dissertation, and the sources are listed there.

First, many communities used sources other than those listed by Drinov. For example, large cities serving as central markets often relied on the intizap or special tax on the sale of cattle to help finance schools. Other communities taxed vehicles crossing bridges to raise money for their schools. Indeed, the list of alternatives was remarkable in diversity, and rare was the community that could depend only on one or two means of school financing.

Also, at least two of the four sources cited by Drinov were no longer dependable. The war's fury had destroyed much of the property both of the Church and of the communities,[41] necessitating heavy investments for reconstruction. Drinov's Temporary Statute made no recognition of these new and difficult realities. Moreover, the communities found their resources strained even further by a host of new obligations and taxes imposed on them by the Provisional Government. These

---

[41] Jireček, Glavno izlozhenie, p. 6 et passim; the archives of the Department of Public Instruction in the Bulgarian Central State Historical Archives (TsDIA), F. 405, op. 1, ae. 3, contain only a few scattered reports on destruction caused by the war in certain villages, not enough to indicate how much Drinov knew. It was the Glavno izlozhenie of Jireček in 1882 that gave the first complete picture of the extent of the destruction.

obligations ranged from the support of local militia to welfare services such as orphanages and hospitals.[42] On top of all this, Drinov and the Department of Public Instruction urged the communities to build new schools in order to allow for the achievement of universal, mandatory primary education. Drinov's incomplete attention to these factors were to cause extreme difficulties for future Ministers of Public Instruction.

In fairness to Drinov and his advisors, however, it must be noted that they recognized the need for clarity and a precise determination of the financial responsibilities of the communes. Article 1 of the Temporary Statutes, in fact, stated that a more complete and detailed regulation would be issued after a full study of the needs and condition of the people.[43]

Despite his willingness to leave the financial concerns of the schools in the hands of local officials, Drinov was not so willing to leave all school affairs in their jurisdiction. He often reiterated his position that the instructional aspects of public school affairs

---

[42] Bulgaria, Ministry of Internal Affairs, "Zakon za obshtinite i za gradsko upravlenie," Dŭrzhaven vestnik, IV, 117 (1882), 924-930.

[43] Bulgaria, Department of Public Instruction, "Privremenen ustav, Uchilishten sbornik, p. 5.

should remain entirely in the hands of the government which would exercise this control through a network of provincial school inspectors.[44] Nor did he rule out the eventuality that the state would or could establish and operate its own schools, specifically institutions of secondary education.

One of the important tasks of the government with respect to the schools came in the area of establishing uniform curricula. Before 1878, schools had been established by individuals or communities with little attention to the affairs of schools in other Bulgarian cities and towns. By 1878, hundreds of schools had been established with no relation to each other and with each school distinguished by its own system of instruction, style of curriculum, etc. Certain features were similar to each other, of course, in terms of a general model such as the Lancastrian schools. But the variations from village to village in even this type of school were so great as to cause concern to such reform-minded individuals as Nesho Bonchev and Marin Drinov.

---

[44] See especially Drinov's unpublished report to the first Prince of Bulgaria, Alexander von Battenberg (1878-1886), in BIA, F. 111 (Marin Drinov), op. 1, ae. 22.

To correct this situation, the Temporary Statute issued by Drinov called for a uniform system of public primary schools consisting of three categories. Each of the three categories would have its own course and length of instruction, its own goals, and would be tailored to the ability of each inhabited area to support such a school. The first category of school was called the primary (pŭrvonachalno) and had a three-year (i.e. three grades) course of instruction. The second category of schools was the intermediate (sredno) school with a two-year course of instruction. The third category was based on the "chief" (glavno) school.[45] The course of instruction would last four years, but the course for the first two years of the chief school duplicated exactly that of the intermediate school. This was due to the somewhat complicated scheme envisioned by Drinov for the actual location of each category of school. Drinov proposed that his administration work very hard to ensure that every Bulgarian community have a primary (category I) school. Meanwhile, an intermediate school with its two-year course of instruction would be opened in the wealthier communities. However, large cities and towns would open

---

[45] Bulgaria, Department of Public Instruction, "Privremenen ustav," Uchilishten sbornik, pp. 5-7.

a four-year chief school instead of an intermediate one.
The chief school would provide during the first two
years the same curriculum as that of the intermediate
school in the rest of the country, plus an additional
two years. Obviously, not every child would be able
to attend such schools.[46]

Each of the three schools had its own goal. The
first category (primary) schools would provide all
Bulgarian children with the basic skills of reading and
writing. The second category or intermediate schools
would amplify that knowledge. The third category or
chief schools would allow students privileged enough
to attend the opportunity of completing their primary
education.[47]

It was in reference to these primary schools,
especially those in the first category, that Drinov
first publicly formulated his plans for compulsory,
universal primary education for the citizens of the
Principality. Part I, Section A, article 9 of the
Temporary Statutes commanded that henceforth all
children of both sexes in the Principality had to complete a primary school (i.e. category I). While

---

[46] Ibid., pp. 7-8

[47] Ibid., pp. 1-7.

Drinov's motives may have been beyond reproach, it is questionable whether the authority of his Department, as defined by the already-mentioned instructions to Dondukov-Korsakov, allowed for such a far-reaching mandate. In any event, Drinov did succeed in writing this provision into the Constitution of Tŭrnovo when he served on the Constitutional Committee. Again, this policy caused considerable discomfort for later Ministers of Instruction when the government, unable to enforce this provision, was held up to scorn and derision on the floor of the Sŭbranie.[48]

The curriculum for each of the three categories of schools was described only in very basic terms. The first category of schools taught not so much specific subjects as general areas: catechism, religious and secular readings, writing, and arithmetic, and church singing, where such instruction was possible. The intermediate school curriculum added to this list such subjects as Bulgarian history and geography, natural science, and drawing. The chief school's curriculum

---

[48] This criticism arose often, see for example, Bulgaria, Narodno Sŭbranie, *Stenograficheski dnevnitsi na vtoroto obikonveno narodno Sŭbranie, pŭrva redovna sesiia* (Sofia: 1881), session of May 21, 1881, pp. 530ff.

was slightly more refined: world history, catechism, old Bulgarian language and Russian, geography, physics, practical geometry, and physiology. These chief or _glavni_ schools thus preserved one of the reasons for naming them chief schools in the first place, i.e. they taught the major sciences (_glavni_ _nauki_). Incidentally, the number of years or classes in each of the schools was three for the first category, two for the intermediate, and four for the chief schools.

One of the major problems with this three-tiered school structure was that it did not follow a logical progression of one to the other. That is, the student did not necessarily pass through each of the three categories in sequence. This was due to the fact that article 22 of the Temporary Statutes provided that the chief schools could accept students from either the primary or the intermediate schools. (If a student proceeded from the primary school directly to the chief school, he started in the first year; in contrast, a student proceeding from the intermediate school to the chief school started in the third year.) This provision blurred the lines between the second and third category of schools and also tended to make the intermediate school useless.

These three categories of primary schools were to provide the basic education for Bulgarian citizens. But the needs of a sovereign state required that at least some of its citizens have the specialized training necessary to run a modern state. The Department of Public Instruction expressed its desire, in July, 1878, to establish several good secondary educational institutions (recalling Nesho Bonchev's recommendations).[49] Drinov was aware that a few schools somewhat answering to the description of secondary educational institutions already existed such as the gymnasia in Gabrovo and Plovdiv. But he thought that these were inadequate for the simple reason that the education provided by them was too general and broad, with the result that the students were not properly prepared for later entry into universities and professional schools.[50] (Since these schools did not exist in their own country, Bulgarian students had to receive their higher education

---

[49] Dondukov-Korsakov, "Otchet," in Muratov, Dokumenti, pp. 159-160. See also the Journal of the Sessions of the Council of the Russian Commissar in Bulgaria, session of July 25, 1878, document 95, in Nikitin, Osvobozhdenie Bolgarii, III, pp. 180-181.

[50] Drinov, report to Alexander von Battenberg, BIA, F. 111 (Marin Drinov), op. 1, ae. 22.

in Russia, Western and Eastern Europe, or Robert College in Istanbul.) Drinov proposed to correct the situation by opening secondary schools with a strictly defined character and curriculum.

Accordingly, at the same time that plans were being made for the primary schools, similar arrangements were initiated for the opening of several technical and non-technical gymnasia. Drinov proposed as early as July, 1878, in a meeting of the Administrative Council, that two classical gymnasia be opened in Gabrovo and in Sofia. The Sofia gymnasium would be maintained from the general expenditures of the Russian Provisional Government, while the Gabrovo school would be maintained by the interest on capital funds already bequeathed by private individuals. This, of course, was a reference to the fund established in 1835 by V. E. Aprilov and N. S. Palauzov. Only the two lower classes (out of a planned seven) would be opened at first in each school.[51] Similar proposals were made at the same time for the establishment of technical gymnasia, but exact locations were not specified. In the autumn of 1878, however, a set of programs and regulations was issued for both types of gymnasia.

---

[51] Dondukov-Korsakov, "Otchet," in Muratov, Dokumenti, p. 159.

Both of the classical gymnasia (so called because of the emphasis on classical languages) were opened in January, 1879. Work towards the opening of the Gabrovo school was not extremely complicated because of the already existing institution there. But the projected school for Sofia required more attention. Drinov, at first, wanted to entrust the matter to the person then serving as Inspector of Public Schools in the Sofia district, Iosif Kovachev. The latter, however, complained that he was already overburdened with his duties as inspector, and the position instead went to Georgi Stamenov. Stamenov had been educated at Moscow University and, until the recent war, had been teaching in a gymnasium in Moscow. The Sofia gymnasium opened with an enrollment of 90, while the one in Gabrovo, under the direction of Raicho Karolev, opened with 109 students.[52]

A very detailed program for both of these schools was published in September, 1878, with the title Program for the First Two Classes in the Classical Gymnasia. This curriculum showed a strong concern for the study

---

[52]Khristo Krŭstev, Ivan Stefanov, et al., eds., Iubileina kniga na pŭrva Sofiiska mŭzhka gimnasiia, 1878-1929 (Sofia: 1929), pp. 30-32.

of languages, both classical and modern. The languages offered were Latin, Bulgarian, and French. However, the category entitled Bulgarian is misleading for part of the exercises in the teaching of Bulgarian required the translation of Latin and French phrases into Bulgarian. The students in the first and second years combined had 40 hours of lessons each week (not counting physical exercise). The study of these three languages accounted for 20 hours or 50 percent of this total. The rest of the time was devoted to the study of arithmetic, penmanship, drawing, catechism, and geography, as well as to physical exercises.[53]

The curriculum devised for the technical gymnasia differed significantly from that of the classical schools. Three such technical schools were opened by the initiative of Drinov: one in Varna in September, 1879, with an enrollment of 49 students in two classes; one in Kiustendil in October, 1879, with three classes and 77 students; and one in Lom in October, 1878, with two classes and 47 students.[54] The goal of these

---

[53]Bulgaria, Department of Public Instruction, "Programma na pŭrvite dva klassa v klassichna gimnaziia," September 21, 1878, Uchilishten sbornik, pp. 25-27.

[54]Jireček, Glavno izlozhenie, p. 30; Krŭstev and Stefanov, Sofiiska gimnasiia, pp. 31-36.

technical schools, as stated in article 1 of the Temporary Statutes for the Real Schools, approved by Dondukov-Korsakov in October, 1878, was not only to give students a general education but also to prepare them for entrance into polytechnical and other specialized schools.[55] It was understood, of course, that for students who so desired such education, travel abroad was necessary. No such schools yet existed in the Principality.

In line with the goals stated in the statutes for these schools, a heavy emphasis was placed on scientific, mathematical, and mechanical subjects. Latin was not offered; however, a student could choose between German and French for the required foreign language. The subject receiving the most attention was mechanical drawing. Out of a total number of 24 class hours in the third year of study (excluding physical exercise), 14 hours or nearly 60 percent of the time was spent on mechanical or scientific subjects. The remaining time was used to study history, language, penmanship, and religion.

A goal of both the technical and classical

---

[55] Bulgaria, Department of Public Instruction, "Programma za purvite dva klassa v klassichna gimnaziia," Uchilishten sbornik, p. 55.

gymnasia, as stated in their programs, was to prepare students for higher education. To this end, a sum of 60,000 leva was designated by the Imperial Commissioner to be distributed as stipends for study abroad by the Department of Public Instruction.[56]

Along with the classical and technical gymnasia, Drinov also provided what amounted to secondary schools for the education of the Bulgarian clergy. Both Drinov and Dondukov-Korsakov were concerned about the limited education that most members of the Bulgarian clergy had received and the sloppiness of many of the priests in celebrating the liturgy.[57] Thus, Drinov made preparations for the opening of theological seminaries, one in Samokov and one in Liaskovets at the Saints Peter and Paul Monastery. A theological seminary had existed in Liaskovets (near Tŭrnovo) for a brief period immediately before the War of Liberation. Bishop Hilarion of Makariopolis (1812-1875) had prepared the foundations of the school which opened at the Saints Peter and Paul Monastery in 1874 with five grades. It closed

---

[56] Bulgaria, Department of Public Instruction, "Ot Otdela na Narodnoto Prosveshchenie i Dukhovnite Dela," Uchilishten Sbornik, p. 55.

[57] Dondukov-Korsakov, "Otchet," in Muratov, Dokumenti, pp. 120-121, 160-161.

in 1877 because of the outbreak of war. Church officials in the city of Samokov had also attempted to open a seminary and invited the first director of the Gabrovo gymnasium to help set up the institution. Neofit Rilski declined the invitation because he was too busy with other school-related work, and the project never materialized.[58]

The theological seminary opened by Drinov in 1878 had as its director Eustatius of Pelagonia, a former bishop of Bitolia. The initial enrollment was 43 students. Unfortunately, the school suffered student morale problems from its first year of existence and foundered. According to the director of the school, the students constantly rebelled because they did not like the food served, did not like to submit to discipline, and did not like to be awakened in the morning by bells like cattle.[59]

The other seminary, established in Liaskovets, also in 1878, fared much better. Prince Cherkasskii himself had attempted to reopen the school before his

---

[58]Tsonkov, Razvitie, pp. 180-182.

[59]Josef Konstantin Jireček, Bŭlgarski dnevnik, 1879-1884, trans. from Czech by Stoian Argirov, (Sofia: 1930), I, pp. 27ff.

death (in March, 1878), but the gift of 1,500 rubles he gave to the school for this purpose proved insufficient and was used instead for back pay to teachers.[60] When the school opened in 1878, it was with an enrollment of 76 students in a preparatory class. In searching for a director of the school, Drinov had consulted with Exarch Joseph, and both decided the position of Rector should be offered to the highly respected Vasil Drumev, whose clerical name and title was Clement, Metropolitan of Tŭrnovo (formerly Metropolitan of Branitsa). Vasil Drumev (1840-1901) was already an important figure in Bulgarian culture. He had received his education in theological seminaries of Odessa and Kiev and had been instrumental in establishing, along with Drinov, the Bulgarian Literary Society in Brăila, Romania, in 1869. In fact, he had served as president of the Society from 1869-1873, while editing its journal and teaching at the Bulgarian School of Brăila. He had also been active writing a novelette and a drama, as well as scholarly items. He was appointed Metropolitan of Tŭrnovo also in 1878 and, for this reason, attempted to refuse the position of Rector of the Liaskovets

---

[60] Stanimir Stanimirov, *Nashite dukhovni uchilishta* (Sofia: 1925, p. 5.

seminary. But after Drinov promised to find an assistant, he relented and served in this capacity until 1884.[61]

In opening all of these secondary schools, whether theological, classical, or technical, Drinov encountered a variety of problems, some of which have already been mentioned. But no problem was more severe than that of finding teachers of any kind, let alone well-qualified ones.

One of the areas in which the Bulgarian city and village communes had especially neglected their self-appointed duties was that involving the teachers. Thus, it is ironic that the same law (the Temporary Statutes) which had laid the financial burden of the schools on the communes had little to say about teachers in general, let alone commune-teacher relations in particular. The lot of the teacher in pre-1878 Bulgaria had never been a very secure, comfortable, or prestigious one. And this undesirable situation did not disappear magically

---

[61] Tsentralni Dŭrzhavni Istoricheski Arkhiv (TsDIA), F. 405 (Department of Public Instruction and Religious Affairs), op. 1, ae. 2; Vasil Drumev, "Autobiographical Notes," in BIA, F. 146 (Vasil Drumev), op. 1, ae. 1; Vasil Drumev, "Avtobiografichni belezhki," Dukhovna kultura, XXXI, 9-10 (11910), 2-10. See also Iurdan Trifonov, Vasil Drumev--Kliment Branitski i Tŭrnovski: zhivot, deinost' i kharakter (Sofia: 1926), pp. 5-69, 81-95ff.

with the establishment of an independent state. Abused
by the peasants and ridiculed by the chorbadzhi (local
notables), the teacher lived in poverty and the constant
need to search for a new position. This was especially
the case in many communes which hired their teachers
only from St. Demetrius' Day (October 26) to St.
George's Day (April 23), after which they were released.[62] The teachers were also often the victims of
the frequent and protracted political squabbles among
the various factions of the communes (for example, the
disputes between the esnafi or guilds and the chorbadzhi). Insufficient and infrequent pay exacerbated this
already unfortunate situation. It was no wonder that
with the rise of an administration and bureaucracy in
Bulgaria and its corresponding need for educated people,
the teachers saw the possibility of a more secure and
better-paid existence and flocked to the capital.[63]

---

[62] That these practices were still prevalent in Drinov's time is evident from the inspectors' reports collected in Nikola Ivan Vankov, Iz Arkhivata na Ministerstvoto na Narodna Prosveta (Sofia: 1905), especially pp. 83-85.

[63] Raicho Karolev, notes on policies of the Drinov administration, in ABAN, F. 62k (Raicho Karolev), op. 1, ae. 8. Karolev wrote at the top of this document, "Podgotovka na uchiteli i pedagogicheski uchilishta sled osvobozhdenieto." It was obviously research for his own policies when he was Minister of Public Instruction, 1884-1885.

This, in turn, depleted the reserves of available teachers for the schools.

The basic school law of the Drinov period, the Temporary Statute, addressed few of these problems effectively, if at all. Through these Statutes, Drinov provided that only persons who had completed study at a chief (i.e. four-class) school and who had a general knowledge of instructional method would be hired as teachers in the public schools. He left the financial management of school affairs in the hands of the communal school boards. These school boards, existing from the time of the struggle for the Exarchate in the 1860s, had traditionally managed the assets, income, and expenditures of community-supported schools. Unfortunately, they also mismanaged affairs, especially in matters concerning teachers' salaries. It was not unusual for teachers to go for long periods without pay. Aware of this, Drinov decided to strip the school boards temporarily of all responsiblity in respect to paying teachers. This power was invested instead, for the academic year 1878-1879, in special provincial school councils. The school boards also lost some privileges in the matter of hiring teachers.[64] From that point on,

---

[64] Bulgaria, Department of Public Instruction, "Privremenen ustav," Uchilishten sbornik, p. 17.

the provincial school inspectors (one for each of the five provinces) were also to assist in hiring teachers. Drinov directed the inspectors to consider the following questions when reviewing candidates for teaching positions: (1) Do they have a legal right to teach?; (2) Do they have the requisite moral qualities, ability, knowledge, etc.?; (3) Do they enjoy the esteem of students and society?; and (4) Are they paid sufficiently for their labor? The inspectors were further charged with weeding out the inexperienced teacher for counseling and with firing the unreliable or incorrigible ones.[65]

Considering the magnitude of the problem concerning the teachers, these provisions in the Temporary Statutes did not effectively deal with the situation. In fact, these brief remarks on the teacher situation noted above seem rather superficial. This is rather puzzling since Drinov was familiar with the general conditions in Bulgarian schools and since many of his top advisors had served as teachers themselves. There are, however, some possible explanations. First, Drinov may not have been sufficiently informed on the

---

[65] Ibid., p. 9.

continuation of the poor situation simply because the number of inspectors was entirely too few to carry out the duties entrusted to them. And although their number was increased to fifteen in May, 1879, many of their reports did not reach Sofia until after Drinov had left office; thus, his successors had to deal with these problems.[66] Second, the Department's policy of encouraging school openings unwittingly increased the shortage of teachers--the more schools opened, the greater the financial burden and the greater the need for teachers. It is quite possible, however, that Drinov was familiar with the situation only too well but decided to address the issues involving the teachers one by one, as they arose. In any event, the Department did indeed have to face the unpleasant realities at the end of the first academic year.

In a circular issued by Dondukov-Korsakov in March, 1879, the Provisional Government gave indication that reports were beginning to filter in on severe problems concerning the teachers in the community-supported schools. The matter eventually reached the attention of the Imperial Russian Commissioner.

---

[66] Dondukov-Korsakov, "Ob inspektsii narodnykh uchilishch," Uchilishten sbornik, p. 29.

Dondukov-Korsakov advised the governors of the provinces that according to information supplied him by Drinov and confirmed by an enquiry under the direction of General Gresser, the teachers in many of the public school had not received any pay whatsoever for several months. The Imperial Commissioner blamed the situation on local authorities and listed three measures to rectify the situation. First, the governors were to have the administrative councils of each province look into the budgets of the city councils in their provinces to see what provisions had been made for school aid. Second, where sums designated by a city council did not cover school expenses, the governor was to urge the community to levy a tax to provide the balance, according to the system outlined in the Temporary Statutes. Finally, city councils were henceforth to make sure that adequate amounts of money were set aside or provided for well in advance.[67]

Several months later, the Department of Public Instruction was forced to confront the whole problem once again. In another circular to the governors, Drinov cited a list of abuses of the teachers by the

---

[67] Dondukov-Korsakov, "Tsirkular ot Imperatorskii Ruski Komisar v Bŭlgariia do Gubernatorite," Uchilishten sbornik, p. 29.

communes, singling out the extremely low pay and the practice of hiring teachers only from St. Demetrius' to St. George's Day (October to April). He warned that given the many new careers opening up to bright young people, only poorly qualified ones would be willing to accept the high calling of a teacher with the low remuneration of the job. Such people, however many were available, would be of little use to the schools.[68] Drinov complained that the Department of Public Instruction had done its share, and now it was up to the communes to do something to alleviate the situation. He ordered that henceforth the teachers were to be engaged for an entire year and paid during the summer months, at which time the teachers would be obliged to attend pedagogical courses and special congresses. Teachers were to be paid with regularity and according to minimum pay scales.[69]

Drinov also acted to ameliorate the shortage of teachers by setting up temporary pedagogical courses to occur in the summer months. He had earlier dismissed the need for such courses by suggesting that the

---

[68]Bulgaria, Department of Public Instruction, "Tsirkular do Gubernatorite," *Uchilishten sbornik*, p. 41.

[69]*Ibid*.

secondary schools the Department was setting up would fill this need. Also, in order to correct the teacher-drain caused by the establishment of a bureaucracy, he entered into negotiations with some of the more outstanding former school teachers in the hopes of getting them to forsake their government jobs and return to teaching. Without listing names or figures, Drinov noted that many felt inclined to accept this proposal.[70] Nevertheless, these actions were not enough. One year later he found himself forced to reverse his position on pedagogical courses.

In June of 1879, the school inspectors were ordered to compile lists of all the inexperienced or poorly trained teachers in their respective districts, as well as of any one with an inclination towards becoming a teacher. These individuals would then be required to attend the new pedagogical courses. Henceforth, no one was to be given a teaching position who was unprepared for it. However, to provide an incentive, he added that all those who successfully passed the courses would be eligible for deferral from

---

[70] Dondukov-Korsakov, "Otchet," in Muratov, Dokumenti, I, p. 118.

mandatory military service.[71] Along with the circular came the Statute for the Temporary Pedagogical Courses. This statute gave the inspectors full authority over the operation of the courses, including the right to decide who had to attend and who did not. The course was divided into both theoretical and practical sessions, all to take place in the better-equipped city schools. Upon graduation from the course, each student would receive a certificate which henceforth would always be demanded before anyone was hired for a teaching position.[72]

Drinov's aim in establishing these pedagogical courses was twofold. He wanted to improve both the professional standards and the material condition of the teachers. The main focus of attention was on the village schools. Budget expenses for the project, according to Drinov, came from the money which the Imperial Commissioner had earmarked for study abroad and within Bulgaria.[73] In a further effort to improve

---

[71] Bulgaria, Department of Public Instruction, "Tsirkular po rabotata za pedagogicheskite kursove," Uchilishten sbornik, pp. 37-40.

[72] Ibid.

[73] Drinov, report to Alexander von Battenberg, F. 111 (Marin Drinov), op. 1, ae. 22.

the material position of the teachers, a sum of 50,000 leva was used to create a pension fund for poor and disabled teachers who had served at least 20 years and were either too old or too sick to continue their duties. A special provision allowed the funds to be used to help the survivors of teachers who had suffered at the hands of the Turks during the War of Liberation.[74]

The Department of Public Instruction's primary activities during its short term of operation centered around, but were not limited to, schools, teachers, and curricula formation. Certainly, the instructions to Dondukov-Korsakov at the beginning of his administration had very narrowly defined the activities of the educational department to setting up, and caring for, the schools. But Drinov did not hesitate to step outside that boundary. Important initiatives were made to set up a national library and museum and to rejuvenate the Bulgarian Literary Society of Brăila (Romania) in the hopes of eventually bringing it to Sofia.

While still serving as Vice Governor of Sofia, Drinov had enlisted the aid of his superior, Governor

---

[74]Ibid.; Bulgaria, Department of Public Instruction, "Tsirkular po rabotata za pedagogicheskite kursove," Uchilishten sbornik, p. 55.

Alabin, in collecting money and books which would serve as the nucleus of a state library. The Sofia library continued to occupy Drinov's attention after he became Director of Public Instruction. Drinov had become the president of a special library committee which, at a meeting in June of 1879, decided to ask the Provisional Administration to take the library (still a private institution) under its wing.[75] Dondukov-Korsakov issued orders to this effect in the same month. He set up a budget for the library and placed it on the register of the Department of Public Instruction. Drinov, in turn, named Georgi Kirkov (1828-1929) as the first official librarian and donated 42 of his own valuable books to the institution.[76]

Drinov similarly attempted to rejuvenate the Bulgarian Literary Society. Drinov had helped to establish the Society in Brăila, Romania, in 1869,

---

[75] Marin Drinov, correspondence concerning the National Library, BIA, F. 111 (Marin Drinov), op. 1, ae. 24; on the history of the National Library, see Raicho Raichev, "Narodnata biblioteka v Sofia," in Iubileina kniga na grad Sofia, 1878-1928 (Sofia: 1928), pp. 156-158ff., and Veliko Iordanov, Istoriia na narodnata biblioteka v Sofia (Sofia: 1930), pp. 19-26.

[76] Bulgaria, Department of Public Instruction, "Doklad," Uchilishten sbornik, pp. 56-57.

along with Vasil Drumev. The organization had lapsed into inactivity during the war years, and Drinov called a meeting of the organization in Brăila on November 28, 1878. Todor Ikonomov represented Drinov and the Department of Public Instruction at the convocation, which ended with a decision to transfer the Society to Sofia, along with all relevant libraries and archives.[77]

Two other important matters occupied the attention of Marin Drinov during his brief tenure of office in the Russian Provisional Administration, and both of these matters had significant importance for the future of Bulgarian education. One was his work on the project to establish a constitutional government in the country. The other was his efforts to bring a young Czech scholar, Josef Konstantin Jireček, to Bulgaria to assist in the work of arranging Bulgarian school affairs.

The Czech scholar in question, Josef K. Jireček, was one of the most important and fascinating figures in all of Eastern European historiography. He was born in Vienna on July 24, 1854, into an extraordinary family

---

[77] Ivan Snegarov, P. Miiatev, et al., eds., Dokumenti za istoriia na Bŭlgarskoto knizhovno druzhestvo v Brăila, 1878-1911 (Sofia: 1966), II, pp. 3-4; Drinov, report to Alexander von Battenberg, BIA, F. 111 (Marin Drinov), op. 1, ae. 22.

of scholar-politicians. His father was Josef Jireček, a noted Slavic scholar, and his mother was Bozhena Šafárikova, daughter of Pavel Josef Šafárik (1795-1861), one of the most important historians of the Czechs and Slovaks.[78] Jireček's father had held several high positions in the Austro Hungarian Empire, including the Ministry of Education. The Jireček household itself was a major center of Slavic scholarship, where Jireček's father, his uncle Hermengild, and his Šaráfik relatives maintained the library of Slavonica which would stir the imagination of the young man.[79]

Jireček received his early education in Austria and attended the noted Theresianum gymnasium in Vienna from 1864 to 1872. Upon graduation, he planned to attend the Charles University in Prague. Before leaving for Prague, he happened to make the acquaintance of several important Bulgarians, members of an ethnic group that would occupy much of his attention for the rest of his life. Vienna was an important center of

---

[78] Stoian Argirov, "Zhivot i deinost na Konstantin Irechek," (preface to) Jireček, Bŭlgarski dnevnik, I, pp. v-xii.

[79] Ibid.; for bibliography of sources on the life and activity of Jireček, see Petŭr Miiatev, ed., Iz Arkhiva na Konstantin Jireček (Sofia: 1953), I, p. 39.

trade and culture for a small Bulgarian colony located there, and two of the individuals he met were already quite important in Bulgarian circles. These were Vasil D. Stoianov (1839-1900) and Grigor Nachovich (1845-1920). Both would play important roles in the future Bulgarian state. At this time, they both encouraged Jireček's interest in Bulgarian studies.[80] In Prague, where Jireček enrolled in the faculty of philology with a concentration in history, he met even more Bulgarians. It was here that he met Marin Drinov, who was soliciting support in the city for the growing Bulgarian movement for independence.[81] Jireček's intense study of history and his work in reviewing books on Balkan affairs written by other Europeans impressed upon him the fact that one group of Balkan people was not very well known or understood, and that was the Bulgarians.[82]

---

[80] Jireček, letter to the Odessa Bulgarians, as cited by Vasil N. Zlatarski, in his introduction to Jireček's Istoriia na Bŭlgarite, trans. by A. Diamandiev and Ivan Raev (Sofia: 1929), p. xi.

[81] Vasil N. Zlatarski, "Deinostŭta na Dr. Konstantin Irechek v Bŭlgariia. Po sluchai na 50 godishninata mu," Periodichesko spisanie na Bŭlgarskoto knizhovno druzhestvo, LXVI (1905-1906), 6.

[82] Miiatev, Iz Arkhiva, p. 39; see also letter of Grigor Nachovich to Jireček, July 23, 1872, in Miiatev, Iz Arkhiva, I, p. 50.

Intrigued by his own lack of knowledge about the Bulgarians, Jireček began to collect, in 1872, materials for a bibliography on Bulgarian antiquities and four years later published, in Czech and German, a complete history of the Bulgarian people from ancient times to the beginning of the nineteenth century.[83] The publication of the first scholarly history of the Bulgarian people was an important political as well as cultural event for the Bulgarians, especially since their history was now available to Western Europeans in a major language.

Bulgarians were quick to realize the significance of Jireček's work, especially since its publication coincided with the first risings against the Turks. He was soon inundated with telegrams of congratulations and of gratitude, as well as with requests to act as a spokesman for the Bulgarian people. He also received offers to translate his study into Bulgarian from the Bulgarian Literary Society and from the Odessa colony of Bulgarians. The latter wanted the work to appear in Russian so that the Russians would know better the

---

[83] The Czech language version, Dějiny Národa Bulharského, appeared in the summer of 1875, while the German language version, Geschichte der Bulgaren, appeared in January, 1876. Jireček wrote both versions himself.

history of the people for whom they would be asked to shed their blood. A Russian translation appeared in 1878.[84]

One result of all of this effort by Jireček was a closer relationship with leading Bulgarians, but most of all with Marin Drinov. The two entered into a correspondence that subsequently became an important source for future historians. Drinov, in fact, had urged the Bulgarian Literary Society to publish Jireček's work in Bulgarian. He also had written to assure Jireček that his work would remain the most important history for a long time to come.[85]

In a letter to the Odessa Bulgarians, acknowledging their telegram of gratitude, Jireček remarked that all those turning their attention to Bulgaria because of the events of the April Uprising of 1876 would discover a diligent, industrious, education-loving people who only needed, for their greater prosperity, a better

---

[84] Zlatarski, introduction to Jireček, Istoriia, p. xii; Nikola Palauzov, letter to Jireček, August 25, 1877, in Miiatev, Iz Arkhiva, I, p. 130.

[85] Marin Drinov, letter to Jireček, November 14, 1876, in Miiatev, Iz Arkhiva, II, p. 131; Drinov, letter to Bulgarian Literary Society in Brăila, February, 1876, in Drinov, Sŭchineniia, III, pp. 234-246.

administration of their national affairs.[86] At least one Bulgarian, Marin Drinov, was convinced that one area of the country's affairs that especially needed good administration was that of education. Drinov was also convinced that given Jireček's intimate acquaintance with Bulgarian cultural needs and conditions, he was eminently qualified to assist in the arrangement of Bulgarian school affairs in the formative years of the nation's existence. Accordingly, Drinov had proposed to the Imperial Russian Commissioner, Prince Cherkasskii, as early as 1877, that Jireček should be invited to help set up the Department of Public Instruction.[87] The Imperial Commissioner, as well as the rest of the Chancery, agreed, and an invitation was extended to the young Czech through Konstantin Stoilov. Meanwhile, however, the Treaty of Berlin reduced the period of Russian occupation from two years to nine months.

---

[86] Jireček, letter to Odessa Bulgarians, in Zlatarski, introduction to Jireček, Istoriia, p. xii.

[87] Zlatarski, "Deinostŭta na Irechek," pp. 6-7; see also G. Todorov, "Obshtestveno-politicheskata deinost na prof. M. Drinov po vreme na osvobozhdenieto na Bŭlgariia ot tursko igo," in Izsledvaniia v chest na Marin Drinov, ed. by Aleksandŭr K. Burmov, Dimitŭr Angelov, and Ivan Duichev, (Sofia: 1960), pp. 52-55.

Both Jireček and Drinov deemed nine months insufficient guarantee of position, and the matter ended.[88]

Nevertheless, Drinov began a campaign to convince young and politically influential Bulgarians to invite Jireček to Bulgaria after the proclamation of an independent state when the Russian occupation ended. He solicited a promise to this effect from Konstantin Stoilov, the personal secretary to the newly elected Prince of Bulgaria, Alexander. Drinov had by this time decided to return to his teaching position in Kharkov for reasons of health, as well as a desire to return to his scholarly activity. He wished to ensure that the work of education and school affairs would be in capable hands.[89] In the spring of 1879, Jireček received a formal invitation, and negotiations began in earnest in the autumn. Jireček insisted on a contract to protect his right to return to his teaching position at Charles University and also to ensure leave for

---

[88] Jireček, letter to Marin Drinov, August 7, 1878, in Josef K. Jireček, Korespondentsiia s Marin Drincv, ed. by Vladimir Sis, (Sofia: 1924), p. 189. (Hereafter cited as Sis, Korespondentsiia). Zlatarski, "Deinostŭta na Irecheck," p. 6.

[89] Zlatarski, "Deinostŭta na Irecheck," p. 6; Todorov, "Obshtestveno-politicheskata deinost," p. 69; Cyril Black, The Establishment of Constitutional Government in Bulgaria, 1878-1885 (Princeton: 1934), p. 157.

research and travel.[90] Both of these desires were incorporated into the contract, as well as a special provision allowing him to accept a high position in the Bulgarian government yet remain a citizen of Austria-Hungary. He received the position of Executive Secretary in the Ministry of Public Instruction when the contract was promulgated by royal decree on November 1, 1879.[91] He received an annual salary of 10,000 leva, an investment that proved well made, considering the important role Jireček was to play in the Ministry of Public Instruction.

The other matter that occupied Drinov's attention during his stay in Bulgaria was the work to produce an administrative structure for the state that would come into existence when Russian forces left the country. The work of devising this structure had begun even before Russian troops entered Bulgaria. Cherkasskii, while Imperial Russian Commissioner in 1877, had ordered the compilation of information relating to Bulgarian affairs so that he and his advisers would be

---

[90] Jireček's contract is in his archives, ABAN, F. 3 (Jireček), op. 1, ae. 7-8. Zlatarski also published some of the provisions in "Deinostuta na Irechek," pp. 8-9.

[91] Miiatev, *Iz Arkhiva*, II, p. 35.

well-informed when it came time to fashion a governmental structure for Bulgaria.[92]

When Dondukov-Korsakov succeeded Cherkasskii upon the latter's death in March, 1878, he also began to study Bulgarian affairs and to search for a model for a constitution (Organic Statutes). His desire to select a model from a country similar to Bulgaria led him to believe the Serbian Constitution of 1869 would be an excellent guide to his own work of writing Organic Statutes for Bulgaria.[93] But before proceeding much further, Dondukov-Korsakov decided to solicit the advice of leading Bulgarian laymen and clergy. He devised a questionnaire in October, 1878, which requested their opinions as to what form the national assembly should take, what religion the royal family should profess, how elections should occur, etc.[94] Drinov was one of those who received the questionnaire, and

---

[92] Black, *Establishment of Constitutional Government*, pp. 52-53. The collected materials were published in five volumes in Bucharest in 1877 under the title *Materialy dliia izucheniia Bolgarii*.

[93] Black, *Establishment of Constitutional Government*, p. 59.

[94] The questionnaire was first published by Drinov in the journal *Grazhdanin*, I (1904), 346-363. The questions, as well as Drinov's replies, are also in his *Sŭchineniia*, III, pp. 178-185.

his replies were so thorough and scholarly that
Dondukov-Korsakov decided to incorporate many of Drinov's
suggestions into the Organic Statutes. Drinov, convinced that his fellow Bulgarians were not ready for
full parliamentary democracy, had suggested a trial
period of seven years for a national assembly. He proposed indirect rather than direct election of deputies
to the assembly and concluded that the first prince
elected could be of any faith, but that in the future,
the royal family would have to be Orthodox. Dondukov-Korsakov not only utilized these suggestions but also
put Drinov in charge of translating the Organic Statutes
into Bulgarian from the original Russian.[95]

Even as the work of translation began, elections
were held for an assembly of Bulgarian notables to
convene in the ancient capital of Tŭrnovo in February,
1879. That assembly, the Constituent Assembly, selected
a fifteen-member committee to consider the Organic
Statutes submitted by Dondukov-Korsakov. Drinov was
also instrumental in the work of the Tŭrnovo Constituent

---

[95] Drinov, "Izrabotvaneto na Bŭlgarskata Konstitutsiia. Neshto ot moite spomeni za tova delo i za moeto uchastie v nego," Sŭchineniia, III, pp. 164-175.

Assembly although he was not part of the fifteen-member Constitutional Committee.[96] Nevertheless, in a speech to the Tŭrnovo Assembly, he argued for primary education to be free, mandatory, and universal for all Bulgarian citizens. The Assembly was convinced by his pleas and adopted the proposal which became article 78 of the Tŭrnovo Constitution.[97]

The final form of the Organic Statutes as accepted by the Tŭrnovo Constituent Assembly in February, 1879, became known as the Tŭrnovo Constitution. The Tŭrnovo Constitution became almost instantly a focal point of political struggles between the fledgling political parties. It was important to Bulgarian educational affairs for several reasons. First, the Constitution marked the beginning of a new organ charged with educational affairs--the Ministry of Public Instruction.

---

[96] Ibid. Drinov's right to participate in the Assembly was challenged by some of deputies since he was a Russian subject, but he was granted special permission to participate by the Assembly.

[97] Zhecho Atanasov, "Prosvetnata deinost na Marin Drinov prez Vremennoto Rusko upravlenie," Godishnik na Sofiiski universitet; filosofsko-istoricheski fakultet, LI, 2 (1957), 63. All references to the Tŭrnovo Constitution will be to the official text as it appears in Bulgaria, Ministry of Justice, Godishen sbornik ot zakoni prieti ot Tŭrnovskoto Uchreditelno Narodno Sŭbranie prez 1879g (Sofia: 1887); article 78 appears on p. 13 of this text.

This organ, unlike the Department of Public Instruction which preceded it, would have to work within a parliamentary system of government. In the Bulgarian context, this served both to stabilize and to disrupt educational affairs and policies. Stabilization came in the form of clearer lines of authority and greater leeway for the government in systematizing Bulgarian education. Disruption came in the form of fighting among the different political factions over whether or not to support fully the provisions of the Tŭrnovo Constitution, especially the provisions which set up a National Assembly (<u>Narodno Sŭbranie</u>), complete with directly elected deputies and full legislative initiative. The Conservative Party did not, in general, believe the Bulgarian people were ready for such broad democratic provisions and responsibility, while the Liberals insisted the people had proved their ability to manage their own affairs during the long period of Turkish rule. The real crisis over the Tŭrnovo Constitution occurred in May, 1881. Prince Alexander von Battenberg had sided with the Conservative views, especially because the Tŭrnovo did not provide the extent of authority he believed a prince should have.[98] Also the Liberals insisted that the Prince should be kept to a very limited role in the country's affairs. Therefore, in May of 1881, Alexander I executed a coup d'état in which the Tŭrnovo Constitution was suspended. This touched off a furious opposition movement by Liberals and their supporters which disrupted the country's political affairs for several years. Governments rose and fell at an alarming rate to the extent that in the period of 1879 to 1885, there were eleven different Ministers of Public Instruction alone.[99] While some of these changes were

---

[98] The best sources on the political disputes from 1878-1885 are Simeon Radev, Stroitelite na sŭvremanna Bŭlgariia, 2 vol., (Sofia: 1973); Ilcho Dimitrov, Kniazŭt, konstitutsiiata, i narodŭt (Sofia: 1972). The best, and only, work in English is the Black volume, Establishment of Constitutional Government cited previously.

[99] The eleven men and their tenure of service were: Todor Burmov (July, 1879); Grigorii Atanasovich (July-October, 1879); Vasil Drumev (October, 1879-March, 1880); Ivan Giuzelev (March-November, 1880); Petko R. Slaveikov (November-December, 1880); Mikhail Sarafov (November, 1880-April, 1881); Josef K. Jireček (May, 1881-June, 1882); Georgi Teokharev (June, 1882-March, 1883); Dimitŭr Agura (March-September, 1883); Dimitŭr Mollov (September, 1883-June, 1884); Raicho Karolev (June, 1884-August, 1886). Biographical details and explanations as to how each one came to and left the office will be given as each Minister is mentioned in the text. Also Chapter Eight presents a survey of the personal impact of the more important Ministers of Public Instruction.

due simply to reshuffling of portfolios in the various cabinets, most were caused by political infighting. (The effect of this will be discussed in later chapters.)

The Tŭrnovo Constitution was important for two other reasons in regard to educational affairs. One of these, of course, was the inclusion of the provision calling for universal mandatory primary education for all citizens of the Principality. This item would present the new Ministry with a great challenge but would also be used by some deputies in the Sŭbranie to criticize the Ministry for its failure to achieve headway in attaining the goal. The other important consequence of the Tŭrnovo Constitution was that the Ministry charged with educational affairs emerged more streamlined than the Department of Public Instruction had been under the Russian Provisional Government. Drinov's Department had also been responsible for religious affairs. However, by the provisions of the Tŭrnovo Constitution, these duties (i.e. religious affairs) were placed in the hands of the Minister of Foreign Affairs and Religions.[100] This had the effect of freeing the Ministry of Public Instruction from entanglement in the

---

[100] Article 42 and article 161 of the Tŭrnovo Constitution, Bulgaria, Ministry of Justice, Godishen sbornik, pp. 7,23.

thorny religious problems that would eventually spring up in the transition from Ottoman control to Bulgarian control. This provision also made the Ministry of Foreign Affairs and Religions responsible for the school affairs of the religious minorities such as the Jews, Moslems, Catholics, and Protestants.[101]

Besides these three general impacts on educational affairs, the Tŭrnovo Constitution had a few specific provisions that directly affected the work of the Ministers of Public Instruction. One of these was article 65, which limited all state, provincial, and communal (municipal) positions to Bulgarian subjects. This caused difficulties not only for the Ministry of Public Instruction but for all government agencies since the shortage of native trained personnel necessitated importing foreigners to fill administrative positions. However, another article (number 66) allowed foreigners to accept positions, but in each and every instance, the approval of the Sŭbranie had to be obtained.[102]

Another important specific provision was the establishment of the Ministerial Council, an organ of

---

[101] Ibid., p. 7.

[102] Ibid., articles 65 and 66, p. 10.

government which shared power with the Prince. All of the Ministers belonged to the Council, and all had the right to summon it into session. Each act of legislation had to be approved by the Ministerial Council. The decisions of the Ministerial Council were, in fact, resolutions issued on the authority of a legislative act and in execution of the provisions of such an act.[103] The Ministers of Public Instruction would work closely with this organ of government especially in matters concerning the spending of special funds in the budget of the Ministry of Public Instruction.

The Tŭrnovo Constitution left it up to each Ministry to define its internal order and structure. Most of the ministries did compose and publish their respective internal statutes, but the Ministry of Public Instruction never did so.[104] However, the records of the Ministry do indicate that it followed the same structural organization as in other ministries. In

---

[103] Ivan Sipkov, Legal Sources and Bibliography of Bulgaria (New York: 1956), p. 16. All Bulgarian legal terms will be translated into English according to the suggestions of Sipkov in this work.

[104] All of the other ministries published their internal statutes in the Dŭrzhaven vestnik. There is no record of any such statute being published for the Ministry of Public Instruction either in the Dŭrzhaven vestnik or in the Ministry's own gazette, Ucheben vestnik.

other words, it had an Executive Secretary, a Section Chief, Archivist, aides, etc. Each of these officers had specific duties. Those duties can fortunately be described to some extent because of a memorandum written by Jireček (Executive Secretary of the Ministry) in June, 1880. This memorandum was entitled "A Statute for the Internal Organization of the Ministry of Public Instruction" and was Jireček's proposal to that effect.[105] While it cannot be ascertained that this project ever became the actual statute (since no record exists of it being used), the memorandum gives a clear impression of the kinds of duties that might have been expected of each of the officers of the Ministry.

Jireček was extremely brief in describing the duties of the Minister. The memorandum stated simply that the Minister possessed full and final authority in the administration of all the affairs of the department. All letters, whether incoming or outgoing (with the exception of those dealing with insignificant matters) were to pass through the Minister's hands.[106]

---

[105] Jireček, "Pravilnik za vŭtreshnata organizatsiia na Ministerstvoto na Narodnoto Prosveshtenie," ABAN, F. 3 (Jireček), op. 1, ae. 1125, pp. 1-2.

[106] Ibid., p. 1.

The duties of the Executive Secretary (Jireček's own position) were enumerated in much greater detail. The Executive Secretary, according to Jireček's plan, would replace the Minister in the latter's absence, verify and initial all incoming and outgoing letters, maintain up-to-date lists of the Ministry's personnel, and administer any scientific enterprises in the Principality. This official also supervised the affairs of the national library and museum and activities for the preservation of antiquities. He had a role in the appearance of scientific publications and in the compilation of programs, regulations, and circular letters issuing from the Ministry. The scope of the responsibilities of the Executive Secretary, claimed Jireček, should also have included the submission of the Secretary's opinion, in writing if possible, on various school questions, the supervision of teaching materials and aids, the control of those governmental stipendists who were studying abroad, and the annual (if not more frequent) personal inspection of all governmental schools in the Principality. Finally, the Executive Secretary was to supervise the archives of the Ministry and, according to the notes in the margin of Jireček's memorandum, to supervise the acquisition by the library of the Ministry of all textbooks, various pedagogical works, and journals.[107]

Jireček's scanty attention to the position of Minister was significant considering the enormously important role he was to play in the Ministry under the first several Ministers. Jireček was Executive Secretary at the time and may have been most concerned with describing his own responsibilities as well as those of his subordinates. Another possible explanation for the brevity of the description of the Minister's office, of course, was that since the Minister possessed full and final authority, little else needed to be said.

After the Executive Secretary's position, the memorandum went on to outline the duties to be performed by the Section Chief (Nachalnik na otdelenieto). This officer opened and dated all incoming correspondence. He then was to indicate in writing his decision regarding any action to be taken on a particular matter and pass the letter on to the Executive Secretary or the Minister. In very important matters, however, the Section Chief would leave this decision-making process to his superiors. After a resolution had been proposed and approved, the Section Chief was expected to

---

[107] Ibid.

implement and enforce the decision. He was also expected to draft advisory memoranda to the Executive Secretary and the Minister and to sign the final copy (either alone or in addition to his superiors). The Section Chief was also given major responsibility for the Ministry's finances.[108]

To the Archivist of the Ministry of Public Instruction were delegated the tasks of registering all incoming letters, forwarding them to the Executive Secretary, and filing them after appropriate action had been taken. His duties also included maintaining a catalog of affairs and recording all outgoing papers. The copyists of the Ministry also worked under his direct supervision. (So meticulous was Jireček's description of this position that he even included a detailed set of instructions on the manner in which correspondence and other papers were to be folded.)[109]

Lastly, Jireček detailed the duties of the two Chief Inspectors. These individuals were to make inventories of all educational establishments and districts during the summers and report to the Minister on their findings. The Inspectors were also expected to

---

[108] Ibid., p. 2.

[109] Ibid.

give their opinions on textbooks and on educational equipment submitted to the Ministry, as well as to supervise the preparation of new textbooks and to discuss the merits and faults of various ministerial programs. This discussion, suggested Jireček, would occur within a five-member council composed of the two Chief Inspectors, the Executive Secretary, the Section Chief, and the Minister. The council was to meet no more than three times a week.[110] Despite these elaborate provisions for the Chief Inspectors, there is no evidence from any source that these two offices were, in fact, ever filled. In budget hearings in the Sŭbranie for 1880, the Minister of Public Instruction at the time, Ivan Giuzelev, mentioned the offices and defended attempts to eliminate them as unnecessary. The items were kept in the budget but evidently never filled. The offices disappeared without notice or fanfare somewhere between 1880 and 1883. The offices of Chief Inspector never appear in any reports, documents, or further budgets of the Ministry.[111]

---

[110] Ibid.

[111] Bulgaria, Narodno Sŭbranie, Stenograficheski dnevnitsi na II-oto Obiknoveno Narodno sŭbranie, pŭrva redovna sesiia, session of May 31, 1880, p. 672.

The central organ of the Ministry also had its share of lower functionaries and secretaries, but Jireček did not define these jobs. Except for the offices of the Chief Inspectors, the apparatus described by Jireček remained basically unchanged until 1883, when a School Council was added.

Whether or not the officials of the central organ of the Ministry of Public Instruction performed their duties exactly as outlined in Jireček's draft for an internal statute, the structure he described did exist from the very first months of the Ministry's existence in 1879. The first government of the Bulgarian Principality was installed on July 5, 1879, with Todor Burmov, the publicist and diplomat, becoming the first Prime Minister. Most of the members belonged to the Conservative faction, causing immense disappointment to the Liberals who immediately worked to reverse Alexander's decisions.[112] Burmov also held the portfolio of Public Instruction until that was turned over to Doctor Georgi Atanasovich (1821-1892) on July 26, 1879. Atanasovich was a native of Svishtov, where he

---

[112] Marko D. Balabanov, "Todor S. Burmov," Letopis na Bŭlgarskoto knizhovno druzhestvo, VII (1906), 84-119; T. N. Boichev, Iubileina istoriia na 25 godishninata Bŭlgariia (Sofia: 1903), p. 220; Radev, Stroitelite, I, p. 163.

had received his primary education. He finished his
secondary education in Athens, then went on to Paris to
study medicine. He practiced medicine in Bucharest and
taught the subject at the university in Bucharest from
1852 to 1878. In the meantime, he used his money and
influence to help arrange school affairs back in his
native Svishtov. In 1878, he was summoned to Bulgaria
to help arrange the first government and accepted the
Ministry of Public Instruction in July, 1879. He left
the position in October, 1879, when the government of
Burmov was dismissed by Prince Alexander I, and
Metropolitan Clement of Tŭrnovo was installed as Prime
Minister and Minister of Public Instruction until new
elections could be arranged. Atanasovich did not
accomplish anything during his brief term of office
because of the intense political infighting caused by
the Liberals' dismay that they had not held enough
offices in the country's very first government.[113]

Marin Drinov had been offered the position of
being the country's first Minister of Public Instruction,
but he had declined the post. He had given up an

---

[113] N. R. Ovsianyi, Bolgariia i Bolgari (St.
Petersburg: 1900), p. 70; Georgi Khristov, Svishtov v
minaloto (Svishtov: 1927), pp. 221-225; Radev,
Stroitelite, I, p. 163.

excellent teaching position in Kharkov University and longed to return to his research, which he did in July, 1879. When Jireček informed him that certain newspapers in Europe claimed that Drinov was fleeing Bulgaria to get away from the political struggles that were then beginning between Prince Alexander I and the Liberals, Drinov denied the rumors.[114] He informed Jireček that he was eager to return to his teaching and research, but also he was worn out from the intense and sometimes frantic efforts to set up a government within the nine months stipulated for the Russian occupation by the Treaty of Berlin.[115] Whatever the reason for his leaving, Drinov's departure and the beginning of a constitutional government signalled a new era for Bulgarian educational affairs. Drinov had not managed to deal adequately with every problem that had confronted him during the nine months he held office. The worsening state of communal school finances was one example of problems left unsolved. But Drinov had prepared the outlines, if not the actual foundation, on

---

[114] Jireček, letter to Marin Drinov, June 25, 1879, (N.S.), in Sis, Korespondentsiia, p. 199.

[115] Drinov, letter to Josef K. Jireček, May 28, 1879, in Miiatev, Iz Arkhiva, II, pp. 145-146; also, Todorov, "Obshtestveno-politicheskata deinost,", p. 69.

which the work of a constitutional Ministry of Public Instruction in the independent Principality could begin.

CHAPTER THREE

FIRST CONCERNS OF THE NEW MINISTRY

Rebuilding the Communal School System

Many of the problems confronting the newly organized Ministry of Public Instruction were in fact very similar to those which had troubled the Department of Public Instruction under Marin Drinov. But the new Ministry was now acting in a permanent capacity and within the framework of parliamentary politics.

Three especially urgent concerns confronted the new Ministry and constitute the subject of this particular chapter. These concerns were: (1) the problem of the publicly supported schools (the community schools), (2) the problem of the severe teacher shortage and the poor training of those teachers who were available, and (3) a need for graduates with secondary and higher education in the face of student poverty and inability to attend even the free schools. These were not the only problems facing the Ministry in these first several years of the 1880-1885 period. Difficulties also arose in matters of student discipline, housing, personnel problems, equipment and supplies, etc. But the three problems of community schools, teacher shortages, and student financial aid occupied a disproportionate amount of the Ministry's attention in the first years of its existence.[1]

The first problem, concerning the publicly supported schools, revolved around financial difficulties. An increasing number of communities found themselves unable to support their local school or schools as they had done in the past. Partly this was due to the destruction and financial losses caused by the war. It was also due, however, to the new responsibilities shouldered by the communities with the coming of independence. They now had legal obligations to provide a broader range of municipal services (telegraph, roads, hospitals) than ever before. Another potential aspect of this issue was that of centralization of school control in the hands of the Ministry, an eventuality that neither the Ministry nor the local officials especially cared to see materialize.

Up to 1878 and for a while beyond this date, the Bulgarian communities employed several methods of school

---

[1] These other problems, as well as more important issues that arose later, will be discussed in appropriate places in other sections of this thesis.

financing, some being quite unusual. Rare was the community that employed just one system of school financing, rather most of the communities had to use a combination of means. For all of the communities, the income from Church sources was of major importance. The most important and most commonly used sources of school financing can be divided into the following categories:

1. contributions from churches
2. tax on the sale of cattle (<u>intizap</u>)
3. real estate holdings
4. voluntary contributions
5. special taxes (on bridges, roads, etc.)

The most important source up to 1878 came directly and indirectly from the Church. First, many of the schools, whether public or private, were located in Church-owned buildings or courtyards, thus defraying the costs of real estate rental or purchase. Second, outright financial contributions, mostly emanating from plate-passing at Church services, covered many other expenses. Unfortunately, accurate records of the actual percentages of the school budgets coming from Church sources are nonexistent.[2] But evidence of how crucial

---

[2] The sources that do exist are very sketchy. These include school budgets for specific communities, reports of school inspectors on financial conditions in

church support really was can be seen from several sources. First the Instructions for the Provincial School Inspectors of 1881 mentioned this source in the following manner:

> Before the war, the schools were mostly supported by the churches, and since the teachers were remunerated, in general, with extremely low pay, these revenues were completely sufficient in many places to maintain the schools. After the war, these revenues again furnished significant sums for the existence of the schools, even in the face of higher prices. But recently steps have been taken to resolve the question of what part of these resources will go to the schools (of course, they /now/ exceed the limits of the churches' resources). As soon as the question is resolved, instructions will be issued to the inspectors by the Ministry.[3]

A special study of school financing by Jireček, then Executive Secretary of the Ministry of Public Instruction, to the Minister at the time, Metropolitan Clement, cited Church support as being the most crucial factor up until 1878.[4] After 1878, when the

---

villages applying for aid, church histories (such as those by Stanimir Stanimirov). All of these sources will be cited in this chapter and will be listed in the bibliography.

[3] Bulgaria, Ministry of Public Instruction, "Instruktsiia za Okrŭzhnite Uchilishtni Inspektori," (1880), Dŭrzhaven vestnik, III, 13-15, 17-19 (1881).

[4] Jireček, "Zapiska za naredbata na narodnite uchilishta v Bŭlgariia," (March, 1880), ABAN, F. 3 (Jireček), op. 1, ae. 1125, pp. 4-6.

communities began to inundate the Ministry of Public Instruction with pleas for aid, one of the most frequently cited reasons for insolvency was the inability of the Church to contribute its former share to local school needs. These needs, in turn, were rapidly burgeoning due the Ministry of Public Instruction's own policies urging expansion of existing facilities and the contruction of new ones.[5]

Another widespread method of school financing was through a tax on the sale of cattle. This tax was called *intizap*, from the Turkish. Some school systems, such as those in Dobrich, financed their schools entirely from this system.[6] Needless to say, this system was most popular in areas where major bazaars or marketplaces were located, such as Samokov, Tŭrnovo, and Gorna Oriakhovitsa.[7]

Many communities had to resort to other systems of local school financing. The system of holding real

---

[5] Jireček, *Glavno izlozhenie*, p. 14.

[6] Bulgaria, Ministry of Public Instruction, School Council, "Izvlechenie ot zasedaniiata na Uchebniiat Sŭvet," *Ucheben vestnik*, III (July, 1883), 45; Vasilev, *Ucheben sŭvet*, p. 45.

[7] Bulgaria, State Council, session of August 24, 1883, TsDIA, F. 708 (State Council), op. 1, ae. 559.

estate for the use of, or in the name of, local schools was fairly common, but took several different forms. In some cases, plots of land usually under cultivation, were earmarked for the use of the schools. That is, all the grain or hay or other crop grown on this particular land would be sold, with the profit from the sale going to the schools. Sometimes a pasture was rented out or a fee charged for its usage, and the proceeds were turned over to the schools, such as in Nikopol.[8] However common the system of real estate, it is true that it was much more widespread in the eastern section of the Principality, where economic and agricultural life was more developed than in the western part.[9] It was no accident that in the eastern half of the country, especially around Shumen, Gabrovo, and Tŭrnovo, educational affairs were more developed and more widespread. For example, in the Vrachansk province and the Oriakhovsk province, both in the western part, no real estate at all was held for the schools. In the province

---

[8] Bulgaria, State Council, session of June 5, 1882, TsDIA, F. 708 (State Council), op. 1, ae. 260. After the war, disputes and confusion arose over the ownership of abandoned Turkish lands, much of which was confiscated by the State. Some communities eventually sued the government to regain usufruct that had existed under the Turks.

[9] Jireček, Glavno izlozhenie, p. 15.

of Vidin, in the northwestern part, only about five acres of fields were set aside for the schools.[10]

In some cases, these real estate holdings were the results of bequests by prominent wealthy citizens and were specifically designated for the use of the schools in a particular locale. The most famous example of this is the Gabrovo gymnasium and school system which were aided by the gifts of Aprilov. Thus the fourth major source of school financing was voluntary contributions from private citizens. Sometimes this took the form of voluntary taxation. In only a few cases, such as Gabrovo, did this form of school support furnish the major share of the community's educational expenses.

Other sources of private and non-Church donations were the guilds (esnafi), the local notables (chorbadzhi), and merchants abroad mostly in Odessa or Romania. The organization and collection of private, as opposed to Church, funds gained prominence during the period in which Bulgarian education became more and more secularized. Ironically, this system became even more widespread after the successful completion of the struggle for a national Church, when local self-governing bodies (nastoiatelstva) were set up. These local self-governing

---

[10] Ibid.

units eventually set the pattern for the later school board (uchilishteno nastoiatelstvo) which administered the various financial resources of the local schools as well as the local schools themselves. In fact, the local school boards eventually began to solicit funds from the various sources.[11]

Alongside the more common means of school financing just described, a few communities adopted somewhat more unusual techniques. The city of Samokov at various times levied a tax on vehicles and animals crossing the bridge over the Iskŭr River, the money going to the schools. A suburb of the same city used a tax on a local fountain for support of its school.[12]

Finally, besides these various types of school financing, some schools used a head tax on each child attending the school. This custom was actually carried over from the cell schools which had always charged a slight fee for lessons. However, arrangements were often made to accommodate children from poor families.

---

[11] See Khristo Khristov's excellent work for a discussion of the development of the "Church-school" boards, Khristov, Bŭlgarskite obshtini.

[12] Samokov, City-Communal Administration, ODA, F. 41K (City of Samokov), op. 1, ae. 523, p. 42

All of the above-described systems worked moderately well up until 1878 and had allowed an impressive number of communities to support local schools. But the war and the new economic and political situation existing after independence caused a breakdown in this pattern of self-sufficiency. The Ministry found itself flooded with petitions from these local communities asking for partial or total support for their schools. This flood of requests and what to do about them was one of the chief headaches of the Ministers of Public Instruction after 1880. There were several reasons for the breakdowns in local school financing.

Some of the causes of financial difficulties were beyond the control of the communities or the Ministry of Public Instruction. However, some of the causes were, in a sense, man-made in that they were the result of new political and social realities.

The sheer destructiveness of the war of liberation was the most immediate and most important reason for the financial problems confronting community schools. The destruction was widespread and severe both to school and Church property.[13] This was a double blow because not

---

[13] The best (and most official) account of the destruction caused by the war is Dondukov-Korsakov's in Muratov, *Dokumenti*, pp. 106-169.

only was real estate itself damaged, but also an institution that had been a traditional source of support--the Church. For the many poor communities that had built a school, however, humble, and staffed it with one or two teachers, however poorly trained, this was fatal to the continued existence or operation of such schools. It was the single most predominant factor cited by the communities that appealed to the Ministry of Public Instruction for assistance. A typical request was that made in a petition from the citizens of Panagiurishte to the Ministry of Public Instruction in August, 1883:

> From the voluntary contributions of our industrious but still impoverished citizens we have undertaken to build once again the burned-out school and with God's blessing have, in fact, already begun; however, we have no means whatsoever /now/ to finish alone the work on the school, since our inhabitants still have not recovered from the end of the recent war....[14]

This request is very similar to hundreds of others filed with the Ministry between 1880 and 1885.

The problem of rebuilding was exacerbated by soaring costs for building materials and construction workers, both of which were not only in scarce supply but also in great demand.

---

[14] Bulgaria, State Council, session of August 24, 1883, TsDIA, F. 708 (State Council), op. 1, ae. 559.

Rising costs and damage to property were not the sole factors hindering the communities' continued successful financing of schools. The communities now had to face new pressures owing to the existence of a national central government. New laws, passed by the government, defined a precise list of duties for the communities, duties ranging from road maintenance and militia recruitment, to more traditional services such as support of schools and orphanages. Ironically, the Ministry of Public Instruction helped add to the burden by its efforts to improve teacher pay and the conditions of the school buildings, and especially by its efforts to promote the goal of compulsory, universal elementary education. These goals, despite their admirable intent, presented many of the poorer or wartorn communities with staggering obligations, which they were ill-prepared to meet.

Even many previously well-ordered communities began to find their resources stretched to the breaking point. Gabrovo, for example, found its famous system of trust funds weakened by inflation and rising costs. Tŭrnovo's three-grade mens gymnasium had been supported by a combination of funds from Church, esnafi, school taxes, real estate holdings and trust funds. But now these were not enough, and the levy on each student (i.e. the head tax or tuition) had to be raised.[15]

Finally, some communities actually compounded the already poor conditions by going overboard in their zeal to establish or to improve educational facilities. Some school boards, such as that of Gabrovo, added new grades or embarked on ambitious new construction programs, without adequate planning. Again, this may have been the result of the Ministry's own exhortations to the communities in favor of rapid development and expansion of primary and secondary education--especially in the rural areas. Jireček had made it an important function of the school inspectors to urge the communities to build more schools. Later ministers continued this trend, such as Minister Dimitŭr Agura, who in 1883 issued a circular letter reminding the inspectors of the government's continued desire to expand the public schools. "The desired goal," explained Agura, "is for our communities, a large part of which were badly hurt in the last war and are still poor to be able to put

---

[15] Gabrovo, City-Communal Administration, "Protokoli na zasedaniiata na Gabrovskoto gradsko-obshtinsko upravlenie," sessions of February 3 and November 10, 1881, ODA, F. 5 (Gabrovo), op. 1, ae. 49, pp. 58-59, 74-75.

themselves in order and to construct the most needed buildings for the communal schools. The mandatory education prescribed by the Constitution is unfeasible without this condition."[16]

The result of this policy was a vicious circle in which the Ministry urged people to build and to maintain more and more schools, stressing the need of education for the progress of the new Bulgarian state. The communities responded, but found they could not support the undertaking, once begun, and turned to the Ministry of Public Instruction to bail them out of these worthy but unaffordable schemes.

The consequent flood of requests were all very much like this one from the village of Staropatitsa, (Kulska county), relayed by the Ministry of Public Instruction to the State Council in April, 1883:

> Having become aware of the great need of a new school building in the village of Staropatitsa, (Kulska county), the community there, with the consent of the school board, decided to proceed quickly with the construction of a new building which will cost around 6,000 leva total. The community alone, however, is not able to

---

[16] Dimitŭr Agura, Circular Letter no. 697 of March 28, 1883, Ucheben vestnik, I, 1-4 (1883), 148-149; Georgi Teokharev, "Zapiska na Ministerstvoto na Narodnata Prosveshchenie vŭrkhu nineshnoto polozhenie na uchebnoto delo v Bŭlgarskoto kniazhestvo," Ucheben vestnik, I, 1-4 (1883), 18-30.

/contribute/ to that goal of more than 3,000 leva and therefore petitions the Ministry of Public Instruction, through the Vidin provincial inspector, to grant it the necessary sum of 3,000 leva.[17]

This predicament was described by many other communities in hundreds of such letters to the Ministry of Public Instruction.

Eventually the Ministry had to confront the problem seriously because the petitions caused an enormous demand on its time, money, and personnel. The increasing difficulties of the community schools raised the specter of centralization of all schools under the control of the Ministry of Public Instruction, which was opposed by all of the Ministers in this early period for financial and philosophical reasons.

Centralization was raised by the first man to analyze thoroughly the entire problem of local school financing, Jireček. In 1880, at the request of the Minister of Public Instruction, Metropolitan Clement, Jireček drew up a detailed analysis of the situation along with a range of possible solutions. This document entitled "Notes" is of critical importance because many of the suggestions of the Czech scholar were eventually made law.

---

[17] Bulgaria, State Council, session of April 29, 1883, TsDIA, f. 708 (State Council), op. 1, ae. 382.

Jireček began his brief with the observation, "There is no question that it is extremely necessary that the material support of the schools be assured and the teacher be freed from his present uncertain and indefinite position, which in no way corresponds to the new condition of things in liberated Bulgaria."[18] In other words, such conditions were unacceptable in a country embarking on a course towards efficiency and modernization.

Jireček labeled the failure of the communities to support their schools as sad, but in the very next sentence, he defended them by pointing out that "in general the rights and duties of communities and of the [provincial] councils are not firmly defined."[19] The Bulgarian community was not as well-defined an administrative unit as in other countries, and many of the lines of authority between mayors, clerks, courts, and councils were still unclear. In some cases there were no precise guidelines on the authority of some of these units.[20] Obviously, he was hinting at the need to shore

---

[18] Jireček, "Zapiska," ABAN, F. 3 (Jireček), op. 1, ae. 1125, p. 6.

[19] Ibid., p. 5.

[20] Ibid., p. 5.

up the communities by writing detailed regulations for the local organs of government.

Also Jireček expressed his concern for the unevenness of development across the country. This was a point he raised several times both in this memorandum and in his <u>Glavno izlozhenie</u>. In the memorandum to Clement, he traced the history of public support for local schools but pointed out that: "Progress or lack of it depended on the material condition of its commune and the attention which was paid to the training of its children."[21] The problem was that the western half of the nation was not only materially less prosperous, but as Jireček pointed out in his <u>Glavno izlozhenie</u>, the regions were also characterized by different attitudes. These attitudes reflected the historical experiences of the two regions. The western part was primarily agricultural, and education was deemed of little use. The eastern part, however, had been a crossroads of trade between Central Europe, Russia, and the Near East. The Black Sea ports were especially important mercantile centers, and their influence had been felt far inland. Education was vitally important in commercial affairs, and this had ramifications in the present time. Jireček

---

[21] <u>Ibid.</u>, p. 4.

observed:

> The eastern half of the Principality is different in attitude from the western half. There, educational affairs are completely rooted, and a school is considered a necessity in each village. There, the people thought of their children's education without much urging, concerned themselves with the welfare of the schools, and were overjoyed with their success.[22]

How could Bulgaria stabilize local school finances and overcome the geographical discrepancies? Jireček examined some of the foreign system of public schools for a possible answer. The centralized system of local school support employed in Serbia, Bulgaria's neighbor, was considered but dismissed as an inherently undesirable way of supporting schools. Jirecek was referring to an 1855 law in Serbia which terminated all current school taxes and substituted a uniform levy out of which a fund was established for schools, teachers, and so on. Jireček disliked this system because it bureaucratized teachers and the communities lost all their rights in school affairs but kept all their duties.[23] The result was a loss of public interest in local school affairs.

---

[22] Jireček, Glavno izlozhenie, p. 14.

[23] Jireček, "Zapiska," ABAN, F. 3 (Jireček), op. 1, ae. 1125, p. 7.

Jireček advised against such a system but realized that some amount of government control or supervision might be necessary. But the most free and progressive arrangement, thought Jireček, was one where the schools remained purely "communal" (i.e. in every sense of the word), supported by the communities with the help of a communal tax and where the government had only minor control. He recognized that this system often depended on the good will of the commune and on the rise or fall of local commerce. But these defects could be overcome by adding or providing for special school aids to supplement the communal tax, such as: (1) Church property, if the school and Church works were united (Church lands or houses, votive candles, etc.) and (2) special school real estate designated by the community or private persons (fields, houses, taverns, shops, etc.). This method, claimed Jireček, was strongest and healthiest because the schools did not exist on the basis of a changeable or voluntary collection but on certain capital. Jireček pointed out that he believed this system was largely responsible for the flowering of school affairs in England, Switzerland, America, Germany, and Greece. Most importantly, however, this system was already being introduced in Gabrovo, Vratsa, Svishtov, and other cities, so evidence existed that it could work in Bulgaria.[24]

What Jireček did not say in his report to the Ministry of Public Instruction was that the Ministry had already been urging the establishment of permanent real estate holdings among the communities. This did come out in the Glavno izlozhenie (published in 1882), where he mentioned the Ministry's efforts to encourage the establishment of real estate in the schools' names. But, again, the most progress was made in the east, where positive attitudes toward education prevailed. A special problem, claimed Jireček, was that of the small hamlets where there was much deserted and unworked space. This, however, would be eliminated slowly as the population grew and as popular wealth rose in value.[25]

Besides this proposal to Clement, however, Jireček was also instrumental in facilitating the passage of a law on communities. Evidence exists to suggest that Jireček even helped write this law which was passed in

---

[24] Ibid., pp. 6-9; Jireček, Glavno izlozhenie, p. 15. Jireček's sweeping generalizations were not always correct, of course. His inclusion of America is especially curious in that his information on the American system of education was vague at best.

[25] Jirecek, Glavno izlozhenie, p. 15.

1881. (A temporary law on communities had already been issued in August, 1879, to combat abuses of power, arbitrariness, and confusion by local officials.)[26]

Many of the proposals advanced by Jireček found themselves formulated into law soon afterwards or under various ministers between 1880 and 1885. Jireček was not the only one who dealt with these problems or proposed solutions, although he did more than anyone else. Soon after his proposal, the Ministry of Public Instruction embarked on a series of actions to shore up the local school financing system. It became official policy to encourage the communities to set aside real estate from which the proceeds would be used to fund the local schools. This method of stabilizing the situation received vigorous endorsement through laws which defined the duties of the communities more succinctly.

An important admission of guilt by the Ministry of Public Instruction was made in the Instructions for the Provincial School Inspectors, in article III entitled "Extension and Opening of the Schools."[27] The Ministry

---

[26] Dŭrzhaven vestnik, I, 4 (1879), 1.

[27] Bulgaria, Ministry of Public Instruction, "Instruktsii za Okrŭzhni Uchilishtni Inspektori," Dŭrzhaven vestnik, III, 14 (1881), 108.

admitted in so many words that a reckless quest for overnight achievement of compulsory, universal primary education might prove disastrous. Thus a critical policy was laid down when the Ministry of Public Instruction stated that:

> By law, every community and every inhabited area must have a primary school, but practical application of this regulation depends on various local conditions, and the desired goal can be reached only after many years. For now, school progress must be oriented to the goal of having one well-constructed school with good teachers in every small area (of, for example, one square mile), with this network of schools to be expanded each year.[28]

While this was still rather an ambitious goal, these specifications provided at least a more reasonable yardstick for school growth.

The section on school finances was equally realistic and flexible. It actually suggested, rather than mandated, various methods of school financing, as long as whatever means used would provide adequate and certain year-round support. Recognition was made as well of local customs such as the harvest tithe.

---

[28] Ibid. Jireček or an editor used the expression one square mile (edna kvadratna milia) for the designated area. There is no question that the term was used incorrectly or without understanding how small such a unit actually is. It may be, perhaps, that he meant per heavily inhabited area, but that is not a valid deduction on the basis of the information given.

A first attempt to define strictly the financial duties of the communities was made during the term of office of Ivan Giuzelev. A law project entitled "Basic Law on Public Schools" was submitted to the National Assembly. The law had been written by Jireček in consultation with participants at a meeting of Bulgarian pedagogues held by Metropolitan Clement.[29] Basically, this law would have defined the responsibilities of the communities more succinctly. But the law never was passed because it died when the Sŭbranie was dissolved in November, 1880.

However, a year later in 1881, the definitive regulation on this subject emerged as part of the Instructions for the Provincial School Inspectors. By this time, Jireček was in control of the Ministry completely, which accounts for the incorporation of so many of his ideas into legislation.[30]

Each community was required to finance its own schools, and now each school budget had to estimate and to designate precise sums for school support.

---

[29] Jireček, Bŭlgarski dnevnik, vol. II, p. 18.

[30] Jireček became Minister of Public Instruction in May, 1881, and resigned in June, 1882. The reasons for the rapid changes of ministers and the circumstances surrounding them will be discussed in Chapter Six.

The expenses of the schools had to be arranged as to allow the regular pay of teachers for designated periods. Jireček also included orders to school inspectors to make sure that the communes, especially the urban ones, did not spend beyond their means for their schools and did not rush unnecessarily into undertakings which would cause large deficits.[31] This, of course, was to counter the problem mentioned already of schools eager to comply with the Ministry of Public Instruction's urging to build more schools.

The chief sources which the communities could draw upon for financial support were listed as: (1) income from real estate and capital funds designated by the communes for the schools or bequeathed by private individuals, (2) a portion of Church income, (3) occasional voluntary gifts, and, if the first three did not suffice, (4) the commune was obligated to levy a compulsory tax in money or in kind.[32] Further suggestions on how the communes might finance their schools showed that Jireček had researched the problem well and was

---

[31] Bulgaria, Ministry of Public Instruction, "Instruktsii za Okrŭzhni Uchilishtni Inspektori," Dŭrzhaven vestnik, III, 15 (1881), 114.

[32] Ibid.

aware of unusual local customs or situations. For example, he knew that many communes were claiming as their own lands abandoned by the Circassians, and he suggested that one part of this newly found community wealth might be put aside for the schools.[33] In another case, he called attention to the existence of common lands which could be rented to individuals for gardens, the income to be earmarked for the schools.[34]

Most importantly, he was aware that at harvest time some school boards invited commune members to donate some of the produce gathered at harvest to the school board, which in turn would then sell it for the benefit of the schools. Jireček, in a note to this article,

---

[33]Ibid. The Circassians (Cherkezi in Bulgarian), a mountain people of the northern Caucasus region, belong to the Caucaso-Iberian language group. During the 1860s, many of the Circassians fled the area when Russian troops finally seized control. They went first to Turkey and eventually many settled in Bulgaria. Since Circassians had joined the Turkish irregular troops (Bashi-Bazouks), so hated by the native Bulgarians, they were forced to flee once again with the advance of Russian troops invading Bulgaria in the Russo-Turkish War of 1876-1878. Their abandoned lands in Bulgaria were the objects of several law suits between local communities and various central government agencies (especially the Ministry of the Interior) who laid claim to the lands.

[34]Bulgaria, Ministry of Public Instruction, "Instruktsii za Okrŭzhni Uchilishtni Inspektori," Dŭrzhaven vestnik, III, 15 (1881), 114.

gave the inspectors advice on how to solicit funds from these sources. Jireček instructed the inspectors to plant the idea that every good-hearted, patriotic villager only naturally would wish to donate some of his harvest to the schools, especially if the year had been a good one. Also, Jireček knew of the custom in some villages at harvest time to gather wine and to toast the men who had been married in the year just passed. The inspectors should suggest that the wine not be drunk but instead be donated to the local school. He noted that in the village of Cherkovna (near Varna), a portion of the wine gathered on this occasion in 1880 had been donated to the local school. The same custom was developing in the Shumen area.[35]

The law also suggested other events that might easily become, through the prompting of the local school inspectors, traditional occasions for donations to the schools, such as weddings, name day celebrations, public lectures, lotteries, and theatrical presentations.[36]

If all these devices failed or were nonexistent, then the community was obliged to collect a school tax from its members in money or in kind. The amount owed

---

[35] Ibid.

[36] Ibid.

or outstanding was to be collected in one general collection, selected and carried out by special commissions for levying the necessary sum on members of the commune. All members of the community were required to pay, whether or not they had children. A provision was made to allow a tax in kind for the benefit of those parts of the country which were rich in agricultural goods but in little else.[37] For those who wished to pay in money, it had to be delivered on time, that is, no credit was allowed. And when the collection was in money, it had to be done together with the collection of the state taxes or whenever the inhabitants were furnished with ready money. For example, in areas where the villagers worked abroad, then the tax would be collected in the spring upon their return. In cities, the money had to be collected regularly in appointed periods. It was suggested that the most appropriate way would be at the same time during which the state and community taxes were collected, preferably all at the same time, with no special distinctions made. The city would then designate from these collections the necessary sum in the annual budget that would be used for the schools.[38]

---

[37] Ibid.

[38] Ibid.

131

Those not paying the tax would be fined a double tax. Most importantly, administrative authorities on the provincial and county levels were instructed to assist the communities in the execution of these stipulations.

A special provision was made for mountain villages and sparsely settled areas:

> In places where villages are small and isolated or where in the environs of the villages there are cottages sprinkled among the forest and mountains, the villages must support one school in their midst for each of the surrounding villages. The expenses for such schools, of course, will be paid by the neighboring villages.[39]

The exact center of such neighboring villages must always be well-defined. Many hardships would still ensue due to the location of the school far away from other villages. In an unusual passage, the authors of the provision suggested that in setting up these special mountain schools, officials should keep in mind systems used in Alpine countries in Europe, such as Norway, Sweden, and Switzerland, all of which used circuit teachers.[40]

As for large cities with outlying quarters, a separate school would have to be opened in any such

---

[39] Ibid., no. 14, 109.

[40] Ibid.

quarter that was so far removed that the students had difficulty attending classes in the city. (This was to take effect, however, only if the number of such students was significant.) Also, if any one grade in any school had more than 60 students, then a parallel grade had to be opened.[41] Finally, the law stipulated that the expenses for all schools within the borders of any one community, urban or rural, would have to be borne by the entire community.[42]

In another step aimed at the furtherance of stability and predictability in school financing, the Ministry of Public Instruction sought to stipulate definitely what sum would be contributed by the Church. Although the Church was encouraged to make any contribution it could, a special law in February, 1881, granted the Church a total monopoly of the production and sale of wax candles with the stipulation that one candle factory had to be set up in each county, and two thirds of the clear profit from the sale of the candles had to be used for the support of the local schools. The remaining one third could be retained and

---

[41] Ibid.

[42] Ibid.

utilized by the Church.[43] This regulation proved to be very helpful to the communal schools.

Also a law was passed regulating the use of funds obtained by the tax on the sale of cattle (intizap), another traditionally important source of funds for many communities. This law formalized the old custom and controlled its usage. But most importantly, all but a tenth of the proceeds now went to the provincial administration in which the community was located. These collected funds were placed under the control of provincial councils which, with the agreement of the mayors in the province, used them for the construction and maintenance of provincial hospitals and schools in appropriate locations.[44]

In another subtle move, concealed in a law on school inspectors, the Ministry assumed control over all trust funds and bequests made to the communal schools.[45]

___

[43] Bulgaria, Ministry of Public Instruction, Ukaz 146, February 20, 1881, Dŭrzhaven vestnik, III, 12 (1881), 90.

[44] Bulgaria, Narodno Subranie, "Zakon za pravoto koeto shte se vzima pri prodazhbata na domashen edŭr dobitŭk," approved by Ukaz 174, December 5, 1880, Dŭrzhaven vestnik, II, 9 (1880), 2.

[45] Bulgaria, Ministry of Public Instruction, "Instruktsiia za Okrŭzhni Uchilishtni Inspektori," Dŭrzhaven vestnik, III, 15 (1881), 115.

All such gifts and bequests now came under the special supervision of the government, with the intent of assuring that they were well-administered and would not be prematurely exhausted. The Ministry also wished to assure that such funds would be used according to the terms stipulated in the will of the donor.

Thus in a series of measures, the central government and the Ministry of Public Instruction mapped out a road to greater financial stability and security for the nation's public schools. However, it was some time before these well-conceived measures could effectively be put into practice. Meanwhile, the single most effective and frequent weapon used by all of the Ministers of Public Instruction from 1880 to 1885 was to dole out huge sums of money. The Ministry itself did not accurately keep track of exactly how much was spent on aid to the communities in this period. Minister Teokharev reported to Parliament that from 1879 to 1882 about one million leva had been spent on financial aid to the communities, with about 150,000 leva being spent in the year 1882 alone. These figures agreed with those cited by Jireček, in his <u>Glavno izlozhenie</u>, of about 300,000 leva per year since 1879, with a drop in 1882 to about one-half the amount or 150,000 leva. That figure rose a bit in later years to around 200,000 leva. All told, the figure for 1879 to 1885 would be approximately 1,600,000 leva.[46]

The Teacher Crisis

Of all the critical issues facing the various helmsmen of the Ministry of Public Instruction during the 1880-1885 period, perhaps none was more frustating and more devoid of a reasonable solution than that of the teacher shortage. The problem surrounding the teacher cadre was actually not one of a mere shortage, but the attendant causes of shortage and the results stemming from them. Nor was it a problem involving manpower alone, because in many cases people could be found to fill the existing gaps. Instead the difficulties ensued from the hopeless inadequacies of these hastily recruited teachers.

Some of the difficulties connected with being a teacher already have been discussed in the section on Drinov. The most significant was the drain of

---

[46] Teokharev, "Zapiska," p. 22; Jireček, Glavno izlozhenie, pp. 17-18; Tsonkov, Razvitie, p. 201. My acceptance of these figures is based on my own examination of the sessions of the Ministerial Council from 1880-1885 where all such expenditures by the Ministry of Public Instruction had to be approved. These archives have already been cited as Bulgaria, Ministerial Council, TsDIA, F. 284 (Ministerial Council).

intellectuals from teaching to government service. Before 1878, the only occupation open to well-educated Bulgarians was the teaching profession. One could, however, also become a priest. In fact, although it is impossible to cite even rough figures, it seems that many teachers were priests and vice versa. After the Liberation, many new opportunities arose for educated people, and they did not hesitate to abandon their previous duties in favor of the prestige, security, better pay, and better living and working conditions of government employ.

The government's need for educated people was extreme and drew talent from the countryside and from Bulgarian communities abroad. Even the Ministry of Public Instruction itself was responsible for tearing talented individuals away from promising teaching careers to serve as policymakers and administrators in the Ministry's central offices in Sofia.

Meanwhile the independent status of the country introduced a hitherto nonexistent drain on manpower reserves--a standing army. Previously, Bulgarian males did not face military duty, and, in fact were forbidden to carry arms. But subsequently, all males were subject to the draft, including teachers.

The teacher shortage would have been a serious matter even in the days before independence. But it presented yet a greater dilemma thereafter, since the country was about to embark on a scheme to expand educational opportunities and facilities.[47] The effects of the drastic shrinking of the pool of available expertise were immediate and traumatic.

The ranks vacated by the more experienced teachers were occupied, if at all, by young, unseasoned, poorly-educated replacements, many of whom were barely literate. This was hardly a promising start on the road to the goal, proclaimed in the Tŭrnovo Constitution, of universal elementary education. It was a terrible handicap to the work of the Ministers of Public Instruction at the time in serveral ways. First, it slowed the progress of upgrading the teachers' lot. The Sŭbranie was not inclined to expend more money, considering the caliber of people flooding into the many newly vacant teaching positions. It led to an inability to expand secondary education facilities, since the graduates of schools with such inadequate teachers were not equipped to enter

---

[47] This same dilemma, by the way, existed in Eastern Rumelia; see N. Markov, "Doklad na Starozagorskii prefekt pri otvarianieto na glavnii sŭvet," Maritsa, October 2, 1881, pp. 5-6 and October 6, 1881, pp. 5-6.

more advanced institutions. The Ministry of Public Instruction was impelled, therefore, to pour more money than it could afford in the long run into remedial or new teacher training programs. The Ministry was also forced to import foreigners to fill important teaching posts. And it hampered the Ministry of Public Instruction's ability to demand successfully more government money from Parliament, as the Sŭbranie members were able to cite the weaknesses in the teaching cadre and the lack of progress as excuses to limit or to cutoff funds.[48]

This new situation was compounded by the continuance of older difficulties, including that of the age-old conflicts between teachers and local authorities and the continuing abuse of teachers by the people in the countryside. The major task then was to solve each of these difficulties in a short time and with very limited resources, both fiscal and physical.

---

[48] See debates on the policies of the Ministry of Public Instruction in Bulgaria, Narodno Sŭbranie, Dnevnitsi na II Obiknoveno Narodno Sŭbranie, pŭrva redovna sesiia, session of May 31, 1880, pp. 665ff.; and Dnevnitsi na III Obiknoveno Narodna Sŭbranie, pŭrva redovna sesiia, session of February 9, 1883, pp. 1-4ff. Henceforth the official reports of the proceedings of the Narodno Subranie will be cited as Stenograficheski dnevnitsi na (no.) ONS. Thus, a citation to the third Narodno Sŭbranie in its first regular session would appear as Stenograficheski dnevnitsi na III ONS, pŭrva redovna sesiia.

Minister Ivan Giuzelev initiated an attempt to solve many of these problems, or at least to mitigate some of them, in his law project which was submitted to the Sŭbranie in 1880. But the project failed when Parliament dissolved. From this point onward, the Ministry of Public Instruction had to grope for other ways of aiding teachers. Minister of Public Instruction Raicho Karolev, looking back on this period (he took office in 1883), described the situation after the failure of the 1880 Giuzelev projects. Karolev claimed that:

> The Ministry found it necessary to establish with instructions, circular letters, and regulations that which should have been established by law. This activity by the Ministry was unconstitutional, but faced with the lack of necessary /law/, the Ministry could not otherwise proceed--to the detriment of its work, since at that time the school order was not yet conclusively formed and regulated, so that misunderstandings often occurred between the Ministry and its subordinate directors and teachers, or between directors and teachers themselves.[49]

The Ministry did little at first to overcome manpower shortages although an obvious first step would have been to request that teachers be exempted from military service. But no serious efforts were made to achieve this exception before 1883. In January, 1883,

---

[49]Karolev, "Podgotovka na uchiteli," ABAN, F. 62K (Raicho Karolev), op. 1, ae. 8, p. 9.

the issue of teachers and military service came before both the Ministerial Council and the Sŭbranie.[50] The Minister of Public Instruction at that time was Georgi Teokharev. On January 3, 1883, the Ministerial Council decided that all teachers in the public schools who presented documents from a pedagogical school, from a temporary pedagogical course, or at every least from some three-class school, or who had been teaching for at least two consecutive years could fulfill their military obligation on the following basis within five years. Those teachers affected would enter the annual military call-up on a general basis, but would be freed immediately on leave with the obligation to appear in the particular units of soldiers which would be indicated to them on the fifteenth of the following May. As part of these units, they would serve from May 15 to September 15 annually until they had served the equivalent of the normal two-year period of active service. If such public school teachers were to leave their profession before their release from their period of duty in the reserve, however, they would be called back into the army where

---

[50]Bulgaria, Ministerial Council, session of January 3, 1883, TsDIA, F. 284 (Ministerial Council), op. 1, ae. 145.

they would complete their terms of duty.[51]

The Ministerial Council passed this proposal and in a reversal of usual procedure sent it to the Sŭbranie. (Normally, proposals flowed in the opposite direction.) The proposal touched off a debate concerning the need for such a deferment. The Minister of War at the time was a Russian, General Aleksandr Kaulbars, and he was not enthusiastic about the release of men, although he recognized the seriousness of the teacher shortage. Kaulbars eventually endorsed the Ministerial Council's proposal, calling it an equitable decision of the issue. He urged, however, that it be tried for five years and then reassessed.[52]

One of the deputies, Shivachov, tried to amend the Ministerial Council's resolution by adding a phrase giving provincial school inspectors the right to issue credentials attesting to the qualifications and good behavior of the teachers.[53] But several deputies objected, pointing out the possibilities of abuse. It was defeated.

---

[51] Ibid.

[52] Stenograficheski dnevnitsi na III ONS, pŭrva redovna sesiia, January 3, 1883, p. 218.

[53] Ibid., pp. 219, 223.

The debate which followed on the original proposal submitted by the Ministerial Council revealed the incredibly poor understanding held by some of the representatives as to the structure of the national school system and the issues involved.

The proposal specifically concerned the teachers in the public schools, as opposed to teachers in government schools. One deputy, Tsachev, asked whether the proposal applied to cities as well as villages, and a fellow deputy, Nachovich, expressed doubts that it did. At this point a deputy, Shivachov, berated the ignorance of the two deputies who did not understand the meaning of the term narodnite uchilishta (i.e. schools, whether rural or urban, that were supported by the communities alone). Other deputies rebuked the Minister of Public Instruction Teokharev for being absent as usual.[54] Some deputies complained that the proposal was not entirely equitable because it did not apply to government teachers. The schools at which this latter group of teachers were employed closed in June and reopened in September, while public schools had much longer vacations, closing usually in March or April and reopening in October. Also protest was made that

---

[54] Ibid., p. 224.

untrained village teachers needed time to attend pedagogical courses. Deputy Nachovich answered that these untrained teachers would be allowed to attend pedagogical courses--only trained teachers would be taken into the military.[55] After all objections were stated and accommodated, the Ministerial Council's proposal was accepted, and a potentially serious obstacle to overcoming the teacher shortage was removed.

But other equally serious obstacles remained, especially where the teachers' working conditions and living conditions were concerned. The teachers' status in the eyes of community leaders remained low, and they continued to be poorly paid and publicly abused, especially in the rural areas. The fact that many of these newer post-1878 teachers were poorly qualified failed to improve matters. All of these conditions prompted the succeeding ministers to launch a variety of programs to overcome these obstacles to the development of Bulgarian education.

A particularly thorny problem, and one never successfully solved, was the traditional peasant hostility

---

[55]Ibid., pp. 220-221. While figures are nonexistent, teachers in government schools were far outnumbered by their counterparts in the much more numerous public schools. In this sense, the law certainly covered the majority of teachers.

in certain areas to the teaching cadre. A strange paradox throughout Bulgarian history was that the very same peasants who made great sacrifices to help support a local school often made life miserable for the people, or more appropriately, the person who ran it. This was not true, however, in all areas of the country, and the difference seems to be due to the financial well-being of the area and its exposure to outside influences. For example, the eastern portion of the Principality (especially the Shumen area) was noted for its progress in school affairs and for the enthusiastic support of its citizens for such matters. The western half was less developed economically, and the dispersion of schools and literacy rates reflected this. But no part of the country really was free from peasant hostility to schools. Incidents of belligerent attitudes were plentiful, some amusing, some quite tragic.

When, for example, in a village near Kiustendil, the school inspectors opened a school, the villagers hid their children. When they finally did bring their children to school, the mothers pulled out their own hair "and with tears, cursed the ones guilty of opening the school."[56] A former teacher, Dobre Ganchev, reported

---

[56] Jireček, Glavno izlozhenie, p. 12.

that parents thought it great fun to deliver their children to school with derisive verses, such as:

> Teacher I give him to you to teach
> To make him a human being.
> Beat his hide,
> But teach him.[57]

The peasants, as well as local priests and officials, had an unfortunate tendency to look upon teachers as their personal valets or slaves. This was, however, practically a tradition and, to some extent, the teachers' own fault.

Even before the Liberation, many teachers had supplemented their incomes with some agricultural activities. This became even more pronounced after 1878, when more professionally-minded people abandoned their work and were replaced by others who did not consider teaching their major livelihood but engaged in other occupations such as farming, bee-keeping, etc.[58] In many instances, however, this outside work was not voluntary and was extremely vexing to the more dedicated educators.

---

[57] Ganchev, Spomeni, p. 3. The verse rhymes in Bulgarian in a way difficult to convey in English. The Bulgarian version reads: "Daskal, dovam ti da go nauchish, chovek da go napravish, kozhata mu smŭkni, ama go nauchi."

[58] Nikolov, "Poiava i razvitie," pp. 50-64; Karolev, "Podgotovka na uchiteli," ABAN, F. 62K (Karolev), op. 1, ae. 8, p. 5.

The school inspector from Shumen province, Iliia Blŭskov, who carried on a vigorous struggle nationwide for reform, reported that:

> In many of our villages, the teacher is kept as a field hand; everyone is his master and all order him around. One yells, 'Hey teacher, go sit in the school and watch the kids; another comes upon him and says, 'I don't need a school--I have no child, have nothing--but I help pay you just to have someone around for village work and to help figure our taxes as long as we have to pay them to the tax collector.'[59]

Teachers in small villages especially were often left without pupils when the peasants decided not to send their children to school for the flimsiest of reasons. (Most village schools made provisions for the sowing and harvesting periods in their schedules.) The teachers were called upon to help in every manner of church and village work, including sowing and reaping crops, writing letters, gathering and figuring taxes, making candles, and so on.[60] One chore considered particularly onerous by the teachers and which was quite widespread in rural areas (but also occurred in some cities) was that of church singing. Again this was a carryover from a

---

[59] Iliia Blŭskov, "Nuzhdata ot revis'or inspektor nad selskite uchilishte," Uchilishte (Ruse), III (1873), 145, 153, 162.

[60] Ibid., p. 146.

previous era when priests and chorbadji had powerful influence in all local affairs but especially over the schools. Looking back on his education in Liaskovets in the 1860s, former teacher Dobre Ganchev recalled that "Teachers were changed frequently, almost every year. Reasons varied. Either he didn't please the priest, was not able to keep order in church, his voice was unpleasant, or the chorbadzhi found him objectionable."[61] Despite the fact that teachers frequently complained about these duties and expectations, it seems that at least some teachers actually helped to make the situation worse. Again looking at the national scene, Blŭskov reported that some teachers urged simple peasants to hire them as teachers because they had good voices and could sing in church. Blŭskov inveighed against this practice as being very damaging to all concerned, since eventually the villagers would realize that they had no need of teachers who hauled their children to church to sing and to lose precious time. As Blŭskov described it, after a few years of such inconsequential activity, the peasants would become upset and begin to pressure the teacher. The peasants reasoned, according to Blŭskov, that if this was "education," they they might as well keep the

---

[61] Ganchev, Spomeni, p. 1.

children at home for pressing farm work and, as a result, withdrew their children from the school.[62]

The issue of outside work, whether or not voluntary, was raised several times in the Sŭbranie. Giuzelev's law on education had proposed to allow teachers to fulfill other village work if this was mutually agreeable. This caused sharp retorts from deputies who had been teachers. Deputy Rangel Kostov explained that outside work led to a vicious circle. From his own experience, villagers valued him as a teacher, but when the time for harvest came, they forced him into village work while the school stood empty. Then when examination time came and the students failed, the teachers were roundly condemned. Singing in church was tolerable, he claimed, but teachers should not be made to work in the fields. Giuzelev agreed and changed his law which, of course, failed, and the situation continued unabated.[63]

In 1883, Minister Teokharev, not very well liked by either teachers or government officials, reported that he was putting more emphasis on church singing lessons so that future teachers destined for village schools

---

[62] Blŭskov, "Nuzhdata," pp. 146, 147, 162.

[63] Stenograficheski dnevnitsi na II ONS, pŭrva redovna sesiia, May 21, 1881, p. 533.

would be able to sing in the churches. This only exacerbated the situation. The problem was not solved until Karolev outlawed outside work in 1884[64] and made sure this provision was obeyed.

Karolev also effectively dealt with a more dangerous aspect of peasant intrusion into disciplinary matters in the schools. Although such instances of peasants taking things into their own hands were very rare, they were nonetheless damaging to the morale of teachers. Corporal punishment in schools had been outlawed in 1880, yet random incidents continued to occur.[65] A vicious incident in 1885 of outsiders entering a school and beating students caused a vigorous effort to enforce already existing laws. Besides the useless cruelty and negative effects of corporal punishment, Karolev was concerned because the incident had significantly weakened the prestige and authority of the teacher in the eyes of the populace and the students.[66]

---

[64] Teokharev, "Zapiska," pp. 18-19.

[65] Raicho Karolev, circular letter 1054 to provincial school inspectors, May 6, 1885, in Nikola Balabanov, Sbornik s otbrani okruzhi ot osvobozhdenieto do kraia na 1942 god. I (Sofia: 1943), p. 681.

[66] Ibid., pp. 681-682. The official records hint that the peasant intruders were upset about something the students had done and never been punished for, but that is the extent of details on the case.

On the positive side, however, a report to Parliament in 1883 noted that the number of children attending school was almost double that of 1870, and, despite the fact that in the western, agriculturally-oriented provinces an especially poor attitude towards education still existed (particularly towards schooling for girls), the situation was not hopeless. Teokharev told the legislators:

> But in general, the populace everywhere understands that a man in the new times has to know how to read and write. A very good influence in this respect was shown by discharged soldiers, especially where some of them have become village mayors.[67]

However beneficial the influence of ex-soldiers, the future of Bulgarian education could not rely on this medium of promotion and correction alone. More concrete and immediate measures were needed, and these came in the form of improved and expanded training of new teachers, control over the caliber of those entering the profession or already there, and better living conditions, i.e. wages. Many of these programs were improvements upon, or expansions of, efforts begun under the Russian administration.

In the summer of 1879, Marin Drinov set up an emergency system of pedagogical courses with the dual

---

[67]Teokharev, "Zapiska," p. 19.

purpose of providing a pool of available manpower for the future, as well as to remedy the woeful training of many of the "teachers" at this time. This effort did not make a significant dent, and another "temporary" pedagogical course was opened the next summer (July 5-August 24, 1880). Raicho Karolev noted that the course was urgently necessary "since the majority of the teachers at the time were people almost illiterate or only with a primary education."[68]

Action to overcome this situation did not stop with Drinov, but not much was achieved in the period from 1880 to 1885. The ill-fated Giuzelev period saw an attempt to improve teacher training facilities. Before Giuzelev, only temporary pedagogical courses had existed, although some of these had become semi-permanent. By 1880, three of the four-grade state schools were being called "teachers seminaries." One of these seminaries was in Dobrich but was transferred to Silistra in September, 1880. The other seminary, originally in Belogradchik, was also transferred in 1880, but to Tsaribrod. A third teachers seminary, in Dupnitsa, was

---

[68] Karolev, "Podgotovka na uchiteli," ABAN, F. 62K (Karolev), op. 1, ae. 8, pp. 7-10.

closed in 1881.[69] Meanwhile, the year 1880 also saw the establishment for the first time of permanent schools oriented specifically towards producing teachers. These schools, each with a one-year course, opened in Vratsa and Shumen. Second- and third-year courses were not opened till 1885. In the interval, the Vratsa school was transferred to Kiustendil.[70]

Both of these schools were established largely along the lines desired by Jireček, who wrote a memorandum on the matter in June, 1880. In this memorandum (eventually used by Giuzelev), Jireček urged immediate establishment of two pedagogical schools, noting that up until that point there had been no such institutions and that primary school teachers were trained in the existing primary schools or sometimes in the middle schools. "And afterwards," he commented,"/they/ have no pedagogical training, without which primary education depends entirely on the personal aptitude of the teacher and on his common sense."[71] He recommended that the schools

---

[69]Dŭrzhaven vestnik, II, 96 (1880), 1.

[70]/D. Teodorov/, Purvi godishen otchet za sŭstoianieto na uchebnoto delo na Silistrenskoto dŭrzhavno triklasno pedagogichesko pŭrvonachalno uchilishte za prez 1896/1897 godina (Sofia: 1897), p. 16.

[71]Jireček, "Zapiska za naredagogicheskita uchilishta v Kniazhestvo," ABAN, F. 3 (Jireček), op. 1, ae. 1125, p. 92.

be established in the western and eastern parts of the country, each with a one-year course, which could later be broadened into additional annual courses. The major need was for <u>any</u> kind of training for teachers in primary schools. He objected, however, to proposals by Giuzelev's advisers to open the western pedagogical school in Dupnitsa. The plan afoot was simply to add another year to the program of the existing three-year government school in Dupnitsa. Jireček's objections (which held sway in the end) centered around the tenuous border location of the school, the harsh climate of the region, its distance from important centers, and its lack of convenient accommodations for the expected large numbers of students from Kiustendil, Samokov, and Sofia.[72] He suggested Samokov instead because of existing facilities and the closer proximity to three-grade and primary schools.[73] Finally Jireček wanted entry requirements for the new schools. Each student should have three years of education beyond the basic four-year primary school, no matter where or in what type of school. If this was not possible, the student should be tested by entrance examinations to determine his basic knowledge

---

[72] Ibid.

[73] Ibid.

of: (1) catechism, (2) Bulgarian grammar, (3) arithmetic, (4) geometry, (5) geography, (6) general world history, (7) natural history and physics, (8) drawing, (9) penmanship, (10) singing, and (11) gymnastics.[74] Many of Jireček's suggestions were eventually fulfilled. The Dupnitsa location for the western school was abandoned, although it was moved to Vratsa instead of Samokov as Jireček had wanted.

The two full-fledged pedagogical schools of Shumen and Vratsa were opened under the authority of the so-called "Omnibus Law" of December 24, 1880, during the short-lived administration of Mikhail Sarafov. This "law," incidentally, was the first of many legal pronouncements by the Ministry of Public Instruction that were actually unconstitutional, since they lacked parliamentary approval. In any event, the two schools were designated as one-year courses with a second-year course to open four years hence. Also meeting Jireček's suggestions, only students who had finished a three-grade school or who showed the necessary knowledge on the entrance examination would be admitted. Further, all students had to be at least 17 years old and male (although this latter provision was ignored for the most

---

[74] Ibid., p. 94.

part, and women were admitted).[75] However, teachers who were not fully qualified could be accepted into the school if they had a record of good educational work.[76] This ostensibly was due to the other teacher training reforms that were also part of the "Omnibus Law."

Besides the two regular pedagogical schools, certain provisions were made for other forms of emergency teacher education. The law provided that if at least ten children in the Sofia classical gymnasium or the real gymnasium in Lom, Kiustendil, or Gabrovo appeared inclined to become primary school teachers, a one-year pedagogical course could be opened at each of the schools with a supplement of one or two more teachers. Also, if the Ministry of Public Instruction deemed it suitable, a one-year pedagogical course could likewise be opened at the Tŭrnovo girls gymnasium before the start of the 1881-1882 school year. The same provision designated 56,000 leva and 75 stipends to cover the expenses of these special contingency courses.[77]

---

[75] Boris Ivanov, "Istoricheski pogled vŭrkhu sistemata za podgotovka na nachalni uchiteli u nas," Narodna prosveta, XIII (November, 1957), 53-61.

[76] Ibid.

[77] Bulgaria, Ministry of Public Instruction, "Zakon za preustroistvo na pravitelstveni uchilishta," Dŭrzhaven vestnik, II, 96 (1880), 1.

Another law in May 21, 1880, confirmed these measures, but also called for follow-up training in temporary vacation courses opened in 1881 in Sofia, Kiustendil, Trŭn, Svishtov, and Vidin and again in 1882 in Sofia, Ruse, Svishtov, Lovech, Oriakhovo, Trŭn, Kiustendil, Varna, the village of Koilovtsi (Pleven area), and in Gorna-Orekhovitsa.[78]

Karolev reports that at the same time all these measures were taken, the Sofia womens gymnasium was being turned into a teachers seminar for women teachers. There is no indication, however, that such a school ever functioned and produced any teachers.[79]

Despite the existence of only two regular schools and a constantly varying number of special pedagogical

---

[78] Karolev, "Podgotovka na uchiteli," ABAN, F. 62K (Karolev), op. 1, ae. 8, p. 10.

[79] Ibid., p. 8; K. Bogdanov, Otchet na Kiustendilskoto dŭrzhavno pedagogichesko triklasno i obraztsovo uchilishte za uchebnata 1899-1900 godina (Sofia: 1901), this report has useful background material for the first years of the school's existence; Iacho Brŭshlianov, Otchet na Shumenskoto dŭrzhavno pedagogicheskoi triklasno uchilishte za uchebnata 1897-1898 godina (Shumen: 1898), again, this is the first official report ever submitted for the school but contains information on the earlier years; Dimitŭr Angelov, "Raport vŭrkhu sŭstoianieto na dŭrzhavnoto pedagogichesko uchilishte v Vratsa," Ucheben vestnik, I, 1 (1883), 100; Ivanov, "Istoricheski," p. 54.

courses, the situation was still better than that of Eastern Rumelia where out of the six planned schools only one was opened in Kazanlŭk in 1883.[80]

Minister Teokharev, in his report to the Sŭbranie in 1883, noted that at the beginning of the approaching school year the teaching cadre would be furnished for the first time with people prepared for their work in the newly-opened pedagogical schools of Shumen and Vratsa. He cited a figure of 27 teachers coming from the Vratsa school and 60 from the Shumen school, which figure included 22 female teachers. The presence of female teachers was due the fact that in 1882, a parallel course for women had been established at the Shumen school. (As originally planned, the two schools were to have been only for boys.)[81]

It was in this same report of 1883, that Teokharev mentioned the continuance of special summer pedagogical courses for already practicing village teachers in eight locations. The locations and enrollments were as follows: Sofia, 124; Kiustendil, 124; Trŭn, 152; Oriakhovo, 49; Lovech, 88; Svishtov, 101; Ruse, 69; and Gorna-Orekhovitsa, 165; for a total of 872. Teokharev drew

---

[80] Ivanov, "Istoricheski," p. 53.

[81] Teokharev, "Zapiska," p. 22.

the attention of the assembled delegates to plans for a model primary school to be set up in the two pedagogical schools, as well as at the womens gymnasia in Sofia and Tŭrnovo. This would help provide training in methodology rather than just in theory.[82]

Teokharev's report to the Sŭbranie is illuminating in that it reveals the awkward imbalance of efforts to train teachers. The two pedagogical schools, set up at some expense, were turning out paltry numbers of graduates, while the summer courses for already practicing teachers were training or upgrading many times more. It is hard to imagine these numbers doing much to alleviate the problem. But the goal, as mentioned by Jireček, was to give at least some training to however few so that at least a start could be made. In this respect then, some progress was made.

The two schools, however, were plagued with a variety of problems ranging from a lack of supplies and poor housing to more serious ones of a poor knowledge of grammatical Bulgarian on the part of the students and even to a student rebellion at Shumen. The Teachers Council at the Vratsa school, for example, found it

---

[82] Ibid.; Karolev, "Podgotovka na uchiteli," ABAN, F. 62K (Karolev), op. 1, ae. 6, p. 12.

necessary to set up a special collection of some Bulgarian books selected for style in the hope of improving the knowledge of the students in their own language.[83]

All of these measures appear quite insignificant, but since no figures exist on the number of teachers needed, it is not possible to assess accurately how much or how little the schools and special summer courses offset the shortage. But it is significant that foreign teachers had to be brought in to fill the gap. Also, Bulgarian students returning from abroad were often pressed into the service of the schools. In this connection, Jireček wrote to Drinov in July, 1880: "For teaching positions, we look whenever possible for people with university educations.... Young people are returning from abroad. We took them and several Czechs, one to each school." He also listed some of the Bulgarian students returning from abroad and the high positions in which they were being placed: Spas Vatsov in the Lom school, Mikhail Sarafov in the Sofia gymnasium, and Todor Ivanchov as director of the Kiustendil school.[84] Each

---

[83] Angelov, "Raport," p. 101.

[84] Jireček, letter to Marin Drinov, June 22, 1880, in Sis, ed. Korespondentsiia, p. 205.

of these also eventually held high positions in the central administration of the Ministry. Some "foreign" teachers were imported from Eastern Rumelia, but in such cases credentials were carefully checked.[85] In 1883, however, the Ministry evidently became worried about the illegality of hiring foreigners, since the Tŭrnovo Constitution expressly forbade it without the consent of the Sŭbranie in every case. Dimitŭr Mollov (Minister from September, 1883-July, 1884), in submitting a request to the Parliament for the approval of hiring a Greek subject as a village teacher in Vratsa, explained that he was well aware of the consitutional provisions requiring approval of the hiring of foreigners. He was equally aware that the law had been circumvented and ignored by a loose interpretation of the constitutional ban on foreigners being hired for state or communal (obshtestvenna) work. Since obshtestvenna could also be translated as "social," foreigners were hired with the understanding that their jobs were in the realm of social (and not communal) work. Mollov enforced the constitutional provision in its clearly intended meaning.[86]

---

[85] Bulgaria, Ministerial Council, session of March 10, 1884, TsDIA, F. 284 (Ministerial Council), op. 1, ae. 274.

[86] Stenograficheski dnevnitsi na III ONS, vtora redovna sesiia, November 17, 1883, p. 21.

Sometimes foreign teachers were hired for special skills. For example, in 1884, the Ministerial Council heard a report from the Ministry requesting permission to seek in Moscow someone experienced enough to set up lessons in silk manufacturing.[87] Undoubtedly, the practice of hiring foreigners to teach continued with or without Sŭbranie approval.

If progress in improving the pedagogical training of the teachers was difficult to provide, so was financial improvement. The existence of teaching seminars and pedagogical schools at least gave the Ministers the ability to tighten hiring regulations in the communities by requiring that no one could be hired who did not have credentials recognized by the Ministry.[88] These credentials were defined so as to allow the hiring as a teacher of anyone who had finished a regular pedagogical course, who had studied in a three-class school, who had taken part in a temporary pedagogical course and received a certificate for good work, or anyone who was able to show that his knowledge and abilities had been

---

[87] Bulgaria, Ministerial Council, session of January 14, 1884, TsDIA, F. 284 (Ministerial Council), op. 1, ae. 244.

[88] Bulgaria, Ministry of Public Instruction, "Instruktsiia za Okrŭzhnite Uchilishtni Inspektori," Dŭrzhaven vestnik, III, 18 (1881), 138.

acquired through long experience and successful teaching (rather than in a higher school). Provincial school inspectors could grant these people the credentials of pedagogical courses, but only if the person had a clear and unreproachable past and was at least 18 years old.[89]

Inspectors were warned in this law and in circular letters to be extremely careful in issuing and accepting credentials and to report any abuses to the central authorities.[90] Strengthening the hand of the inspectors helped, in the opinion of the Ministry, to assure that better-qualified teachers would be hired.

These better-qualified teachers had to receive commensurate compensation, however, if they were going to remain at, or even seek, the kinds of positions for which they had trained. The Ministers thus fought very hard on the floor of the Sŭbranie to assure adequate pay, in line with the higher standards and qualifications which the Ministry was also trying to achieve. The Ministry of Public Instruction had direct control of the wages for teachers in state-operated schools, whereas

---

[89] Ibid.

[90] Ibid., pp. 138-139. In several cases, villagers had ejected regular teachers and substituted some of their own sons, in the hope of aiding them to avoid military service.

it was limited in what it could do for the teachers in the communal schools. On the one hand, it could demand that the communes pay teachers regularly on the basis of contracts. On the other hand, economic conditions varied so greatly throughout the Principality that it would have been extremely difficult to set minimal pay scales for each region, let alone for the entire country. Therefore, the communes continued to determine the wages for teachers in their own schools.

During Drinov's tenure of office, the issue of pay for teachers had been a continuous headache, as well as the subject of several stern missives to provincial and communal officials. The issue at the time was not so much poor pay as it was the frequent lack of it at all. Drinov's efforts, supported by Dondukov-Korsakov, had centered around motivating the communes to allot adequate reserves of money in yearly budgets and to contractualize the financial arrangements between communities and teachers so that the teachers would have legal evidence in the event of non-payment.

These efforts were continued in the period of 1880-1885, with varying degrees of success. The provincial inspectorate regulation of 1881 put some teeth into what had previously been only vague warnings about communal responsibilities to the teachers. The provisions of this regulation included discussions of the background of the problem which threw interesting light on the subject. These discussions revealed that the ministerial officials recognized that teaching conditions, as well as salaries, until that time were extremely varied according to the local conditions and to the attitude of the inhabitants towards schools and learning. Since no law on teachers' salaries yet existed nor was likely to exist for some time, the inspectors were charged with preventing the communes from paying insufficient wages to their teachers. The inspectors were instructed to make sure that the teachers were paid in money or kind an amount which would allow them to live decently.[91] (Also, the inspectors were not to intervene without coming to an agreement with the provincial council and with people who knew the province well.) Finally, the Ministry of Public Instruction singled out the irregular paying of teachers as the most important stumbling block in the path of school development.[92] The best process for eradicating the problem would be to ascertain the reasons for the irregular remuneration--a task also

---

[91] Bulgaria, Ministry of Public Instruction, "Instruktsiia za Okrŭzhnite Uchilishtni Inspektori," Dŭrzhaven vestnik, III, 15 (1881), 115.

[92] Ibid.

entrusted to the provincial school inspectors.

Should the best efforts of the provincial authorities and the school inspectors fail to achieve results, the teachers were given the right to sue the negligent community either in local courts or the provincial court, a right that proved quite useful to the teachers.[93] Furthermore, the minimal contents of teaching contracts were now stipulated. The contracts had to be of a duration of at least one year, with pay periods specifically designated, and the communes were obliged to guarantee that no work would be imposed, with some exceptions. For example, a small village could rightfully ask a teacher to perform letter-writing duties as long as such work did not interfere with teaching duties.[94]

In 1881, the heretofore random system of issuing pensions was also formalized. From then on, teachers could apply for and receive pensions only under certain conditions for old age, illness, or merit. The applicants had to prove how many years they had taught as well as their inability to work or to otherwise sustain themselves. All pensions were granted by petition only, and, in continuation of Drinov's policy, widows of

---

[93] Ibid., p. 116.

[94] Ibid., no. 18, p. 139.

teachers killed fighting the Turks in the War of Liberation were also eligible for pensions. In 1882, eleven people received pensions ranging from 300 to 1,800 leva per annum; eight were former teachers, two were the widows of teachers.[95]

The Ministry often found its efforts to provide better pay and working conditions for both the state and communal teachers thwarted by the Sŭbranie. Time and again, ministerial officials were forced to lobby and to argue vigorously to maintain or to raise by meager amounts the teachers' salaries, while Sŭbranie deputies worked in direct contradiction to these efforts. Giuzelev, for example, in his budget for 1881 wished teachers who worked as school directors to be paid an extra 1,500 leva, especially at the mens gymnasium in Sofia. He argued that the gymnasia were the highest educational institutions in the country, and thus it was crucial that people be found with corresponding education to teach and to direct the establishments.[96] Supporters of the measure added that anyone acquainted with school

---

[95] Ibid.; Teokharev, "Zapiska," p. 22; Liuben Georgiev, "Dobri Chintulov, naroden uchitel," Narodna prosveta, XII (September, 1956), 63.

[96] Stenograficheski dnevnitsi na II ONS, pŭrva redovna sesiia, May 31, 1880, pp. 669-675.

affairs knew how difficult it was not only to work all day with children, but also to bear responsibility for an entire establishment. The argument fell on deaf ears as the Sŭbranie consistently quashed attempts to recruit better skilled people. On one such occasion, Stambulov (who later became a controversial prime minister) challenged the inconsistencies between the pay scales for female and male teachers. Stambulov asked the already exasperated Minister of Public Instruction whether or not he ever intended to include female teachers in the discussion of the budget. Giuzelev answered affirmatively, saying that male teachers would, of course, be paid higher rates. Stambulov remarked that such a policy was absurd in view of the crucial need--especially since some women had completed their education in Europe, even at the university. Giuzelev tried to argue that female teachers could not teach some subjects, mathematics, for example. But Stambulov persisted. "It seems to me," he continued, "that a male gymnasium student received the exact same education as a female gymnasist. We cannot look upon women as inferior to men."[97] These views received little support, however, from his fellow deputies.

---

[97] Ibid.

It is difficult to gauge exactly what effect the Ministry's fight for higher wages for state teachers had on the conditions of the communal teachers. Figures are nonexistent, and even the Ministry itself had little idea what sums were being paid to the communal teachers, except that these sums were inadequate and infrequently granted. Yet the differences must have been striking for several deputies in the Sŭbranie actually spoke against higher pay for state teachers because it would make it all the more difficult for the communes to find qualified teachers.[98] That is, the better qualified individuals would seek the state positions. Again it was Stambulov who lashed out at the huge sums lavished on the state-operated schools, while the communal ones went begging. He warned that a pay of 4,000 leva per annum just for junior teachers in state schools would force the communities to pay just as much, which few communities could afford to do. Others agreed and added that the already hard-pressed rural primary schools would not be able to compete with the salaries paid to teachers in the government schools.[99]

---

[98] Stenograficheski dnevnitsi na II ONS, pŭrva redovna sesiia, May 31, 1880, pp. 671-672.

[99] Ibid.

Precise figures are available on wages for state teachers. For example, in 1880 the director of the Mens Gymnasium in Sofia received 6,000 leva per annum, a senior teacher 5,000 leva, and a junior teacher 4,000 leva. (By contrast, a clerk at the same school received only 1,200 leva.) These wages were generally the same for all gymnasium teachers throughout the Principality, except for women teachers who received less. At the Tŭrnovo womens gymnasium, for example, the female teachers (senior and junior) received less than 4,000 leva.[100] To put all these figures into perspective with the pay of other professionals, the Minister of Public Instruction in the same year was paid 10,000 leva, the Registrar at the same Ministry received a salary of 2,400 leva, while in other professions, a provincial court president was paid 5,000 leva.[101]

The Ministers of Public Instruction, from Giuzelev in 1880 to Karolev in 1885, never succeeded in wresting from the Sŭbranie the pay scales they wished to implement. Sŭbranie deputies cited everything from lack of funds, to avoidance of competition with communal

---

[100] Ibid., pp. 665-675.
[101] Ibid.

schools to reduce the amounts requested by the ministers in their budget proposals. In fact, in 1883, state teachers suffered pay cuts, despite furious lobbying by Ministry officials to avoid this setback.[102] Nevertheless, state teachers continued to be better off than their colleagues in communal schools. Ironically, in that same year, the Ministry spokesman in the Sŭbranie claimed that if the communes were competing with state schools for good teachers, the state schools were competing with Eastern Rumelia and with the government itself, whose higher salaries and better working conditions continued to siphon talented people from the teaching profession. Eastern Rumelia, on the other hand, paid its teachers and school directors as much as 500 leva more for each level than did the Principality.[103]

The issue of teacher pay was one issue never fully resolved in a successful manner. However, the Ministry fared much better with its third crucial challenge, that of helping destitute children attend the free schools, especially at the higher levels.

---

[102] *Stenograficheski dnevnitsi na III ONS, pŭrva redovna sesiia*, February 9, 1883, pp. 6-19.

[103] *Ibid*., pp. 9-10.

State Needs Versus Student Poverty
The Stipend Issue

While the architects of the future of Bulgarian education opened schools at a pace that was bankrupting the communities, a terrible irony was that many students could not afford to attend either the state schools or the community schools. Despite the fact that both types of schools were either free or extremely cheap in terms of tuition, financial obstacles remained for a relatively poor populace still recovering from the war. Clothing, food, housing, and books were some of the incidental expenditures connected with the free education that threatened to defeat the goal of universal primary education. The secondary school situation was even bleaker because these schools, more often than the primary ones, were few and far between and entailed long daily trips or boarding in the city of location. Unfortunately, since the middle and secondary schools were usually located in cities, the extra cost of boarding fell on those who could least afford it--rural students. However, the problem of incidental expenditures for boarding, supplies, and food was not confined to either rural areas or to the secondary school system. Even if a primary school was located in one's own village, there were still books and supplies to be bought. And even city children had to commute or board if a secondary or middle school was not located in their own city.

Many more complications lay in store for those who aspired to higher education, since this by definition meant going abroad. The country desperately needed citizens skilled in all areas of learning and technology, yet could not provide such instruction in the Principality. Thus students had to go to a wide variety of countries to acquire post-secondary education, an unthinkable luxury for all but a privileged few.

Many of these same problems had existed long before 1878 and independence. The tradition of subsidizing education for those who could not afford it was hardly new to Bulgarians. In previous times, cell schools and secular schools had waived head taxes or tuition for indigent students. The famous Aprilov gymnasium established an important precedent with its stipend system designed to prevent the school in Gabrovo from becoming a purely local rather than a national affair. At the same time, Bulgarian merchants began to underwrite all or part of the costs involved in sending young Bulgarians abroad for the purpose of acquiring secondary, university, or specialized educations. Sometimes, as in the case of Panslavists in

Russia, foreigners helped to defray such expenses. The notable efforts of American missionaries at Robert College was another such example.

The establishment of a number of secondary education facilities in the newly independent country did not erase the need of direct student subsidy for reasons already indicated. But more importantly, since no higher education institutions yet existed and the need for people with such training was urgent, the practice of sending young Bulgarians abroad became even more pressing and necessary. However, the Ministry's desire to continue sending students abroad or even to increase the number became a controversial issue involving national pride and priorities in the allocation of funds.

Drinov had encountered no such problems when he established stipends in his administration because he did not have to obtain the approval of a legislative body. His successors, however, ran into some obstacles when the first request was formally made in the <u>Sŭbranie</u> for funds to send Bulgarians to foreign countries. (There was little opposition to funding internal scholarships.)

Basically, opponents of foreign stipends accused the Ministry of squandering money to send a privileged few abroad when that money could have been better used either to build more village schools or preferably to construct higher educational and specialized schools in the Principality.[104]

The giants of Bulgarian education rallied to the defense of foreign stipends. Such seasoned educators or literary figures as Georgi Kirkov, Petko R. Slaveikov, and Ivan Giuzelev made impassioned pleas for understanding and pointed out that state needs demanded continued subsidy for foreign study because while Bulgaria could not provide higher education to its own youth, it desperately needed people with such training and education. Kirkov, former director of the Sofia Mens Gymnasium, argued that there were in Russia alone about 100 Bulgarian students who could not complete their education on their own resources. "We must not regret," he argued, "the 2,000 leva we spend on each student because when he returns fully prepared, the State will have great use of him."[105]

Ivan Giuzelev, the Minister of Public Instruction at the time, emphasized as well the pressing and

---

[104] Stenograficheski dnevnitsi na II ONS, pŭrva redovna sesiia, May 31, 1880, p. 672.

[105] Ibid., p. 673 et passim.

immediate needs of state, but also endorsed the idea of eventual construction of higher educational facilities in Bulgaria.[106]

The best presentation of the case for sending young Bulgarians abroad, however, came from the reknowned poet Slaveikov, who answered the charge that the state lavished great sums of money on a few foreign scholarships while the same amounts could support many new village schools in Bulgaria. Slaveikov carefully explained that while it was true that the villages needed schools and that in many places the schools were operated by malcontents, these problems would in time be overcome, and the schools would not remain in this condition. "But," cautioned Slaveikov, "if we turn our attention only to these schools, then everything will remain in the same place it has up until now. We have entered into a political existence, we have become a state, buth with our /present/ resources, we are not able to forge ahead."[107] He further urged that the amount not be cut even by the smallest amount because that would make it easier to eliminate it entirely the

---

[106] Ibid.

[107] Ibid., p. 673.

next time. Such cutting and elimination could be justified only when they fulfilled pressing state needs.

The Sŭbranie was swayed by the orators and voted the required sums, but a warning had been served on the Ministry, and the message was not lost. Further debates over these issues in Parliament raised the problem of arbitrariness in the granting of all stipends, foreign and domestic. Also several legislators hinted at the possible abuses of the stipends, such as the granting of scholarships to the children of the rich.[108]

The latter problems came under the scrutiny of the methodical Jireček, who devised a well-defined system of administering stipends to cope with abuses as well as with the rising number of applicants. A particularly thorny problem concerned the appropriate action to be taken if a student decided not to return to his native land or resisted entering the state service. Also, some stipends called for repayment, which sometimes was a long while in coming.

Figures on the number of stipends which were distributed are rare for the period of 1880-1882. Jireček

---

[108] Ibid.; Ivan Geshov, "Chinovnicheskii proletariat (Kritika vŭrkhu srednoto obrazovanie)," Periodichesko spisanie na Bŭlgarsko Knizhovno Druzhestvo, XIX (1886), 118.

in a letter to Marin Drinov in 1880, quoted the following figures: 300 state stipends in Bulgarian secondary schools and 62 government stipendists outside the country (presumably all in higher education.) Of the 300 internal stipendists, 75 were from Macedonia, 40 from Eastern Rumelia, 13 from Pirot and Vranje, 7 from Edirne, and 1 from Dobrudzha.[109] All of these areas were outside the borders of the Principality of Bulgaria. Of the 62 foreign stipendists, 32 were in Russia, 10 were in Bohemia and Croatia, 2 in Romania, 1 at Robert College, 4 in France, 3 in Germany, and 1 in Switzerland.[110]

Minister of Education Georgi Teokharev reported to Parliament in 1883 that 28 students were abroad in the school year 1881-1882 and the distribution was as follows:

Moscow	2	Paris	1
Odessa	3	Zagreb	4
Prague	2	Belgrade	1
Saint Petersburg	2	Robert College	1
Leipzig	1	Kiev	4

---

[109] Jireček, letter to Marin Drinov, July 4, 1880, in Sis, Korespondentsiia, p. 205.

[110] Ibid.

Munich 2   Zurich 1

Jena 1   Nikolaev . . . 1

Strasburg . . . 1   Kharkov . . . 1

Thus, 13 were in the Russian Empire and 15 in non-Russian schools.[111] But these figures were only for the Ministry of Public Instruction; other ministries also supported students abroad. For example, in 1882-1883, the Ministry of Public Instruction reported 29 students abroad on its resources and 19 abroad through the funding of other ministries.[112]

Teokharev's report also mentions figures for internal stipends: 351 full stipends and 131 partial stipends for a total of 482. Of these 482, 390 went to male students, 92 to female students. Sixty percent of the recipients were from the Principality, 40 percent from outside. Forty-two of the full stipendists and 33 of the half-stipendists were in pedagogical schools.[113]

---

[111]Teokharev, "Zapiska," pp. 27-28.

[112]Bulgaria, Ministry of Public Instruction, Report to the Budget Commission of Narodno Sŭbranie, February 4, 1883, TsDIA, F. 173 (Narodno Sŭbranie), op. 1, ae. 45.

[113]Teokharev, "Zapiska," p. 27.

The Ministerial Council decided in February, 1885, to limit severely the number of stipends going to Bulgarian students outside the Principality itself. (Most of these "outsiders" were from Macedonia or Eastern Rumelia.) The measure was taken because of the constantly rising number of applicants within the Principality.[114]

Despite the great numbers of internal stipends, it was obviously not enough to keep up with the demand. The Ministry thus had to devise stricter regulations for apportioning the meager amounts available for such aid. In 1883, upon the opening of a special School Council to assist the Ministry in its work, the Minister of Public Instruction Agura cited a law on stipends as a most pressing need due to the steadily increasing numbers of students wanting such aid. Therefore, the School Council, headed by Jireček, set to work compiling the "precise guidelines which Agura begged of them."[115] In actuality, however, evidence

---

[114] Bulgaria, Ministerial Council, session of February 8, 1885, TsDIA, F. 284 (Ministerial Council), op. 1, ae. 355, p. 1.

[115] Dimitŭr Agura, "Otkrivaneto na Uchebniia Sŭvet pri Ministerstvoto na Narodata prosveta," Ucheben Vestnik, I, 1-4 (1883), 107-110.

suggests that most of the "Statute on Stipends" that
came out of the meetings of the School Council was
Jireček's own handiwork. (A detailed list in Jireček's
handwriting in his archives corresponds exactly to a
draft bill on the subject submitted to the School
Council.)[116]

This project, adopted in August, 1883, finally
regulated the entire procedure for obtaining a stipend,
whether for internal or external study. The law on
foreign stipends promised a list would be published
each June in the Dŭrzhaven vestnik, indicating the number and kind of stipends open from the past year ("kind"
referring to half-stipend or full-stipend, as well as
to what field was involved). For the first time, a
complete set of credentials would be demanded from each
and every applicant. Credentials would have to show:
(1) that a student had completed a secondary institution with good grades or that the student had already
been accepted at the institution where he wished to
complete the education desired, (2) that the student
could not pursue higher education on his own means

---

[116] The Ucheben Sŭvet deserves special attention and will be discussed in Chapter Eight. Established in 1883, it helped review texts and formulate policy. Jireček was president of this council from 1883 to 1884.

(as certified by community officials), (3) that the student was completely healthy, as certified by a physician, and (4) most importantly, "that the student is prepared to obligate himself to serve the Bulgarian government for as many years as he has received the stipend."[117]

The actual petition for foreign stipend, moreover, henceforth had to include exact details as to the student's birthplace, his parents and their occupations, on whose resources he had studied up until then, as well as an explanation of what courses he wished to follow and at what institution. The student also had to present a document showing his success in such studies already at the secondary level.[118] The law made it clear that applicants already pursuing studies abroad would be given first consideration so that they could more quickly be put to practical use in the Fatherland; this was an obvious attempt to deal with the criticisms raised in the press and in the Sŭbranie concerning the impracticality of the venture or the aversion of the average student to working for the state on his return.

---

[117] Jireček, "Pravilnik za stipendii v chuzhbina," ABAN, F. 3 (Jireček), op. 1, ae. 1125, p. 61.

[118] Ibid.

Special consideration was also to be given to the children of veterans. These applicants had to furnish the so-called certificate of absolutorium.[119]

In addition, regulations controlled the stipend once it was given to a student. Each recipient had to submit to the Ministry every three months an account of his educational work, including a list of textbooks, lectures, and a description of the progress he was making. Also, the student was obliged to take all examinations and to perform all work as scheduled. Failure to do so without medical excuses would mean divestiture of the stipend from the errant student.[120]

Provisions were made for supplementary aid in the event that the recipient needed unusually expensive books or equipment, but only if the stipendist presented documents, signed by university officials, testifying to this need. Further, at the completion of the studies, the Ministry would verify whether the student had actually purchased such equipment and used it. No mention of how exactly this would be done is made. Each government stipendist had to study French, English, or German intensely enough so as to be able both to speak

---

[119] Ibid., p. 63.

[120] Ibid.

and to write the language. Also, the stipendist could not transfer from one institution to another without permission from the Ministry of Public Instruction.[121] Finally, a hasty note at the end sternly warned stipendists to keep the Ministry informed of every change of address but never to send letters to the Ministry postage due.[122]

The Ministry also instituted similarly tighter controls for the granting of internal stipends. The opening paragraph of the regulation expressed the government's intention that such stipends were to be issued only "to poor and to trustworthy students at <u>state</u> secondary educational institutions in the Principality."[123] State stipends fell into two categories, full or half, and in either case, could only be received by students in the third class or beyond Students in the lower classes could receive temporary aid or in unusual cases, only a half-stipend. Again, announcement of the number and kind of stipends

---

[121] Ibid.

[122] Ibid.

[123] Jireček, "Pravilnik za stipendii pri uchebnii zavedeniia v Kniazhestvoto," ABAN, F. 3 (Jireček), op. 1, ae. 1125, p. 64.

available was made at the end of the school year in the Dŭrzhaven vestnik.[124] The Ministry issued such stipends at the beginning of each academic year, although temporary aid could be granted even after the first semester.

The same proofs of success, impoverishment, and health were required for these stipends as for the foreign study ones. However, instead of submitting these documents directly to the Ministry as in the case of foreign stipends, the applicant submitted them to the director of the school which he wished to enter. The Teachers Council then considered these applications and turned them over to the Ministry along with its opinions on each case.[125] Only in unusual cases of applicants from outside the Principality could petitions be sent directly to the Ministry.

The Ministry then took over the actual decision-making and the distribution, again with several publicly stated preferences in mind. In this case, students of higher grades came first, as well as children of "those deserving the honor of the Fatherland."[126] The

---

[124] Ibid.

[125] Ibid.

[126] Ibid.

Ministry promised to take special care that the stipends were evenly distributed through all provinces and counties, as well as through the rural and urban population.

Although in theory the Ministry of Public Instruction was supposed to have total control over the distribution of all forms of stipends, a severe complication arose when the State Council decided to intervene in the process, with unfortunate results. The problem was connected to the political turmoil in the young state. In May, 1881, Prince Alexander von Battenberg suspended the Tŭrnovo Constitution, and shortly afterwards a new political body, the State Council, was set up to help the Prince rule the state. There was no provision in the Constitution for such actions, and, in short, the State Council was quite unconstitutional and illegal. Nevertheless, it was a political fact of life and could not be ignored. In drawing up the internal regulations for running the State Council, a particularly ominous sentence appeared reserving to the State Council final decisions on all questions regarding outlays for pensions, stipends, aid to schools, and other items for which the Sŭbranie had already designated funds.[127]

With the intention of avoiding all future misunderstandings, Jireček, Minister of Public Instruction at the time (February, 1882), immediately dispatched an angry letter demanding an explanation of this clause and its direct or indirect meaning.[128] The reply to Jireček tersely explained that the article's message was quite clear, and the Ministry of Public Instruction had to forward its decisions to the State Council. It would then be determined whether the aid, stipend, or pension was appropriate and whether it should be granted in the amount specified.[129] This action, to which the Ministry acquiesed, although not with great enthusiasm, was certainly a vexatious interference in the ability of the Minister to dispatch his duties without encumbrance. The clause had several unfortunate effects. First, it set a precedent which, after the abolition of the State Council and upon the restoration

---

[127] Bulgaria, State Council, letter of the Ministry of Public Instruction to the State Council, February 15, 1882, TsDIA, F. 708 (State Council), op. 1, ae. 204, p. 21.

[128] Ibid.

[129] Bulgaria, State Council, letter to the Ministry of Public Instruction, February 16, 1882, TsDIA, F. 708 (State Council), op. 1, ae. 204, p. 3.

of the Tŭrnovo Constitution, the Ministerial Council then used in order to adopt some of the practices in question, including the review of financial outlays.[130] Second, the State Council, and later the Ministerial Council, began to exceed a mere review and began, in effect, to shape and state policy on stipend distribution. At times, decisions of the Ministerial or State Council merely confirmed those of the Ministry of Public Instruction. On other occasions, however, provisions were laid down, riders were attached, amounts changed, or types of scholarships altered. Also, the Ministerial Council took a very active role in deciding what to do with special bequests involving stipends. A case in point involved the Keremitchiev trust set up by Petŭr Khadzhi-Nenkov Keremitchiev for sending young Bulgarians to study in Romania. In this case, the Ministerial Council's aid was vital since the Keremitchiev fund involved extensive legal wrangling in Bulgarian, Russian, and Wallachian courts.[131] The Ministerial Council

---

[130]During the period in which the Tŭrnovo Constitution was suspended by Prince Alexander's coup d'état, the Ministerial Council had continued to exist, but most of its power had been usurped by the State Council. The State Council had been set up by Alexander to bypass the normal constitutional channels.

[131]Bulgaria, Ministerial Council, session of January 16, 1882, TsDIA, F. 284 (Ministerial Council), op. 1, ae. 80, p. 3.

eventually decided that the Keremitchiev fund should be used to support one stipend each for physics or mathematics, animal husbandry, architecture, engineering, women's higher pedagogy, and mining, along with two stipends abroad for philology.[132]

The Ministerial Council also eventually ended up making decisions as to how vacant foreign stipend slots should be filled (i.e. what subject should be studied), and whether or not special requests should be granted.[133] In 1883, a session of the Ministerial Council warned the Ministry of Public Instruction that new foreign stipends should be given only to students who were preparing to become teachers in middle schools of the Principality, doctors, engineers, or other specialties.[134] In time, the Ministerial Council and the Ministry of Public Instruction began to work more

---

[132] Bulgaria, Ministerial Council, session of June 7, 1883, TsDIA, F. 284 (Ministerial Council), op. 1, ae. 180, p. 2, and session of August e, 1884, ae. 321, p. 1.

[133] Bulgaria, Ministerial Council, session of August 17, 1883, TsDIA, F. 284 (Ministerial Council), op. 1, ae. 186, p. 3, and session of October 11, 1883, ae. 196, p. 2.

[134] Bulgaria, Ministerial Council, session of October 29, 1883, TsDIA, F. 284 (Ministerial Council), op. 1, ae. 208, p. 1

closely with one another as in the decision of the Ministerial Council in August, 1884, which defined the new limit of foreign stipends as 1,800 leva each (with extra provisions for test fees). This decision also laid down the measures that were to be taken against students who failed to return to the Principality or to enter state service.[135] A similar joint action in February, 1885, limited stipends of all kinds to only those students who came from the Principality itself, unless the Ministerial Council expressly ruled otherwise; under no circumstances, however, would the graduates of Macedonian schools be accepted into Bulgarian institutions.

All of the measures advanced by the Ministry and other governmental agencies helped smooth many of the difficulties and obstacles in the stipend program. But problems remained. The amount furnished to the foreign stipendists increased from 100 leva a month to 150 leva a month. Occasional letters from stipendists in desperate financial straits during the early years had had their effect. Emanuil Ivanov, for example, a young Bulgarian studying in Munich, wrote to the

---

[135] Bulgaria, Ministerial Council, session of August 20, 1884, TsDIA, F. 284 (Ministerial Council), op. 1, ae. 336, p. 3.

Ministry in September, 1881, describing his pitiful plight. His 100 leva a month stipend was woefully inadequate, which provoked constant worry, which in turn caused him to receive poorer grades. Ivanov asked for a supplementary income, because after all his necessities had been paid for, he was left with only 25 leva with which to live. Other stipendists wrote about difficulties caused by illness, outrageous examination or graduation fees, or expensive texts or equipment. The Ministry, especially under Jireček, eventually made special provisions which were aimed at ameliorating many of these difficulties, but Bulgarian students abroad never received more than subsistence-level stipends.

Problems also persisted with regard to the abuse of the stipend-granting procedure, especially random incidences of wealthy students receiving state aid. These were largely overcome by the new regulations which called for more careful checks on the financial needs of each applicant. Certification of this condition was removed from the jurisdiction of communal officials and placed in the hands of teachers councils, especially as regarded domestic stipends.[136]

---

[136] A good explanation of a typical system in operation can be found in Umlenski, ed., Pŭrva gimnazia

The pool of resources for stipends was enriched by several large bequests earmarked for this purpose, such as the Keremitchiev fund or the Ivan Manafov fund given to the Gabrovo schools in 1883. In such cases, the community and the Ministry would cooperate in all legal matters leading to the disposition and distribution of such funds.[137]

Finally, special funds or societies sprang up with the express purpose of providing *ad hoc* assistance to students not qualifying for stipends yet still in need of aid of some kind. In Gabrovo in 1883, the Teachers Council established a special Society for the Assistance of Poor Students to help such students purchase texts and supplies.[138] All such activity helped not

---

"Neofit Rilski," p. 22ff. The student would submit an application to the director of the school he attended. These credentials would be checked and sent to the teachers council of the same school, which would recheck them, decide whether the applicant would be turned down or receive aid, then forward this information to the Ministry of Public Instruction along with recommendations as to how much aid should be granted.

[137] Gabrovo, City-Communal Administration, "Prepiska s Ministerstvoto na Narodna Prosveta otnosno zaveshtanieto na Ivan Kh. Manafov," ODA, F. 5K (City of Gabrovo), op. 3, ae. 98, pp. 1-10. Manafov had stipulated that stipends be set up to send Bulgarian youths to the Odessa technical gymnasium.

[138] Gabrovo, Technical Gymnasium, "Protokolna kniga na Gabrovoska realna gimnaziia," meeting of October 28, 1883, ODA, F. 150K (Gabrovo Technical Gymnasium), op.1, ae. 1, p. 43.

only to ease the difficulties, but also to call attention to the situation.

The problems surrounding the stipend question were integrally related to the entire debate in Bulgaria over the question of priorities in Bulgarian educational policy. In fact, debate on the stipend issue helped touch off a conflict over much greater issues. Gradually, two camps or points of view emerged in the course of this debate. One group rather idealistically demanded the immediate establishment of universities, law schools, and manufacturing schools. The other group resisted and claimed that the country could not realistically embark on such an ambitious program. The conflict between the two camps caused much frustration for ministerial officials and indicated the atmosphere of opinion regarding the future of Bulgaria that existed at this time.

CHAPTER FOUR

PROBLEMS OF PRIORITY IN EDUCATIONAL POLICY

Realists and Idealists

When criticism of the Ministry's stipend program arose, those in charge at the time responded with promises of better guidelines for the awarding and the administration of the stipends. However, such measures did little to allay criticism of the program. It took a while for ministerial officials to realize that the critics were not aiming their remarks at the stipend system itself, but in fact had much deeper philosophical interests in mind. The controversy over the foreign stipends, especially, was only part of a much broader problem pitting those favoring an ambitious educational program against those who were struggling to set up a rudimentary system. The "Idealists" tended to belong to the Conservative faction in Bulgarian politics, while those on the "Realist" side tended to be Liberals.[1]

---

[1] The terms Realist and Idealist will be used here only for the sake of discussion. While adherents of the respective positions accused each other in these terms, there were never any formally or informally organized groups bearing such names. Realist then refers to anyone urging that the country could realistically only afford to concern itself with the construction of a basic primary and elementary system. The term Idealist refers to anyone rejecting this assumption and

Yet it would be a mistake to attach too much political significance to the clashes between these two antagonistic groups. Liberals and Conservatives could be found in either camp, and many of the people in the Realist camp actually sympathized with most of the demands of, and criticisms by, the Idealists.

On the issue of priorities of post-Liberation Bulgarian educational policies, the Idealists were outspoken critics of the policies of Ministers of Public Instruction such as Giuzelev, Agura, Jireček and Teokharev. Most of the clashes between the two groups occurred on the floor of the Sŭbranie during consideration of annual budgets for the Ministry. Sŭbranie representatives used these occasions quite effectively to question specific educational policies, as well as the general future of Bulgarian education. What kinds of schools would best promote the success of the new nation in every aspect of its existence? What were the most pressing needs of the new state, and how could the schools help meet the challenges? What should be

---

advancing a program of specialized or higher educational institutions to be started at once. Idealists also disliked the system of sending Bulgarians abroad and wished to curb the practice.

the nature of such education?[2] All of these questions were hotly debated, and some were never resolved.

The first such interpellation of the policies of the Ministry of Public Instruction came during the first regular Sŭbranie. Representatives Eremiia Geshov and Petko Karavelov questioned the 60,000 leva requested by the Ministry to send Bulgarian students to schools and universities abroad. Karavelov wondered why such a large amount was being diverted for such usage, in view of the Ministry's efforts to set up good secondary schools. Geshov, who claimed he would support the amount if it proved to be necessary, nonetheless maintained that it was a pity that government-run schools were so inadequate that such sums still had to be spent abroad to compensate.[3] These questions were the opening shots of the debate and were echoed throughout this period. The innocent questions were answered with impassioned pleas by the Minister of Public Instruction Giuzelev and the President of the Sŭbranie, Petko R. Slaveikov. Giuzelev simply pointed out that while

---

[2] Tsani Kaliiandzhiev, Profesionalnoto obrazovanie u nas (Varna: 1925), p. 3.

[3] Stenograficheski dnevitsi na II ONS, pŭrva redovna sesiia, May 31, 1881, pp. 672-673.

Geshov's remarks were true, it was undeniable that Bulgaria had no institutions of higher education, yet desperately needed people with such advanced training. Slaveikov made a more eloquent and poignant defense of such scholarships. He acknowledged that many village schools were then in poor condition but assured the Sŭbranie that it was unlikely that this condition would continue. The future would see great improvements. Meanwhile, the Sŭbranie must not lower the allocation from 60,000 to 45,000 leva, as it had planned to do. Slaveikov argued:

> We have entered political life, we have become a state, yet with our resources, we are unable to advance. Thus, I am of the opinion now that if we reduce the sum from 60,000 to 45,000 leva, there will come a time when the money will be completely eliminated; but for now, we wish to prepare administrators /_deiateli_/ for our own higher educational institutions, so that in time we can open them ourselves; otherwise, we will not achieve our goal. Thus, in the face of all economics, I think that the commission has well considered these sums which perhaps from year to year can be gradually reduced. But for now, let us keep the sum as requested. Otherwise, there will be a loss of the progress which we desire to have in our state.[4]

Finally, these remarks were buttressed by Georgi Kirkov, director of the National Library, who pointed out that the Bulgarian people should regard these

---

[4] Ibid., p. 673.

scholarships of 2,000 leva each as a worthwhile investment. When the student returned home with his higher education, he assured them, the State would make great use of his knowledge.[5]

The Sŭbranie approved the reduced sum, but the battle had just begun. The critics were satisfied that foreign stipends were still needed, but Geshov's question had opened a Pandora's box. The most obvious question was what, if any, steps were being taken to open domestic higher education facilities. But the inquiry did not stop there. In the same session of the Sŭbranie, a delegate asked why so many general gymnasia were being opened when Bulgaria had need of people with much more specialized education, for example, in agriculture. The delegate, Tseko Petkov, in fact, introduced a bill to establish an agricultural school. The motion touched off a heated debate on the need for specialized education, especially when the "Realist" president of the Sŭbranie, Petko R. Slaveikov, urged that the bill be tabled because the timing for such action was inappropriate. This only angered delegates such as Balarev, who advanced the argument that if anything served the real needs of an agrarian country such as

---

[5] Ibid., p. 673.

Bulgaria, it was an agricultural school. Deputy Minkovich further argued that agriculture was the chief source of wealth for the new Principality, and good schools of agriculture would allow the country to exploit its resources effectively. He drew a parallel with America and claimed that American agricultural schools had helped that country advance to the point where even Russia, the breadbasket of Europe, was having difficulty in competing.[6] The motion for the agricultural school failed when its author withdrew it, but one deputy used the failure to lambast the Sŭbranie for its shortsightedness. The delegate, Ianko Brŭshlianov, raised the issue that was to plague the Ministry of Public Instruction again in future parliamentary sessions. "If we look at the present condition," claimed Brŭshlianov, "in which we are found, three years after our liberation, we will see that from day to day one class develops among us, and this class, so to speak, is the bureaucratic one." It seemed to be a common occurence, he noted, for a village boy to acquire a little learning and then go to the city to become a bureaucrat. Brŭshlianov warned, "If we allow

---

[6] Ibid., p. 673.

this state of affairs to continue, it will not be long before we have a special class of bureaucrats." An agricultural school, he implied, might have curbed this tendency.[7]

The theme of a dangerous exploitative class of bureaucrats was stressed even more forcefully in the next session of the Sŭbranie in 1883. Impatience had grown, and the criticisms of the Ministry of Public Instruction's emphasis on general education grew correspondingly sharper and more severe. A particularly black day for the Ministry of Public Instruction came on February 9, 1883, when a deputy to the Third Regular Sŭbranie suggested that in view of the unacceptable policies of the Ministry, the Parliament should make approval of the budget dependent upon the undertaking of certain essential reforms. Another delegate, Dimitur Boshniakov, stood ready to supply suggestions for reform. Again, the focus was on the type of education offered, although other charges were levelled, such as that of the involvement of teachers in politics. Boshniakov sarcastically remarked that he understood education to be something more than simply the production of more useless bureaucrats. Furthermore, he said:

---

[7] Ibid., p. 575.

> We have gymnasia, realschulen, but not one institution in which to study any kind of manufacturing or commerce or industry which /could/ support the country. We have five or six gymnasia or realschulen of which the Fatherland had almost no use; from these /schools/ emerge simply bureaucrats, and they will burden the people rather than provide anything useful for the Fatherland.[8]

Boshniakov urged that a new Minister be hired who would, with the State Council, work out a complete reform of the existing educational institutions to make them more compatible with the needs of the Bulgarian people. He suggested as well that Bulgaria must strive to build, as soon as possible, a higher school or lycée for the instruction of medicine, law, and engineering.

In a final blast, he called again for stricter supervision of stipendists abroad, because not one of the stipendists of 1882 had returned to serve his country. These individuals, he demanded, should be required by law to return.

Other delegates jumped to add their own criticisms to Boshniakov's already thorough treatment,

---

[8] Stenograficheski dnevnitsi na III ONS, purva redovna sesiia, February 9, 1883, p. 2. Boshniakov urged that one good reform would be to turn the Ministry over to a native Bulgarian--a slap at both Teokharev (who was not born in Bulgaria) and at the Executive Secretary, Jireček, who was a subject of the Austrian Empire.

although many of the supporting statements were aimed at the alleged incompetence of the current Minister, Georgi Teokharev.

The points raised by Boshniakov were reiterated throughout the period of 1880-1885 and even after. In his memoirs, Eremiia Geshov, who had touched off the debate, painted a grim picture of the results of too much reliance on gymnasial education at the expense of specialized or technical schools. Geshov dismissed secondary schools then in existence as nothing but factories for the production of bureaucrats. If this continued, there would soon be a dangerous oversupply of already superfluous students. Geshov warned that these hordes of unemployed would form armies and parties to overthrow the government: "like the condottiere of the Middle Ages, they will group themselves around political leaders, and under the banner of some popular idea, they will fight each other for the public money."[9] Geshov pointed to Spain and Greece, where terrible political strife occurred because, with each change of each head of a ministry, went also hundreds or thousands

---

[9] Geshov, Spomeni, pp. 220-224.

of lower bureaucrats. That situation must not be allowed to happen in Bulgaria.[10]

Most of this virulent criticism of bureaucrats was voiced by delegates who belonged to the Conservative faction. There are several possible explanations as to why Conservatives were so upset with the state of affairs. The Conservatives were aware, first of all, that the people tended to identify the new bureaucrats with their counterparts in Turkish times and hence mistrusted them. More importantly, however, the Conservatives represented a strong constituency of traders and more powerful farmers who, in turn, feared and resented foreign intrusions in the Bulgarian economy, as well as the diversion of field workers into schools. Thus, the Conservatives were often articulating the views of particular social groups. Also, as the representatives of the entrepreneurial classes, the Conservatives no doubt realized the need for continued growth and of the availability of people trained in economic and business affairs.[11]

---

[10] Ibid.

[11] N. Aleksiev, Nashata uchilishtna politika (istorichesko izsledvane) (Sofia: 1911), pp. 20-25; Ivan Stamenov, "Ideiata za trudovo vŭzpitanie i obuchenie sled Osvobozhdenieto," Narodno prosveta, XIV, 7 (1958), 88-89; see also, Dimitŭr Blagoev (founder of

Whatever the reasons for dissatisfaction with the burgeoning bureaucratic class, the opponents were few. By this time, most of the Bulgarian intelligenstia itself was part of the bureaucratic structure which, of course, included the Sŭbranie deputies, whether Conservative or Liberal. Nevertheless, the criticisms of the Ministry of Public Instruction on this issue and others stung those who were responsible for the state of affairs.

Those who advanced what might be called the "Realist" position were caught in a very uncomfortable situation. Most of them sympathized with the frustrations of those calling for medical and agricultural schools as well as universities. Many of the Realists, for example, were also members of the Liberal Party, a party conscious of its ties to the revolutionary movement of the 1860s and 1870s. In 1874, one such revolutionary, Liuben Karavelov, had advanced a list of priorities for Bulgarian education which included the establishment of a higher educational institution.[12] Karavelov's

---

Bulgarian Communism), Izbrani proizvedeniia (Sofia: 1950), I, pp. 555, 590, 608. Blagoev, an ex-teacher, believed these calls for professional schools were indicative of the needs of a growing capitalist system in Bulgaria.

[12] Liuben Karavelov, in Nezavisimost, March 30, 1874, p. 190. Karavelov noted that graduates of foreign institutions could not answer Bulgarian needs because

remarks had been made in his journal <u>Nezavisimost</u>, which was also the name used for the biweekly organ of the Liberal Party. In fact, Karavelov's brother Petko helped edit the journal. Continuing in the earlier tradition, an editorial in <u>Nezavisimost</u> (1880) called for the immediate establishment of a "practical school" to train lawyers for government service.[13] Yet some of the same people endorsing such ideas in 1880 soon found themselves in a position of power and under attack for opposing plans to establish such institutions.

The Realist position was determined by what they as individuals considered to be the political, social, and, especially, economic realities of post-war Bulgaria. Those speaking against the idealistic demands of the <u>Sŭbranie</u> representatives consistently stressed that it was the timing and the priority of the proposals to which they objected, not the ultimate goals themselves. On the issue of foreign stipends, for example, Slaveikov, Giuzelev, Kirkov, and others had emphasized that the immediate needs of the state were so pressing that the country could ill afford the

most of the subjects taught in foreign schools were unnecessary "not only for the graduates but for mankind in general."

[13]<u>Nezavisimost</u>, October 29, 1880, p. 3.

gap that would result if a university or other such school were to be constructed with monies earmarked for sending Bulgarians abroad, with no other funds available.[14] To charges that Bulgarian students were not returning, the Ministry could only promise that it would take stern measures to rectify the situation and remind the stipendists to their responsibilities.[15]

The commitment to send Bulgarians abroad for specialized education had been made by Marin Drinov who was in charge of educational affairs during the Russian occupation. Drinov, a lover of classical education, had also been responsible for the emphasis on general education. He did not believe that Bulgaria was ready, financially or otherwise, to provide such education

---

[14] *Stenograficheski dnevnitsi na II ONS, pŭrva redovna sesiia*, session of May 31, 1880, pp. 670-672.

[15] *Ibid*. In an 1883 debate on this issue, deputies Shivachov and Metropolitan Clement claimed to know of many cases in which wealthy students received aid while poorer ones went begging. Metropolitan Clement maintained that communal officials would often give wealthy students credentials testifying to their "impoverishment" in order to keep good relations with the students' parents. Jirecek answered these charges by promising tighter controls and by remarking that poverty was only one factor in the granting of stipends; high grades and strong letters of recommendation were equally important. See, *Stenograficheski dnevnitsi na III ONS, purva redovna sesiia*, session of February 9, 1883, pp. 4-5.

itself and, in 1879, advised Prince Alexander I that it would be at least four or five years before any kind of higher specialized schools could be opened. Drinov also noted that it would take that long for the newly opened gymnasia to produce enough people eligible for such education.[16] While Prince Alexander I may have been convinced, others were not and insisted that such schools be established.

The Realists had many good arguments against meeting these demands, at least for the time being. Some of them have already been mentioned, such as that of pressing state needs. The Realists argued also that Bulgaria was hardly in a condition to set up elaborate specialized schools when the basic schools were still in a very uncertain state. The Ministry of Public Instruction, they pointed out, was hardly able to enforce the compulsory attendance law of the Constitution, and even then, its standards for success were extremely limited. For example, the Instructions for the Provincial School Inspectors outlined what a successful primary education should consist of:

---

[16] Marin Drinov, letter to Prince Alexander von Battenberg, July 3, 1879, BIA, F. 111 (Marin Drinov), op. 1, ae. 22, p. 205.

Given the existing condition, it will be considered sufficient success, if it can be said that each child who has attended primary school has learned freely to read, to write, to count, and to know at least the rudiments of his native tongue.[17]

The Ministry's inability to enforce compulsory attendance also irritated the Idealists who tried to pass laws ordering such enforcement. The Realists argued against such measures. Ivan Giuzelev, Minister of Public Instruction, cried out in anguish over such attempts, "how can we collect all the children [for the schools], when we do not even have a sufficient number of teachers to instruct them?"[18]

Realists constantly stressed the poor condition of the basic schools as a reason for not setting up more advanced ones. Sometimes, as in the case of Georgi Teokharev, this actually took the form of a Minister of Public Instruction pointing out the failures of the Ministry itself as well as of his predecessors. Teokharev claimed that Bulgarian educational affairs had acually become worse since independence because after the War of Liberation, Bulgarian education had

---

[17] Bulgaria, Ministry of Public Instruction, "Instruktsiia za Okrŭzhnite Uchilishteni Inspektori," Dŭrzhaven vestnik, III, 18 (1881), 149.

[18] Stenograficheski dnevnitsi na II ONS, pŭrva redovna sesiia, session of May 21, 1881, p. 534.

been orphaned; that is, claimed Teokharev in a sensational charge, because the intelligentsia had deserted education for more lucrative and prestigious government jobs:

> All those who were the most experienced teachers have entered into state jobs, while those who remained as teacher are young people, not so experienced; some of them /having/ completed only secondary education, and those who finished higher desired better jobs in government.[19]

As for specialized schools, Teokharev agreed that Bulgaria needed such schools. However, he pointed out that Bulgaria also needed the means to open such schools, and it was questionable whether such means existed. He also suggested that the Sŭbranie delegates stop criticizing the Ministry since the Ministry could do nothing along such lines if the Sŭbranie did not allocate funds for such projects.[20]

In this statement, Teokharev raised probably the most important argument against a high priority on specialized and higher schools--the financial argument. The issue was raised on yet another occasion when the

---

[19]Stenograficheski dnevnitsi na III ONS, pŭrva redovna sesiia, session of February 9, 1883, p. 3.

[20]Ibid.

possibility of opening an agricultural school was considered in the Sŭbranie sessions of 1880. A bill was proposed that would establish an agricultural school and allocate 600,000 leva to finance it. Realists such as Mollov, Slaveikov, and Karavelov were aghast that such an action could even be considered. Karavelov, incensed at the unreasonable amounts proposed for such a project, argued that this type of school might be of little use to Bulgaria. Besides, sniped Karavelov, it would be absurd for a small poor country like Bulgaria to build a school so expensive that "its cows will live better than its peasants!" He also cited the example of Russia's Petrovskaia Akademiia, employing 30 to 40 professors but of minimal use to Russian agriculture.[21] Other supporters of the Realist position more calmly argued that such work was better suited for the future, and Slaveikov and Mollov proposed that perhaps for the time being, a trade school could be set up which could be beneficial for the many children who had been orphaned by the war. But anything further was financially impossible at the time.[22]

---

[21] Stenograficheski dnevnitsi na II ONS, pŭrva redovna sesiia, session of May 21, 1880, p. 571.

[22] Ibid.; such schools, called islakhaneta, had existed in Turkish times in Vidin, Ruse, and Sofia, but were no longer in operation.

In the Sŭbranie, the financial argument was the chief weapon utilized against the Idealists. Elsewhere, however, the Realists, especially the Liberals, outlined their own priorities for Bulgarian education. The Liberals argued that other issues which were far more urgent and basic deserved attention; these included: the position of schools in terms of hygiene and construction, class sizes, the securing of well-trained and effective teachers, the dissemination of propaganda to encourage popular support for schools, and studies of changes in literacy rates. These, claimed the Liberals, were the real priorities in Bulgarian education.[23]

Another argument advanced by the Realists was that in terms of future employment possibilities, specialized education might be very restrictive to the student, whereas a broad general education would have less limited opportunities.

Despite objections and resistance to the demands for specialized schools, the proponents of such schools continued their attacks and finally succeeded in having some measures taken to rectify what they perceived to be the errors of the Ministry. Throughout the period

---

[23] "Uchilishta," Nezavisimost, September 3, 1880, p. 3.

1880-1885, several measures were taken to accommodate and to placate the demands of the Idealists. Most of these efforts, however, ended in dismal failure.

In the first session of the second Sŭbranie, a delegate had introduced a bill to establish an agricultural school. This motion had led to the first real clash between the Idealists and Realists. It ended in failure for the Idealists as the motion was voted down. In the next session of the Sŭbranie, however, an attempt was made to partially accommodate the demands of the Idealists. The Minister of Public Instruction himself, Ivan Giuzelev, reminded the delegates of what had transpired in the previous session. He conceded that support for such a school was too strong to be treated lightly:

> The measure, in which this thing was proposed, was so significant, that some deputies displayed a lack of sympathy towards it; but in any case, from the debates it is seen that the larger part of the deputies were of the opinion that it is desirable to open an agricultural school.[24]

Thus, claimed Giuzelev, the Ministry of Public Instruction had studied the issue and had worked out a bill to open such a school in the experimental farm (chiflik) in Ruse. The bill consisted of twelve points.

---

[24] Stenograficheski dnevnitsi na II ONS, pŭrva redovna sesiia, session of November 25, 1880, p. 170.

It would set up a state-financed agricultural school in the state-owned experimental farm in Ruse. The school was to be under the authority of the Ministry of Public Instruction. The course of instruction would last four years and was to be open to anyone who was at least 14 years old and who had successfully finished a primary school. The bill said nothing, however, about curriculum. When Slaveikov asked the Minister of Finance for his opinion of the project, Giuzelev cut him off, aware, no doubt, that the Minister of Finance had vigorously objected to previous attempts to establish such a school. Giuzelev argued that the bill had been approved in the Ministerial Council so no further ministerial comment was needed.[25] The Sŭbranie sent the bill to committee, but it was never passed since the government changed hands only four days later (November 29, 1880), and Giuzelev was replaced.[26]

Nothing further was said or done on the question of specialized schools until the administration of

---

[25] Ibid.

[26] An agricultural school was finally opened in Ruse in 1883. See N. Buchvarov, K. Sharov, et al, Otchet za sŭstoianieto na uchebnoto delo i fermata na dŭrzhavnoto zemledelchesko uchilishte pri grad Ruse prez 1896/97 uchebna godina (Ruse: 1898) for an official account of the school and its progress.

Georgi Teokharev who, in a report to the Sŭbranie in 1883, mentioned that the Ministry of Public Instruction was considering the idea of opening a commerce and trade school in Svishtov.[27] Teokharev knew that a merchant academy had existed very briefly in Svishtov from 1873-1874, financed and run by Dimitur E. Shishmanov. (Shishmanov's son Ivan was soon to be an important figure in cultural and political affairs in Bulgaria.) Shishmanov felt the existing primary schools did little to fulfill this need for practical training and that such schools were necessary to help the development of commerce and industry.[28] Teokharev never attempted, however, to follow up on the idea.

It was not until D. Agura became Minister of Public Instruction in March, 1883, that serious plans were set into motion once again for specialized education. By this time, however, the Conservative Party, which tended to espouse the view of the Idealists, was in power.

---

[27] Teokharev, "Zapiska," p. 25.

[28] Ivan Shishmanov, Pŭrvoto Bŭlgarsko tŭrgovsko uchilishte na D. E. Shishmanov v Svishtov (Sofia: 1903), pp. 1-5. D. Shishmanov wrote his own curriculum and hoped to set up a complete four-year merchant academy along Austrian patterns.

In 1883, the government managed to open three specially oriented schools, but only one of those schools was under the control of the Ministry of Public Instruction. The two others were the result of the efforts of Prince Mikhail Khilkov, a strong supporter of more practical education. He became Minister of Public Works, Agriculture, and Commerce in 1883 and planned for the opening of two schools. One of these schools, which was approved on June 25, 1883, was the long-desired agricultural school in Ruse. The other school was called a "Trade Workshop" and was approved on July 13, 1883, to open in Kniazhevo.[29] Both schools were entirely under the control of the Ministry of Public Works, Agriculture, and Commerce, but the program for the Trade Workshop was submitted to the Ministry of Public Instruction for approval.[30]

The latter Ministry, meanwhile, first under Teokharev's direction, received approval from the Sŭbranie in February, 1883, to open a commercial school in Svishtov the following September. In May, 1883,

---

[29]Bulgaria, Ministry of Public Works, Agriculture, and Commerce, "Zakon za dŭrzhavanata zanaiztchiinitsa," Dŭrzhaven vestnik, V, 74 (1883), 702-703; Aleksiev, Nashata, pp. 30-32.

[30]Bulgaria, Ministry of Public Works, Agriculture, and Commerce, "Zakon za dŭrzhavanata zanaiatchiinitsa," Dŭrzhaven vestnik, V, 74 (1883), 703.

Agura, then Minister, published the statute for the school.[31]

None of the schools fared very well, and the Svishtov school foundered soon after its opening. The problem, as predicted by the Realists, was that specialized schools were very expensive to operate, and the State could not afford to keep them staffed with well-trained personnel. The schools actually competed with the state government for people with such backgrounds.[32] The Trade School was opened again in Svishtov, however, in 1885 under the ministry of Karolev.[33]

During Karolev's tenure of office, an important law was passed which provided for the opening of some professional schools or, at least, classes.[34] But they

---

[31] Stenograficheski dnevnitsi na III ONS, pŭrva redovna sesiia, session of February 9, 1883, p. 21; Aleksiev, Nashata, p. 32.

[32] Aleksiev, Nashata, p. 32.

[33] A statute (ustav) for the school was submitted to the Ministerial Council by the Ministry of Public Instruction on June 7, 1885, and approved on June 28, 1885, see Bulgaria, Ministerial Council, session of June 28, 1885, TsDIA, F. 284 (Ministerial Council), op. 1, ae. 392, p. 3.

[34] Bulgaria, Ministry of Public Instruction, "Zakon za obshtestvennite i chastnite uchilishta," Dŭrzhaven vestnik, VII, 13 (1885), 1-10.

never materialized because the communes were given the opportunity to increase the number of grades in their own secondary schools. The communal officials almost always opted for the expansion of gymnasial (i.e. general education) classes rather than for the addition of specialized or professional classes; the former type of classes were relatively inexpensive to finance in comparison with the more elaborate specialized ones. It was also easier to find teachers to staff the general classes. Equally important, however, was that the communal officials believed that general education classes did not limit a student's employment opportunities but gave him or her an education suitable for a variety of professions.[35]

In any event, throughout the period of 1878-1885, the Ministry of Public Instruction paid little attention to the problem. Even when it did, as in the case of the Svishtov Trade School, its bias was still towards general education. The two schools opened by the Ministry of Public Works, Agriculture, and Commerce were wholly concerned with the specialized nature of the instruction and offered almost no courses in general subjects. In contrast, the Svishtov school, although

---

[35] Aleksiev, Nashata, p. 53.

supposedly a training ground for commerce, still heavily emphasized its relationship to other general education schools. For example, the schools run by the Ministry of Public Works, Agriculture, and Commerce accepted anyone who knew how to read and to write, while the Ministry of Public Instruction's school would accept only those applicants showing a successful completion of a basic primary school education.[36]

One possible reason yet to be mentioned for the heavy emphasis on general education by the Ministers of Public Instruction from 1878 to 1885 is that none of them came from business-oriented backgrounds. They were writers, teachers, historians, or lawyers, or, as in one case, a clergyman. Drinov and Jireček, both enormously influential, were products of classical education and favored the establishment of this type of program in Bulgaria. They could not be expected to take anything but a dim view of technical and trade schools as unworthy of much attention. However, this is a matter of speculation on the basis of their actions, for neither ever spoke against such forms of educational facilities. In any event, little was done in this period to address the issues raised by opponents of

---

[36] Ibid., p. 32.

this aspect of the country's educational policy. But another priority problem was the object of intense concern at the same time; that issue revolved around the degree to which the central government should control all schools, including those at the local level. This issue generated as much intense debate but had happier results in terms of compromise.

The Centralization Issue

The other important priority problem in Bulgarian education at this time, the problem of centralization, caused much less controversy than that of what type of schools should be opened. Yet this problem nonetheless remained a constant one and generated significant debate and discussion.

The crux of the issue was whether or not the State should assume total control and direction over all schools in Bulgaria. This would have been a tremendous break in the tradition of Bulgarian school development. Except for occasional experiments, Bulgarian schools had never experienced centralized control--either native or Turkish. The Turks had taken little or no interest in the educational affairs of their Bulgarian subjects, except to ensure that they did not lead to subversive activities. The Bulgarian higher clergy was not available since Greeks assumed control of those offices. Bulgarian religious affairs were under the loose control of the Patriarch in Constantinople. Since that position was always held by a Greek, the Patriarch naturally favored Greek dominance in Orthodox affairs; this included Greek interference in, and control of, the important clerical positions in Orthodox churches and schools in the Rum Millet. It was not surprising then that the first moves to provide some measure of supreme control over Bulgarian educational affairs coincided with the movement to establish a separate Bulgarian Exarchate; a move that was inspired as much by politics as it was by religion.[37] In fact, two radical members of the Bulgarian intelligentsia, Khristo Botev (1848-1875) and Liuben Karavelov (1837-1879) had suggested in 1873 that Bulgarian school affairs might greatly benefit by the existence of some general supervisory organ.[38] They gave no details on what form

---

[37] The literature on the struggle to establish an autocephalous Bulgarian Exarchate is immense. A classic work is that of Nikov, Vŭzrazhdane na bŭlgarski narod. This is a republication of the original 1930 work. A good modern treatment of the question in its most critical period is Markova, Bŭlgarskoto tsŭrkovna-natsionalno dvizhenie.

[38] Nezavisimost, June 30, 1873, p. 1. This was a substantial departure from their usual insistence that the people be left to themselves in governing their own

or scope such an organ might have. However, when Bulgarian Church aurhorities in the province of Shumen initiated steps in this direction, Karavelov and Botev retreated from supporting such ideas. Their suspicion of the higher clergy as tools of the Turks combined with their fears that such a centralized organ might be used by Ottoman authorities for reasons other than promoting progress in Bulgarian schools.[39]

Botev and Karavelov's fears proved needless because the first attempts to organize school affairs under the aegis of the Church were quite limited and feeble. The Church officials were concerned mostly with trying to establish some modicum of uniformity and some measure of quality control over school affairs in the province of Shumen.[40]

The issue of centralization as faced by the Ministry of Public Instruction after the Liberation had similar elements but involved much deeper issues. The

---

affairs, a position shared by the Liberal Party in post-Liberation Bulgaria. For an outline of the Liberal Party's views on self-government and minimum centralized control, see Tselokŭpna Bulgariia, no. 38, November 30, 1879, p. 1. Unfortunately, the article makes no mention of school affairs.

[39] Nezavisimost, June 30, 1873, p. 1. Chakŭrov, "Liuben Karavelov," pp. 75-84.

[40] Iordanov, L'Instruction publique, p. 20.

similarities were that the Ministry, like church officials in Shumen, discussed centralization as a way to unify school affairs and to control the quality of education. Also, just as revolutionaries viewed the Shumen clergy's attempts to organize with suspicion, so too did the Ministry's proposals meet with mistrust and unease by opponents. Yet the issue of centralization after 1878 was more complex due to the fact that the long tradition of community support and control of the schools had been seriously threatened by the vicissitudes and consequences of war and independence.

Before 1878, certain individuals such as Nesho Bonchev and Marin Drinov had looked at Bulgarian school affairs in a comprehensive manner and suggested changes. Church officials in Shumen had done the same for that province and were genenerally aware that the situation in Shumen province was not unlike that of the rest of the country. But only after 1878 was there a central organ, the Ministry of Public Instruction, that could not only gather facts and statistics to give a view of the entire country's educational affairs but also had the means to make necessary corrections. When the leaders of the Ministry looked at the country's school affairs as a whole, the view was one of intense differentiation. The Ministry, charged with the improvement and advancement of the country's cultural life, saw the terrible imbalances in the nation's schools and universal problems such as teacher shortages. With the communities sinking deeper and deeper into financial difficulties, which caused even wealthy communities to close their schools, the answer appeared obvious--centralize. But while the suggestion was made formally and forcefully, the Bulgarian educational system from 1878 to 1885 remained in a strange situation of symbiosis--neither centralized nor autonomous. The reasons for this situation sheds light on the country's condition at that time.

The first person to control the institution of public instruction, Marin Drinov, was a student of Bulgarian history and thus aware of how well the country had managed to provide schools for its children entirely extemporaneously. He decided not to interfere with this process, believing it to be a spontaneous outgrowth of the people's desire for enlightment.[41]

Drinov's successors, however, did not all believe the traditions of the past necessarily spelled success for the country's future well-being. What had been

---

[41] Tsonkov, Razvitie, p. 199; Chakŭrov, Uchilishtno zakonodatelstvo, p. 37.

appropriate to a backward subject people might not be appropriate to a nation suddenly plunged, independent, into the rapidly changing world of the nineteenth century.

It was Ivan Giuzelev, who took the portfolio of Public Instruction in 1880, who formally opened the debate on whether or not the logical outcome of having a Ministry of Public Instruction should be having a centralized, government-controlled school system. The debate began over suggestions from some circles that the State assume control of teacher appointments; it continued throughout the period and only ended in 1891, when the schools were in fact centralized.

There were indeed many good and logical reasons for centralizing the country's schools, and almost all of these reasons were itemized by the supporters of increased government control, especially in matters concerning the teachers.

In response to the Ministry's own call for public debate of the question, an editorial appeared in the conservative journal Bŭlgarski glas. The anonymous writers lauded the provisions in the Giuzelev project which called for increased supervision by the government over communal financial support of schools and teachers. One part of the editorial exclaimed:

> The material support of the schools does not have to depend on the good will or the greater or lesser attention which the commune pays to the education of its children, but there must be an effective law on official positions passed, so that if the commune does not regularly pay its teachers, the deed will not pass without unpleasant consequences for it. The lack of effective binding force is the principal reason for all our present difficulties.[42]

This argument reflected traditional conservative fears that the people were not ready for self-rule, whether political or financial. But more worrisome was the growing inability of the communes to finance schools, which also raised questions as to how the Ministry was to fulfill the constitutional mandate of compulsory primary education.

The financial problems, however, were not the only questions raised concerning the advisability of letting the communes continue to run school affairs. In a cogent and well-organized essay, also in response to Giuzelev's call, the then Chief Executive of the Ministry, Spas Vatsov, explained why the Ministry had to appropriate more power at the expense of the communes. Vatsov began by taking note of the work of the French student of Balkan affairs, Emile Laveleye, who had made a study of the effects of centralization in

---

[42] "Za Uchilishtata," Bŭlgarski glas, March 27, 1880, p. 7.

Serbian education. Laveleye concluded that Serbia had achieved centralization of political affairs at the expense of popular involvement and independence. There was no genuine interest anymore because the government had removed local affairs from the hands of the citizens.[43] Vatsov, while agreeing that centralization was a risk, even dangerous, believed that in the field of education such a risk was worthwhile. Vatsov's argument was that the independence of the commune should be preserved in all affairs, save educational ones, and he offered four basic reasons for this. First, the central government (i.e. the Ministry of Public Instruction) was in a better position to know the merits of teacher candidates in communal schools. The Ministry's inspectors would evaluate qualifications of candidates since it also set the standards.[44] Second, it was essential that all teachers be grouped into one class with a definite hierarchy, which would serve as the basis of promotion. Without such a national system, there would

---

[43] Émile de Laveleye, La Peninsule des Balkans (Paris: 1888), I, p. 44.

[44] Spas Vatsov, "Koi da naznachava obshtinskite uchiteli za osnovnite uchilishta, Ucheben vestnik, I, 7, (1883), 4.

be no stimulus to progress. If teachers were named by individual communities, there could be no system, and teachers would have to remain where fate had sent them.[45] Third, a good selection of teachers could only be made by a specialist experienced in school work, and most communal administrations were too small to be so prepared and to be able to avoid favoritism.[46] Finally, primary education was a subject of national interest not just local. Why then, asked Vatsov, leave such an important problem as teacher appointments to local powers with their caprice and inexperience? He concluded:

> Without a central organization, it is not possible to have cohesion, it is not possible to have order. Without general supervision, the uncontrolled appointment of teachers will coincide with party interests, to their arbitrary preferences: that is anarchy.[47]

Vatsov's arguments were not without their flaws. For example, there was no guarantee that party interests would not affect teacher appointments by a centralized authority, as if those in power in the nation's capital were somehow immune.

---

[45] Ibid.

[46] Ibid., p. 5.

[47] Ibid.

The opponents of centralization would offer their critique of such views, but Vatsov was not the only one urging centralization, nor were the others necessarily moved by his considerations.

In the Sŭbranie, some deputies urged the Ministry to regulate more closely and to supervise the schools for political or nationalistic reasons. Minister Teokharev voiced the concerns of many over the uncontrolled existence of schools run by foreigners (especially Catholics and Protestants). Some of the objections were xenophobic in basis, but many critics were genuinely concerned about the activities of these non-Bulgarian schools. Teokharev singled out Greek schools in Varna, American Protestant schools in Samokov, and a French Catholic school in Sofia as being in need of scrutiny.[48] Teokharev suggested a special law be passed to give the Ministry the power to regulate the opening and closing of such schools in the future. Teokharev's unvoiced worry was that these schools represented a threat to the sovereignty and uniformity not only of Bulgarian education, but perhaps also to the Bulgarian political entity.

---

[48]Teokharev, "Zapiska," p. 23. The question of non-Bulgarian and non-Orthodox schools within the Principality is discussed in a later chapter.

Also in the Sŭbranie, there were calls for more control of school affairs by the Ministry so that a stricter rein over politically troublesome teachers and students might be established.[49]

A better and more powerful argument, however, was that which stated that if Bulgaria had progressed so remarkably well against terrific odds in education without a central organ of control, then the possibilities under a centralized system were surely much more promising. This in fact was precisely the position of the Minister who finally succeeded in centralizing Bulgaria's school system.[50] Georgi Zhivkov's arguments were no doubt also used before his time (1891). These included the belief that the schools and the government deserved to be one and should not be alien to each other.[51] He was not adverse to local self-government, but only if it was not carried to extremes which could injure national interests. Zhivkov praised the advances in Bulgarian education since 1878, but suggested that:

---

[49] Stenograficheski dnevnitsi na III ONS, pŭrva redovna sesiia, session of February 9, 1883, p. 3.

[50] Georgi Zhivkov, "Izlozhenie na Ministerstvoto na Narodnoto Prosveshtenie," November 1, 1891, TsDIA, F. 104 (Zhivkov), op. 1, ae. 10, pp. 1-2.

[51] Ibid.

> When our people were able to achieve a significant educational equality without any kind of organization, how much higher could it /education/ be then if the possibility had existed long ago to act systematically towards the uplifting of the people through the schools.⁵²

However powerful an argument this finally proved to be, it, and all others related to it, failed in this period to produce a centralized system of schools in the Principality. The opponents of centralization held sway with arguments equally well expressed and just as strongly held.

The opponents of centralization had centuries of tradition behind them and used this argument repeatedly. Yet they recognized that this centuries-old system was faltering. Some of the most carefully constructed arguments against state control of all schools came from Jireček. He realized that in some of the communities, local officials looked forward to centralization as a means of relieving themselves of many worries. But, he argued, once the difficult period was over, those same officials would no doubt strongly decry their loss of autonomy.⁵³ Jireček, without reference to

---

⁵²Ibid., p. 1.

⁵³Jireček, "Zapiska," ABAN, F. 3 (Jireček), op. 1, ae. 1125, p. 7.

Laveleye, endorsed his fears and concerns over the effect of centralization in Serbia where, he claimed, people had lost interest in school affairs. Worse, the teachers were now simply government functionaries whose dedication had declined miserably. The most disheartening aspect of the Serbian plan was that while communities were still obliged by law to finance the schools in their areas, they had no voice in the determination of policy.[54] Another problem cited by Jireček was the confusion and litigation that would certainly result from government control of all schools because many Bulgarian schools, and even whole school systems, were operated on the basis of specially allocated real estate or even from endowed funds. How would such arrangements be affected?[55] Finally, he noted that a special consideration in Bulgaria was the existence of many variations in local school affairs--geographic, financial, and otherwise. In some locales, the schools were very well run (schools such as those in Tŭrnovo and Shumen). In other places, however, there was a negligent attitude towards schools and school affairs. Without expressing

---

[54] Ibid.

[55] Ibid.

this outright, Jireček hinted that the better-organized districts would resent having to share their resources with less concerned communities.[56]

Jireček was not alone in opposing, or pointing out the dangers in, state control of all school affairs. Vatsov, a staunch advocate of centralization, was also aware of some of the inherent dangers. He recognized that in many cases, local officials would know best what kinds of schools and teachers were needed in the vicinity and what local factors might affect school affairs. If the government stripped the communes of too many of their powers, the people might lose their initiative and interest. Furthermore, the position of a teacher in communal schools appointed by the central government might become untenable because of local hostility to his appointment.[57]

Despite the fact that Giuzelev's measures failed, another attempt at increased central control came under the administration of Dimitŭr Agura (1883). This attempt engendered much outright hostility and opposition from the communes and the foes of centralization. Agura launched a systematic drive to tighten ministerial

---

[56]Ibid.

[57]Vatsov, "Koi da naznachava," p. 4.

control over all aspects of educational affairs in the state-operated schools. Circular letters poured from his pen, attempting to curb severely any independent thought or action by the directors and teachers in state educational institutions. This served to stir up much antagonism. Thus, when Agura's bill for a new educational structure was put forth, it met with stiff opposition. Letters to the editor of the newspaper Maritsa, for example, pointed out that Drinov had used as the foundation of the new state's educational system the traditional arrangement of autonomous local school systems; to change it was to court trouble.[58]

Other letter writers attacked the plan to remove the right of teacher appointment from the communes as a poor precedent. To take such a privilege from the control of the communities would cause confusion and eventual disillusionment on the part of the populace.[59]

Opponents of the government's proposed control of textbook selection viewed this move as dangerous because of the possibility of bureaucratic dullness and stagnation. Finally, in a searing blast, a "citizen of the Principality" concluded that Agura was bent on

---

[58] Maritsa, August 16, 1883, p. 1.

[59] Ibid.

controlling everything from the school councils and school boards to text selection and even the opening and closing of schools:

> As we become more acquainted with the issue, we see clearly that the people will retain no other right except that of paying money. The words 'public school' in the title of the bill will have neither meaning nor significance if by some misfortune the administration of these valued institutions becomes as now proposed.[60]

For the communal officials, who also strongly opposed Agura's bill, the memory of their traditional role in Turkish times was still fresh. This sentiment may have blinded them to the fact that most of the communes were increasingly unable to continue that role.[61]

While full-fledged centralization such as that proposed by Agura was defeated every time in this period, neither did the situation remain one of total autonomy on the communal level. What existed from 1878 to 1885 was an anomaly created from the compromise, a situation which in retrospect was probably the only one attainable.

The compromise situation was due to a number of actors, the most important of which was the opposition of Jireček to centralization. However, another

---

[60] Letter to the editor from "A Citizen of the Principality," *Maritsa*, October 21, 1883, p. 5.

[61] Aleksiev, *Nashata*, p. 48.

significant reason was that each side of the debate did not advance its position without some doubt and hesitation. The adherents of centralization were aware of the possible dangers in the system, and the opponents of centralization realized that the situation resulting from the financial difficulties of the communes could not go unabated. Thus, important figures on each side of the question themselves came to the conclusion that perhaps a compromise situation would be best for the present time.

Giuzelev, under whose administration the first moves were taken toward centralization, was against outright government control of the public schools. In arguing against financial support of public schools by the government, he noted that such support would automatically mean that the government would play the chief role in local school affairs, with the communities shunted to the sidelines. Rather, claimed Giuzelev, the school should be administered "in the spirit prevailing up until now."[62] Presumably, this did not rule out government regulation of certain aspects of school affairs, such as teacher training.

---

[62] Ivan Giuzelev, speech to the Sŭbranie, Stenograficheski dnevnitsi na II ONS, pŭrva redovna sesiia, session of May 21, 1881, p. 529.

Jireček, an ardent and persuasive opponent of centralization, nevertheless was greatly disturbed by the sloppiness and lack of professional training on the part of local officials charged with school affairs. He was appalled, for example, that two-thirds of the school board members in Kiustendil were illiterate. He was not adverse to greater government supervision in such situations. In fact, in the end, Jireček supported a trial period of five to ten years during which a moderate amount of centralization would be allowed:

> In the present circumstances, it is necessary to find a middle road between centralization and autonomy which will induce people to a better organization and will develop in them a fondness toward their school. It will be evident after 5-10 years whether it is necessary to turn the administration of the school toward one or the other above-mentioned systems.[63]

Regarding the unsettled issue of who would appoint teachers, Jireček suggested another compromise wherein the communities would nominate teachers for their schools and the Ministry would credentials and confirm or reject the appointment. The community could not freely fire a teacher, however, since only the Ministry, acting

---

[63] Jireček, "Zapiska," ABAN, F. 3 (Jireček), op. 1, ae. 1125, p. 8.

through the local school inspector, could do so.[64]

Vatsov, who was in favor of more government control of school affairs, also suggested a compromise on the critical issue of teacher appointment. He advanced a system based on the Belgian model, according to which the provincial school inspector would nominate three candidates for a vacant communal school position. The communal officials would then select one from this group.[65] Eventually, it was precisely this method of teacher appointment that was employed in Bulgaria.

Compromises were also made in other areas of education between the Ministry and local officials, although unquestionably the communes' previously total control of their own school affairs eroded steadily until finally it was eliminated in 1891. The coexistence of a Ministry of Public Instruction and a theoretically (at least) autonomous school system seems unfeasible until one recalls the centuries of traditional local self-government fostered by the Turks and the political significance attached to this. Yet Zhivkov was probably correct when he claimed in his argument for centralization that "the lack of any supreme leadership, of any

---

[64] Ibid., pp. 8-9.

[65] Vatsov, "Koi da naznachava," pp. 7-8.

central administration of educational affairs was the most important obstacle to its development."[66] The extremely dedicated and competent individuals in charge often felt stymied when it came to eradicating abuses, promoting universal education, and setting reasonable standards of achievement. Yet it was these same individuals who themselves were wary of too much government control too soon.

---

[66] Zhivkov, "Izlozhenie," TsDIA, F. 104 (Zhivkov), op. 1, ae. 10, p. 1.

CHAPTER FIVE

POLITICS AND THE MINISTRY

The public debates and controversies, acrimonious at times, surrounding the designation of priorities in Bulgarian education, paled in comparison to the serious clashes over personalities and politics confronting the Ministry in this critical formative period. Personal and departmental rivalries within the Ministry itself came close to rendering useless the efforts of Bulgarian cultural leaders to inject a certain amount of professionalism into the country's educational system. At the same time, the involvement of ministerial officials and employees in the country's vicious political squabbles marred the public image of the Ministry--much to the exasperation of every Minister in this period from Drinov to Karolev. The internal personnel problems and the external involvements in politics, especially by the teachers, often hampered the Ministers' abilities to execute or to initiate programs and sometimes interfered with the work of the institution.

The Internal Struggles

The problems in the ranks of the Ministry itself ranged from conflicts of personality, rivalry, and jealousy over jobs and duties to protests over unfair practices in appointments. Included as well were differences in the educational backgrounds of the employees, especially between those educated in Western Europe and those educated in Russia. These difficulties were not confined to any particular section of the ministerial bureaucracy but occurred at every level, especially, and unfortunately, at the very highest.

Some of the bitterest and most disruptive personality clashes surrounded Jireček, as might be expected, given his stubborn temperament, his perfectionism, his enormous influence, and his status as a privileged foreigner. In fact, the first public scandal, occurring during the tenure of Ivan Giuzelev as Minister, pitted the Liberal Party appointee against the strong-willed Czech. Giuzelev had powerful connections within the Liberal Party and was appointed Minister of Public Instruction in the government of Dragan Tsankov, which assumed power in April, 1880.[1] Jireček had little but praise for the outgoing Minister of Public Instruction, Metropolitan Clement of Turnovo,[2] but greeted the arrival

---

[1] Aleksiev, *Nashata*, p. 14.

[2] Jireček, letter to Marin Drinov, April 15, 1880, in Sis, *Korespondentsiia*, p. 200.

of Giuzelev with ill-concealed disapproval. Entries in his diary and a letter to Drinov recorded his dismay. Jireček had plied Drinov with letter after letter, denouncing the political struggles around him and describing his apprehension. However, in another letter to Drinov in April, 1880, Jireček demonstrated that, if he did not wish to soil his hands with politics, he was not averse to caustic remarks about people in his private correspondence. He described Giuzelev as a good and hard-working subaltern functionary, but devoid of independence, invention, or original and profound ideas on education.[3] His diary entry, however, was harsher, revealing not only his contempt for Giuzelev, but for all-Russian educated Bulgarians and signaling trouble ahead:

> Giuzelev will be the Minister of Instruction, despite the fact that Karavelov himself, in front of Stoilov, called him an imbecile. Stoilov asked Karavelov, 'How can you believe that such a ministry can be viable?' Giuzelev does not know foreign languages--like the rest of the Russian-trained Bulgarians.[4]

Jireček's hostility to the new Minister was evidently repaid in kind as Giuzelev completely ignored the

---

[3] Ibid.

[4] Jireček, Bŭlgarski dnevnik, I, p. 60. Petko Karavelov was the prime minister at the time, and Konstantin Stoilov, an old friend of Jireček, was not in office at the time.

advice and counsel of the Czech scholar, who as Executive Secretary, held the second highest post in the Ministry. The rift became final and public, however, over the infamous Tashikmanov affair.

Giuzelev had incited deep resentment within the Ministry by appointing his usually poorly-qualified cronies to high positions either in the central administration of the Ministry or to posts in the state-operated educational establishments.[5] An especially scandalous appointment concerned the position of the Department Chief for Primary Schools. As Jireček described it to Drinov:

> Giuzelev, against my wishes, finally appointed to the important post of chief of the Section of Primary Schools an ink-slinger from Eski-Dzumaya--Tashikmanov, who barely finished a few grades in Gabrovo. This appointment has led to great resentment among all the employees and among the entire public (all the other section chiefs are people with a university education).[6]

Jireček launched the offensive by sending a vituperative letter to Giuzelev protesting the poor choice and the failure to consult him in accordance with practices commonly accepted in countries more advanced

---

[5] Dr. Vasil Beron, letters to Jireček of May 26, July 5, August 15, 1881, ABAN, F. 3 (Jireček), op. 1, ae. 62, pp. 1-5.

[6] Jireček, letter to Marin Drinov, June 22, 1880, in Sis, Korespondentsiia, p. 203.

than Bulgaria. He also used the opportunity to protest
the changes that had been made in the critical Bill for
the Public Schools, again without any attempt to solicit
Jireček's opinion. (Jireček had written the original
draft.)[7] The litany of offenses continued with a demand
for explanations as to why he had not been invited to
certain public events which had been attended by national
dignitaries and royalty. Jireček reminded Giuzelev that
he had a contract with the Bulgarian government and
could not be abused so easily. He also called attention
to the shabby treatment accorded him by the "local intelligentsia", and commented:

> Many odd opinions and rumors are directed
> at my person and my intentions--all the product
> of childish Eastern fantasy. Given the unscrupulous and frivolous bases upon which, in the
> East, even wiser and more enlightened people base
> their false notions, it is clear that Bulgarians
> are not well disposed toward me. Not by reason
> of their own observations, but because of the
> malicious agitation of some figures unknown to
> me.[8]

In the original draft of this letter, Jireček offered
his resignation but in a subsequent version changed
that to a demand for a formal reply, by category, to all

---

[7] Jireček, letter to the Ministry of Public Instruction, May 12, 1880, ABAN, F. 3 (Jireček), op. 1, ae. 114, pp. 1-2.

[8] Ibid.

the accusations outlined in his letter. The reply never came.

Instead Giuzelev's supporters went to the Sŭbranie (knowing that the new budget was under consideration) and lobbied to have Jireček's position eliminated. Meanwhile, Jireček submitted copies of his ultimatum to Giuzelev to the press, which caused much turmoil but produced no concrete results because everyone's attention was distracted by the death of the Russian Empress (July, 1880).[9] While the Prince, who doubtless would have supported Jireček, was in Russia for the funeral, Giuzelev and his supporters successfully convinced the Sŭbranie's budgetary commission to eliminate the post of Executive Secretary.[10] The struggle, however, was not over.

Three days after the Sŭbranie commission's decision, the other ministers finally intervened. Jireček informed Drinov that Giuzelev and his supporters were doomed to failure when the commission's actions were

---

[9] Jireček, letter to Marin Drinov, June 22, 1880, in Sis, Korespondentsiia, p. 203.

[10] Ibid.; debates on this position are in Stenograficheski dnevnitsi na II ONS, pŭrva redovna sesiia, session of May 31, 1880, pp. 665-666.

debated on the floor of the Sŭbranie.[11] He was correct; the post was restored by unanimous vote. Jireček believed that the fact that Karavelov and Tsankov were Western-educated had some significance in rallying them to his camp and against Giuzelev, thus ending the growing public scandal. He speculated that fear was among the motives behind this change of heart:

> Fear, before the the public, before Slavdom, and before the Austrian Consulate (I have a contract which, if breached, could give cause for reprisals) were the motives for this reversal.[12]

The victory over Giuzelev was a Pyrrhic one, however; Jireček acquired even more critics and enemies than he had already possessed by virtue of his being a foreigner in a powerful position. He also forfeited a cherished project, the proposed Bill on the Public Schools, which would have been the first comprehensive law on the nation's educational system. The bickering and maneuvers in the struggle between the two men caused the tardy submission of the project on the eve of the dissolution of the Sŭbranie. Thus, the project failed, with unfortunate consequences for Bulgarian education.

---

[11] Jireček, letter to Marin Drinov, September 6, 1880, in Sis, Korespondentsiia, p. 207.

[12] Jireček, letter to Marin Drinov, June 22, 1880, in Sis, Korespondentsiia, pp. 203-204.

Worn out by the struggle, Jireček asked for a two-month leave to travel abroad, a request that resulted in a new imbroglio. Rumors flew that the request for leave was just a pretext and that once out of Bulgaria Jireček would never return. Jireček complained bitterly to Drinov in a letter that sheds light on the continuing problems in the ranks of the Ministry:

> I have entered a position where I have lost all ground: all my projects, programs, regulations, etc. for education have found themselves shelved; all my efforts for reforms remain a voice crying in the wilderness; my right of personal inspection of schools in the Principality is refused; and finally, the bureaucrats in the Ministry itself display against me such inimical behavior that I was forced to request a reshuffling of personnel.[13]

The situation was somewhat alleviated in December, 1880, when Jireček, by special provision in his contract, was given greater control over the governing of the schools. Actual resolution of the power struggle came temporarily when Jireček was appointed Minister in May, 1881. He served as such until June, 1882.

The clash between Jireček and Giuzelev was not by any means the only incident of personnel problems or personality conflicts at this time. It does, however, epitomize many key issues such as the suspect position of foreigners, the results of a lack of civil service

---

[13] Jireček, letter to Marin Drinov, September 6, 1880, in Sis, *Korespondentsiia*, p. 207.

laws, and differences in philosophy on education.

Another important personality clash emerged during the administration of Georgi Teokharev, an obscure figure whose rise to power is astonishing, considering how very little was known about him then or even now.[14] Teokharev quickly became known after his appointment in 1882, however, though not for positive reasons. He irritated all of his colleagues and employees of the Ministry with his slovenly work habits and his utter failure to understand the need for thinking before speaking, especially in politically sensitive times. He was denounced openly in the Sŭbranie and privately by his co-workers for all of these reasons.

While Teokharev's difficulties were attributable to his personality, others had problems due to their

---

[14] Georgi Teokharev was a figure about whom little was known, even in his own time. He was born in Peshtera (date unknown) and studied in Odessa and Moscow. He was among the literary circle of Bulgarian students who published the student literary journal called Bratski Trud. He eventually became a lawyer and in 1881 served as Minister of Justice. In June of 1882, he became Minister of Public Instruction, resigning in March, 1883. He left Bulgaria sometime afterward to practice law in Russia. His date of death is also unknown. See P. Pechev, Pulen ukazatel na zakonite v Bŭlgariia ot Osvobozhdenieto do 30 Iuni 1939 g. (Sofia: 1939), p. 467; Bŭlgarska vŭzrozhdensak knizhnina, I, p. 352; Ivan Bogdanov, Bŭlgarska literatura v dati i kharakteristiki (Sofia: 1966), p. 201; Stoiko Bozhkov, Istoriia na bŭlgarskata literatura (Sofia: 1962), III, p. 352.

political views and were denied positions because of them. The most noteworthy example of this was Mikhail Sarafov who was slated to become Director of the new Statistical Bureau, a department of the Ministry of Public Instruction. Sarafov, a liberal, had received an excellent education in Paris and Zagreb and, by reason of his special training, was certainly the only Bulgarian at the time capable of helping to establish and direct the country's first statistical bureau.[15] This project was greatly desired by many in the Ministry, but especially by the methodical Jireček, who thus appointed Sarafov to the directorship, in spite of his own disapproval of Sarafov's protests against the coup.

---

[15] Mikhail Sarafov was born in Tŭrnovo in 1854 and received a gymnasium education in Zagreb (1871-1878). He returned to Tŭrnovo to teach and joined the Revolutionary Committee there. After his arrest for political activity, he went to Paris and received a degree in mathematics and finance from the Sorbonne in 1881. In that same year, he was appointed Minister of Public Instruction, but held the office for only a few months. Later he became Minister of Finance (1883) and held a series of high diplomatic positions until his death in 1924. He is most famous as the founder and first director of statistical studies in Bulgaria. See Nikola and Ivan Danchov, Bŭlgarska Entsiklopediia (Sofia: 1956), p. 1384; Mikhail Sarafov, "Obshtestvenata i politicheska deinost na Mikhail K. Sarafov po zapiski, belezhki, i pisma, sŭkhraneni v arkhivata mu (1875-1924)," compiled by his brother Konstantin Sarafov, ABAN, F. 17 (Mikhail Sarafov), op. 1, ae. 290, pp. 28-52; B. Sekulov, Nashite pravitelstva i Ministri ot Osvobozhdenieto do dnes (Sofia: 1911), p. 8.

(Jireček may have also favored Sarafov because of the latter's Western education.)

In any event, the appointment immediately became another apple of discord when Jireček's fellow ministers (all conservatives) objected strenuously to Sarafov because of his political views. At one point, Jireček bitterly suggested that the consensus would probably prefer a police officer for the position rather than suffer the likes of Sarafov.[16] The opponents also took steps to have the Sŭbranie severely reduce the salary of the post to ensure Sarafov's discomforture should all else fail. Again, only an appeal to the Prince and the intercession of more enlightened members of the Conservative Party allowed this uniquely talented man to assume the position.[17] This event and others caused another outburst from Jireček to Drinov on the difficulty of achieving educational objectives given the personality politics within the Ministry. Jireček worried about what the public thought of all this bureaucratic

---

[16] K. Sarafov, "Obshtestvenata deinost," ABAN, F. 17(M. Sarafov), op. 1, ae. 290. See also Radev, Stroitelite, I, p. 324.

[17] K. Sarafov, "Obshtestvenata deinost," ABAN, F. 17 (M. Sarafov), op. 1, ae. 290, pp. 86-93; Jireček, Bŭlgarski dnevnik, I, pp. 489-495ff and II, pp. 358, 363.

infighting and claimed that it seemed the new country had adopted as its model of a proper government employee the notoriously inefficient and corrupt Turkish bureaucrat and zaptiia.[18] In another complaint, he noted that the stringent efforts of the Ministry to trace blame to individuals caused many nerve-wracking sessions of tears and hand-wringing with the responsible employees.[19]

One event over which many tears were shed on both sides for very different reasons involved a protracted and acrimonious suit by temporary employees of the Statistical Bureau. While the details of the litigation were insignificant of themselves, the affair reached incredible proportions and eventually involved hearings before the Ministerial Council and the Sŭbranie. (Both ordered the Ministry to pay these temporary employees the housing allowance provided to permanent employees.) The affair illustrates how a handful of disgruntled employees could take advantage of the confused state of affairs regarding the rights and

---

[18] Jireček, letter to Marin Drinov, June 22, 1880, in Sis, Korespondentsiia, p. 205.

[19] Jireček, letter to Marin Drinov, September 6, 1880, in Sis, Korespondentsiia, p. 207.

privileges of bureaucrats to hamper the progress of the Ministry and the invaluable work of statistical data gathering.[20]

The work of ordering and advancing the country's cultural affairs was not held back only by a few highly publicized disputes. Equally vicious disputes simmered and smoldered beneath the surface; although they rarely attracted public attention, they affected work just as devastatingly. Some of these problems were chronic and devoid of solution, such as the mutual suspicions between Bulgarians who had received their higher education in Russia and those educated in the Western tradition. These differences surfaced in debates over curriculum and philosophy of education. A significant number of Bulgarians had been sent to study in Russia, through the combined efforts of Bulgarian merchant colonies and the Panslavists in Russia. However, an equally large group had studied in Western Europe.[21] The two groups had

---

[20] Ibid.; Bulgaria, Ministerial Council, session of March 16, 1882, TsDIA, F. 284 (Ministerial Council), op. 1, ae. 92, pp. 5-6; session of March 30, 1884, TsDIA, F. 284, op. 1, ae. 154, p. 1; session of April 30, 1884, TsDIA, F. 284, op. 1, ae. 293, p. 5; Stenograficheski dnevnitsi na III ONS, pŭrva redovna sesiia, session of December 23, 1882, p. 90.

[21] This new situation was perpetuated by the stipend-granting policies of the new country. For example, in the academic year 1881-1882, out of a total of 32

received educations differing markedly in scope and emphasis. Russian-educated Bulgarians were steeped in religious-oriented subjects and in music, art, and mathematics--all safe subjects in the view of the reactionary educational policies of the Russian empire. Their Western-educated counterparts, by contrast, received a much broader, diverse, and open education.

Also, although many of the Russian-educated Bulgarians had trained to become teachers, few had received any formal pedagogical instruction.[22] This, along with their lack of training in foreign languages, put them at a disadvantage in competition with Western-educated Bulgarians, especially when Jireček was in charge of affairs. Jireček, incidentally, did not reserve his contempt for Russian education alone. He also thought little of graduates of another major source of higher education--Robert College. He claimed the college's curriculum was shallow, especially in the all important classics. In a conversation with Bishop Sinessius of Edirne, he claimed that in regard to

---

foreign stipends, 13 went to students studying in Russia, while 19 went to students in Western Europe or Robert College, see Jireček, Glavno izlozhenie, p. 39.

[22] Naiden Chakŭrov, Istoriia na bŭlgarskoto obrazovanie (Sofia: 1955), I, p. 234.

classicism, "Robert College gave only preparation there to read Buckle and Spencer and believed that this was everything."[23]

Bulgarians educated in Russia had one advantage, however, in that they reflected a general suspicion of Westerners on the part of most of their countrymen immediately after the Congress of Berlin. It had been Western nations, after all, that had imposed limits on their country's borders and had divided it into three sections. However, this feeling was soon replaced by growing concern over Russia's intention to exert control over the new state,[24] a move that caused ill-will even among Russophiles.

Whatever the motivations, Russian-educated Bulgarians tried to undermine attempts to fashion Bulgarian education entirely after Western models, especially with regard to the emphasis on classical languages. This inevitably brought them into conflict with Jireček. They believed that the emphasis on classicism was useless to Bulgarians and held them back from real

___

[23] Jireček, Bŭlgarski dnevnik, I, p. 419.

[24] Noikov, Pogled ot Paisiia, p. 56.

progress.[25] When Bulgarians, trained in the newly completed secondary schools of their own country failed to gain entry into foreign universities because of their lack of proper classical training, this attitude was reversed. Jireček had all along argued for classicism as a necessary condition for opening a university. (Drinov shared this opinion, although he himself had been educated in Russia.)[26]

Coexisting with these differences on educational orientation were numerous conflicts among Ministry personnel over political issues. Also, the scandals and public clashes of personalities described thus far were only major examples against a background of everyday minor disputes throughout the educational organization. A truly serious situation involving the morale and prestige of the Ministry and its employees resulted from an explosive mixture of teachers and politics.

In 1888, the French observer of Balkan affairs Emile de Lavaleye cautioned that the leaders of the new Bulgarian state should adopt neither the American

---

[25] Vatslav Vlcek, "Konstantin Irechek," trans. by S. Velev, Uchilishten pregled, IX (September, 1904), 924.

[26] Ibid.

system of changing all ministers and many employees with every new president nor the Belgian system of allowing new ministers to appoint their own friends and relatives to positions of power. This, he warned, would make the functionaries agents in political struggles, too concerned with maintaining their party in power to work for the public good; Laveleye noted:

> In exchange for the sort of tenure that you accord your functionaries, demand from them absolute honesty, assiduous labor, exact fulfillment of their tasks, but no political services whatsoever.[27]

Bulgarian educators soon had much cause to regret that their country had not followed Laveleye's sage advice, for the political struggles that broke out frequently hurt Bulgarian education, even though educational affairs were not usually themselves the subject of political strife.[28] Nevertheless, the country's enormous political instability had negative repercussions upon the ability of the Ministry of Public Instruction to function effectively and efficiently.

---

[27]Laveleye, La Peninsule, II, p. 78.

[28]Krachunov, Iz Bulgaska, p. 5.

Teachers and Politics

While politics affected the Ministry in many ways (almost always negatively), in no way did it cause more difficulties than when teachers engaged in political activities. The rapid succession of governments saw seven different Ministers of Public Instruction within a two-year period (1880-1882), which severely hampered any continuity of policies and programs. But teacher participation in politics was just as troublesome to the work of the Ministry because such activity dangerously combined anti-monarchical and anti-conservative elements and was, moreover, patently illegal. More importantly, the Bulgarian school system was always attacked whenever the economic, social, or political affairs of the country encountered difficulties. The political parties in power were always ready to hurl accusations against the schools "as hotbeds of corruption, as sources of the very evil against which they were called to combat."[29] The active involvement of teachers in politics only reinforced this unfortunate tendency to blame schools for all ills.

The tradition of teacher involvement in politics, while a relatively new development, was a strong and

---

[29] Aleksiev, Nashata, p. 25.

respected one. The teachers' political appetite was whetted during the eighteenth and nineteenth centuries, but especially during the struggle for the Exarchate and the movement for liberation from Ottoman rule. They had fought against chorbadzhi, Greeks, and Turks in turn. They had opposed the Greeks because they were viewed, rightly or wrongly, as proponents of the elimination or suppression of the Bulgarian national identity. The chorbadzhi incurred the enmity of many a liberal-minded teacher since the chorbadzhi supported Greek authority. These were the days of struggle between the so-called Old (stari) and Young (mladi) factions throughout the Bulgarian-inhabited territories. The Young faction favored the establishment of a separate Bulgarian Church, autonomous from the Patriarch (a Greek) in Constantinople. The Old party, on the other hand, only wished for permission to appoint Bulgarians to episcopal seats and to use the Slavic language in services.[30] Most teachers

---

[30] It is difficult to generalize about the background of the membership of each party, but for the most part, many of the members of the Conservative Party came from the ranks of wealthy merchants, while Liberals drew much of their constituency from the ranks of professionals, peasants, and smaller merchants. See Ilcho Dimitrov, Kniazŭt, Konstitutsiiata, narodŭt (Sofia: 1972); Radev, Stroitelite, especially I, pp. 1-241; and, in general, Black, The Establishment of Constitutional Government.

vigorously supported and had active roles in the Young Party. In fact, one of the most important leaders of the Young group was a Gabrovo teacher, Petko R. Slaveikov.[31] The chorbadzhi usually held the upper hand, however, and succeeded in making life difficult for all teachers, not just activist ones.

Teachers also had a critically powerful role in the long struggle to generate a movement for national existence. In this case, the opening of reading rooms across the country served as a convenient vehicle for the transmittal of cultural as well as nationalist literature.[32] Teachers in regular schools often turned physical exercise periods into military instruction. Finally, teachers were in the forefront of outright revolutionary activities, many losing their lives in the April Uprising and subsequent War of Liberation.

Thus, when the Conservative Party tried to limit severely the right of government employees to engage

---

[31] Nadezhda Dragova, "Dobri Voinikov--vdŭkhnoven vŭzrozhdenski uchitel," Narodna prosveta, XIV, 5 (1958), 90-100; another good account of the activities of the Renascence teacher may be found in Raicho Karolev, Istoriiata na Gabrovskoto Uchilishte (Sofia: 1926).

[32] For a definitive study of the role of the reading rooms (chitalishta), see Chilingirov, Bŭlgarski chitalishta.

in political activities, the results were easily predictable. Many of the government employees were former teachers and, of course, teachers working in state schools also came under the general definition of government employee. Any directive forbidding these people from participating in politics was doomed to failure, especially when there was so much occurring in the political arena to attract the interest of even the most apathetic citizen.

Bulgaria's political troubles, which so interested the teachers, stemmed partly from a lack of experience in parliamentary affairs, especially the fine art of compromise. Added to this was the fact that one of the two political parties, the Conservative, was skeptical about the readiness and the ability of the people to assume participation in government of any kind, let alone one with a parliamentary structure. This was to be the critical issue arousing much heated debate and maneuvering between supporters of constitutional government and its opponents. The conservative view as expressed, for example, in the meetings of the Constitutent Assembly at Tŭrnovo (1878), held that the Bulgarian people were too inexperienced in political affairs and thus should be ruled by a constitutional system favoring a strong prince and an oligarchy comprised of well-educated and affluent citizens.[33] The Conservatives drew their support from many of the same sources as had the Old faction in pre-Liberation times: former chorbadzhi, bankers, high clergy, etc. This was true as well of the Conservative forces in Eastern Rumelia.[34]

The Liberal Party held a completely opposite opinion regarding the advisability of popular government in the newly-established state. The Liberals forged an odd combination of nationalism, radical socialism, and bourgeois democracy into a political platform, buttressed by Montesquieu, rule of law, social contract, and English-style government. The basis of the deep faith in the ability of the people to rule themselves was spelled out simply and clearly in the official Liberal journal:

> Even though our people everywhere was subjected to slavery, the free democratic spirit predominated over them, a fact which even their fierce and cruel enemies understood and appreciated; always they declared their free spirit of self-rule, always their yearnings were liberal, however much these were crushed and smothered.[35]

---

[33] Dimitrov, Kniazŭt, p. 9.

[34] Ibid., p. 8. The Marxist view, incidentally, is that the Liberals and Conservatives were a continuation of the Old and Young factions before the Liberation.

[35] Tselokŭpna Bulgariia, September 19, 1879, p. 1.

In other words, the people had earned their right to self-rule, and the government had to be based on this fundamental premise. Liberals agitated energetically for ministerial responsibility to the Sŭbranie, which was the supreme organ of government. Though the Tŭrnovo Constitution distributed power more evenly than some Liberals would have preferred, the Prince's position was never regarded by the Liberals as anything but decorative.

The Liberal Party also asserted as a basic tenet that poverty would be overcome only when the land was a possession of the entire community. In many respects, it represented the majority of the people, and its ranks were formed from workers, small merchants, progressive intellectuals, and the less affluent peasantry.[36] It was also the Liberal Party which, in 1880, defeated the first attempts to set limits on the rights of government employees to enter politics. The rationale, as explained by Petko Karavelov to the Sŭbranie, was that outside of the government employees, there were few citizens with an adequate education able to comprehend quickly the mechanism of governmental

---

[36] For background on the Liberal Party, see Radev, Stroitelite, I, pp. 141-241; Dimitrov, Kniazŭt, pp. 10-40; Black, Establishment of Constitutional Government.

functions.[37] What Karavelov did not point out was that many of the government employees were either former teachers of present teachers and highly committed to the defense of the Constitution, which the Conservatives sought to eliminate. The opening shot in this struggle against the Constitution was the appointment of a Conservative (Todor Burmov) as Prime Minister, despite the Liberals' greater representation.[38]

In the meantime, the problem of government functionaries and their relationship to politics continued. In the Constituent Assembly, the debate over whether or not government employees could stand for election resulted in a compromise; it was resolved that the employees could not stand for election in the respective provinces in which they worked. Georgi Atanasovich, a Conservative who held the position of Minister of Public Instruction for only one month, later interpreted this to apply to teachers as well.[39] The formal efforts

---

[37] Aleksiev, Nashata, p. 40; Stenograficheski dnevnitsi na II ONS, vtora redovna sesiia, session of December 10, 1880, pp. 250-270.

[38] Dimitrov, Kniazŭt, p. 17.

[39] Georgi Atanasovich, Circular letters of August 18 and October 6, 1879, Dŭrzhaven vestnik, I, 4 (1879), 2-3; I, 10 (1879), 2-3; Bulgaria, Ministry of Public Instruction, "Privremenen zakon za obshtinite," Dŭrzhaven vestnik, I, 4 (1879), 1. This latter law forbade communal employees from becoming a mayor or a mayoral assistant.

to curb more completely the political rights of government employees and especially of teachers did not occur until after the initial uproar following the coup d'état and suspension of the Tŭrnovo Consistution in 1881.

In October, 1881, the Ministerial Council met in secret session to determine how to punish state employees for their anti-government agitation and how to prevent its reoccurrence. The result was a temporary statute forbidding anyone receiving pay from the state's coffers "to take part for any reason in election campaigns, to organize meetings, and to take part in them, to make and to publicize proclamations, to make speeches in public places having political goals."[40] Perhaps aware of the dubious legality of this "Temporary Statute," the Ministerial Council, goaded by the so-called Political Cabinet of the Prince, also decided to recommend that the Sŭbranie draw up precise laws regulating, among other questions, political involvement of state employees.[41]

---

[40] Bulgaria, Ministerial Council, session of October 15, 1881, TsDIA, F. 284 (Ministerial Council), op. 1, ae. 66, p. 2.

[41] Ibid.; a detailed study of the teachers' movement at this time concluded that the deprivation of legal rights to protest forced the teachers into concerted actions which in fact led to the beginning of professional unions, per Nikolov, "Poiava i razvitie," pp. 50-64.

The "Temporary Statute," insofar as it could be enforced, stripped the teachers of participatory rights. This action was confirmed by the Law on State Employees passed by the Sŭbranie in 1882. All of these actions in effect only worsened the situation because they deprived the teachers of a legal and public outlet for their demands. The result was only more frustration, hardened resolve, and the introduction of the struggle into the classroom.

Such measures frustrated the teachers who now carried their complaints and political views into the streets and the classrooms. It was no accident that teachers were in the forefront of agitation against Prince Alexander and the government. When the Prince staged his coup, with the support of the Conservative Party, government workers, at both the local and central level, initiated passive and active protests against the government. These actions included resistance to decrees, refusal to circulate official proclamations and circular letters, "forgetting" to send deputies to greet government officials, and neglecting the courtesy of thanksgiving addresses to the Prince for favors and appointments.[42] The active measures ranged from strikes

---

[42] Aleksiev, Nashata, p. 41; Dimitrov, Kniazŭt, p. 84; The gymnasium at Kiustendil, a hotbed of such

264

and demonstrations to petitions. Teachers participated in all such activities but also organized their own efforts within educational establishments.

On their own ground, teachers involved themselves in widespread activities calculated to express their dissatisfaction with the political state of affairs in the country; they refused to teach, for example, subjects which they deemed reactionary.[43] On the other hand, they did not hesitate to express their own views on political topics to their students. Teachers also attempted to stand for election to various offices and organized demonstrations against the government.[44] Sometimes these demonstrations, which often meant missing classes, involved the students in the teachers' charge. Strikes were a rarely used weapon--although very effective when utilized--but they did occur especially to express sympathy for political activists, whether or not they happened to be teachers. For example, in February, 1882, the President of the Teachers

---

activity, was to become an example when punishment finally was meted out by the Ministry of Public Instruction. See Umlenski, ed., Pŭrva gimnaziia "Neofit Rilski,"

[43] Aleksiev, Nashata, p. 41; Umlenski, ed. Pŭrva gimnaziia "Neofit Rilski," p. 10.

[44] Nikolov, "Poiava i razvitie," p. 55; Aleksiev, Nashata, p. 41; Nezavisimost, June 20, 1881, p. 1.

Council of Sofia, a powerful Liberal, Dragan Tsankov, was arrested by the authorities without cause. The very next day, the Teachers Council, which had never before discussed politics, approved the closing of all schools by strike action until Tsankov was released. If he were not released quickly, the mass resignation of teachers was threatened. The strike lasted several weeks until Tsankov was finally released.[45]

It was not long before such activities on the part of teachers caused repercussions for the Ministry in Parliament, eventually resulting in repressive measures against the teachers. Besides the earlier steps to forbid the teachers from participating in political agitation of any kind, a new election law of 1882 had deprived teachers, as well as all other government employees, of the right to stand for election to the Sŭbranie.[46] That same year saw the first attempts to enforce previously ineffective legislation. In February,

---

[45] Sofia, Sofia School Board, "Protokolna kniga ot zasedaniiata na Uchitelskiia sŭvet pri Sofiiski osnovni narodni uchilishta, 1880-1885," special session of February 8, 1882, SGODA, F. 5K (Sofia School Board), op. 1, ae. 87, p. 46.

[46] Bulgaria, Narodno Sŭbranie, "Zakon za chinovnitsite," Dŭrzhaven vestnik, IV, (1882), 985ff; Nikolov, "Poiava i razvitie," p. 52; Aleksiev, Nashata, p. 40.

the Ministerial Council ordered the mayor of Sofia:

> as he appointed a new Church-School Board, to invite the institution to purge all communal teachers who have taken part in the incitement of students to disorder: in case of disagreement on this by the above-mentioned council, such measures will be referred to a communal council which can be set up for that end.[47]

In that same month, the Ministerial Council issued a terse note to the Ministry of Public Instruction. Noting recent demonstrations in favor of the Liberal opposition leader, Dragan Tsankov, by teachers in the pedagogical school in Vratsa, the Council commanded that the Ministry of Public Instruction "act energetically and strictly against guilty teachers and students with whatever measures necessary for an exemplary punishment."[48] Notwithstanding the harsh orders, the Ministry did not "energetically and strictly" punish teachers until 1883, and then only in response to sharp criticism in Parliament.

The critics in the Sŭbranie charged that the teachers and school administrators were openly encouraging anarchy in the schools. Kiustendil Gymnasium, Gabrovo schools, and even the Saints Peter and Paul

---

[47] Bulgaria, Ministerial Council, session of February 9, 1882, TsDIA, F. 284 (Ministerial Council), op. 1, ae. 85, p. 1.

[48] Ibid.

Seminary were singled out as institutions where teachers filled the heads of students with politics "and preach politics in the street, leaving school work, for which the people pay out such huge sums, on the side."[49] While the teachers and students ran through the streets, claimed the critics, the Ministry watched this depravity unperturbed. At the same time as they attacked, the Conservatives urged that the Ministry be given more direct powers to hire and fire teachers. Rumors were also heard about the reduction of teacher salaries, but this was opposed by even most Conservatives.[50]

Stung by the accusations, the Minister at the time, Teokharev, lamely tried to defend himself by arguing that the politicization of the teachers and the students was a natural reflection of the turbulent situation in the country. "How can students avoid introducing politics into the classroom," pleaded Teokharev, "when that is all they hear their fathers discussing? The Ministry of Public Instruction tries to elect only truly moral people and to select teachers compatible with their duties and calling. But what can we do when

---

[49] *Stenograficheski dnevnitsi na III ONS, pŭrva redovna sesiia*, session of February 9, 1883, pp. 1-2.

[50] Aleksiev, *Nashata*, pp. 43-45.

we have a lack of people?"[51]

Realizing that such apologies would get nowhere, Teokharev's successor, Dimitŭr Agura, took the first internal measures against political activists. On the very first day he took office, Agura issued a circular letter to all of the school inspectors which began by acknowledging that not only did many teachers contumaciously engage in forbidden political activities, but that they were the largest single group of activists in demonstrations for or against the government.[52] Agura also admitted that such activities had resulted in absenteeism on the part of teachers and pupils and was beginning to interfere seriously with education. He reminded the inspectors:

> The Ministry of Public Instruction has always looked with disfavor on this activity among teachers because without doubt it prevents the teacher from fulfilling his designated task and demeans his high calling. Also politics occupies teachers with work which has nothing in common with the verities of learning and cannot be without impact on the still immature students with whose upbringing the teachers are charged.[53]

---

[51] Georgi Teokharev, reply to interpellation, *Stenograficheski dnevnitsi na III ONS, pŭrva redovna sesiia*, session of February 9, 1883, p. 3.

[52] Dimitŭr Agura, Circular letter No. 1089 of May 6, 1883, *Ucheben vestnik*, V-VI (May, 1883), 91-92.

[53] Ibid.

The official policy was now to be that the proper activities of teachers (and inspectors) must be exclusively in the realm of educational affairs. Ministry officials now detailed specific measures designed to curtail any transgression outside this realm, such as demanding from every state school director a list of teachers in his establishment who were absent from classes, however long, without good reason.[54]

The pattern begun by Agura was continued by others, including Jireček, with highly controversial results, especially surrounding school closings. The directors of schools in highly politicized communities such as Gabrovo and Kiustendil were fired when they stood for election. The director of the Sofia *pansion*, G. Uzunov, was dismissed when he refused to introduce what he considered reactionary ideas into the curriculum. Provincial inspector G. Karanov was recalled from Kiustendil for his political writings in defense of the Constitution. In a unique case, the Lom district school inspector was hauled before a military court for agitation in the elections.[55] When firing the director and several other punitive measures failed to curb political

---

[54] Ibid.

[55] *Nezavisimost*, June 20, 1881, p. 1.

activities in Kiustendil, the school was closed in 1883. Jireček, who outlined the proposal for the closing, listed only economic concerns as his motivation. Nevertheless, the Liberals singled him out for especially harsh criticism.[56]

The Liberals reacted vigorously to the Ministry's new policy of reprisals against educators involved in politics. Needless to say, the Liberal Party owed a great debt to the teachers for their invaluable aid in the struggle to restore the Tŭrnovo Constitution.[57] It was understandable then that persecution of teachers should cause the Liberal Party to respond quickly. The Liberal journal *Nezavisimost* spoke out eloquently in defense of the teachers. According to the Liberals:

> The persecution of the teachers has two goals: with their removal will also be removed and uprooted the solid pillars of the Bulgarian constitution, and with this /there/ will also be opened sufficient places in order to find room for Mr.

---

[56] The official history (1959) of the Kiustendil school states that the school was closed because of political activities of teachers and students, especially surrounding the elections to the Grand National Assembly called by Prince Alexander to solidify his anti-constitutional measures, see Umlenski, ed., *Pŭrva gimnaziia "Neofit Rilski,"* pp. 10-11ff.

[57] While the Liberals acknowledged their indebtedness in the successful struggle to restore the Turnovo Constitution, they did not act quickly to restore the political rights of teachers when they returned to power, see Aleksiev, *Nashata*, pp. 54-55.

Jireček's toadies--Czechs from Austria--who since April 27 (1881) have despatched to Mr. Jireček about a hundred petitions for positions.[58]

The vicious slur against Jireček, however, was tempered by more reasoned and reasonable observations. The Liberals pointed out that from Turkish times up until the present, the teachers had been the freest and most independent of all Bulgarians, yet at the same time, most useful to the people. Now, however, their own national government despised them for defending the rights of the people--an activity that no one had belittled in previous times. The journal's editors claimed to receive many letters from the provinces detailing the abuse and persecution of teachers by local officials. Yet all this, claimed the editorials, was nothing compared to the treatment they received from their own supervisors in the Ministry of Public Instruction, who had been instructed to turn recalcitrant teachers over to the military courts.[59]

---

[58] Nezavisimost, June 20, 1881, p. 1. While the Liberals were severe in this instance, they nevertheless maintained a high respect for Jireček's activities in the realm of education, see D. Boshniakov, "Bŭlgarskiiat Dnevnik na Irechek. Bulgariia predi 50 godini, gledana prez ochilata na edin evropeets," Sila, November 4, 1930, pp. 3-4.

[59] Nezavisimost, June 20, 1881. The circular in question was issued by Minister Georgi Atanasovich.

The problem of teachers and politics diminished somewhat after the installation of a coalition government in September, 1883. But the Ministry's image in the eyes of many of its own employees was tarnished, and the effect of the turmoil on the progress of education was incalcuable. The struggle to restore the Constitution may have contributed to the rise of teacher organizations. It is no accident that teachers would be given a far greater role in the affairs of the Ministry, which will be described in Chapter Eight.

CHAPTER SIX

THE MINISTRY AND THE PEOPLE:
THE ROLE OF THE INSPECTORATE

Given the acerbic battles inside the Ministry (which often became public scandals) and the political involvements of many of its employees, the Ministry of Public Instruction needed good people to mend public fences and to help repair damage done to educational affairs or to the public image of the Ministry. This task more often than not fell to the sixteen people holding the office of provincial school inspector. And while public relations was not the only task of the inspectors, it was certainly the most crucial part of their jobs.

Public Relations and the Inspectorate

The creation of provincial school inspectors was one of the most significant events in Bulgarian education stemming from the establishment of a full-fledged educational ministry. The country had never before had a system of school inspection on any level, communal, provincial, or national, before the Liberation. While an attempt was made to inaugurate such a system in Shumen in the 1870s, it never amounted to anything due to Turkish pressures on the would-be reformers. The Shumen program was devised by a specially convoked teachers congress, which decided that the Metropolitan of the area should head the supervision of school affairs in conjunction with teachers congresses. In other words, the basic needs of the schools would be discussed every year at these congresses, with the Metropolitan providing interim guidance. Neither institution, however, had any legal basis for such actions. The same program endorsed measures to promote uniformity of instruction, texts, curricula, and quality of teachers.[1]

These Shumen plans, however, never succeeded, and the first actual inspectorate had to wait until the Russian Provisional Government of 1877-1879. Marin Drinov, Director of the Department of Public Instruction, took the first steps toward a system of school inspection. In his Temporary Statute for Public Schools, he called for the appointment of five persons, each assigned to a special educational section of the country, to inspect schools on a regular basis.[2]

---

[1] Vasilev, *Ucheben sŭvet*, pp. 17-20; Nikolov, "Poiava," p. 51; Zhechev, "Uchitelskiiat sŭbor v Shumen," pp. 77-89.

[2] Bulgaria, Department of Public Instruction and Religious Affairs, "Priturka pri Privremenni Ustav za Narodnite Uchilishta, No. 1, Instruktsiia za Okruzhnite Inspektori," in Marin Drinov, *Sŭchineniia*, III, pp. 75-80.

The duties of these inspectors were defined in the broadest of terms. Their most important task was to check on the credentials and the performance of the teachers, as well as their working conditions, especially matters relating to remuneration.[3] This task received particular emphasis since many short-term pedagogical courses were being set up at the time to provide an adequate supply of teachers; Drinov recognized that many of these would be poorly trained. This job alone would have provided more than enough work for the handful of inspectors. However, Drinov burdened them with the extra duties of establishing a school calendar, ensuring that the specified programs were carried out and enforcing compulsory attendance. The inspector was to act as an agent of the Department of Public Instruction to encourage local officials to furnish the schools with necessary books and supplies. On top of all this, he had to ensure that the physical conditions of the schools were satisfactory and report to the Department of Public Instruction if any community could not adequately care for its schools.[4] Another important task was to ascertain whether or not a given community was

---

[3] Ibid., pp. 76-77.

[4] Ibid., pp. 79-80.

able to open more schools, and if so, to encourage such openings. An additional duty involved mediation in disputes between local officials and teachers. Finally, he had to submit a written detailed report at the end of the school year to the Department of Public Instruction on the conditions (financial and educational) of the public schools in his district.[5]

The duties described by Drinov were all extremely necessary and timely. However, Minister Raicho Karolev, looking back on the first steps taken by Drinov, pointed out the obvious flaws. The program set up by Drinov could not be implemented, he noted, "because the five inspectors did not have the physical ability to visit all the towns and villages in the province since the school districts were extremely large, and this prevented the inspectors from carrying out their duties."[6]

Added to the geographical problem was the fact that even in the brief period of 1878-1880, there was a high turnover among inspectors, and sometimes an educational district would be without an inspector for long periods.

---

[5] Ibid.

[6] Karolev, "Podgotovka na uchitelite," ABAN, F. 62K (Raicho Karolev), op. 1, ae. 8, p. 4; Krachunov, Iz Bŭlgarska, p. 5.

Before long, the whole system became extremely irregular and unworkable and cried out for reform.

When the reforms did come and a new system was developed, it was far more extensive and involved than its prototype under Drinov. The individuals responsible for the reforms, primarily Jireček and Iliia Blŭskov, had much different goals in mind than those envisioned by Drinov. The latter had had no choice but to concentrate as much attention as possible on the critical teacher shortage, and his inspectorate program reflected that overwhelming concern. By 1881, however, the shortage had eased somewhat, allowing current administrations to turn their attention to other pressing concerns that might be alleviated through a nationwide system of school inspection.

One such concern in the 1880s was the tremendous variance between different parts of the country in terms of the quality of the schools and school programs. An editorial in the newspaper Bŭlgarski glas in March, 1880, decried the great discrepancies in school affairs around the nation:

> There are areas where the schools are entirely well-ordered and regularly supported, where the people show a great zeal and genuine diligence towards the schools and a full comprehension of all the good things emanating from a good, general primary education. But there are places, where the schools barely survive, where one encounters

in the people great negligence towards the schools and where the people expect everything from the government and nothing of themselves.[7]

The leaders of the country's school affairs were equally aware of, and concerned about, this circumstance. Jireček blamed part of the situation on the fact that the western part of the country, where education was poorly developed, had lain outside of the great highways and communication routes and was thus less developed in all aspects of culture and commerce.[8] Whatever the reason, the inequalities were evident in the crude statistics on literacy which the Ministry was able to gather by 1881. In eastern provinces such as Shumen and Tŭrnovo the ratio of literate to non-literate adults was relatively high. The figures were:

Tŭrnovo province	1:14
Shumen province	1:50

In western provinces, the figures were quite different:

Vratsa	1:212
Vidin	1:121 [9]

The figures for school attendance, again admittedly

---

[7]"Za Uchilishte," Bŭlgarski glas, March 27, 1880, pp. 5-6.

[8]Jireček, Glavno izlozhenie, p. 12.

[9]Ibid.

rough, reveal the same pattern. In the more advanced provinces of the east, as much as 82 percent of school-age children were enrolled in primary schools, while in the western part, the figures ran in the twenties and thirties, such as in Kiustendil where only 28 percent of the school-age children were in schools.[10]

Attitudes towards education differed tremendously. The western part was primarily agricultural, and peasants tended to resist sending children to school because they were needed for farm chores at home. In exasperation over such attitudes, Jireček wrote to Drinov, complaining that an extremely difficult task lay ahead for Bulgarian educators when it came to convincing some people to support schools. "Many things cannot at all be explained to the people," he noted:

> they do not understand because they have not seen Western European schools and their structure, and in general do not appreciate anything about progress and the strivings for modern pedagogy. Their souls are sunk in domestic prejudices, in mutual mistrust, and in woeful amateurism.[11]

Jireček and eventually others such as Bluskov, Mikhail Sarafov, and Spas Vatsov began to think that a good system of permanent school inspectors was a

---

[10] Ibid., pp. 13-14.

[11] Jireček, letter to Marin Drinov, August 27, 1880, in Sis, ed. Korespondentsiia, p. 201.

possible remedy for the discrepancies and the negative attitudes. Recognizing the futility of assigning five people to cover the entire country, the Ministry raised the number of inspectors to fourteen. The inspectors' school zones were made identical with the new administrative division of the country into fourteen provinces in 1882.[12]

Meanwhile, Sarafov and Jireček began work on a massive overhaul of the entire inspectorate and the instructions pertaining to their duties. From the results of their work, a totally new kind of inspector emerged, one whose most important task dealt with public relations between the Ministry and the people, either directly or through the people's representatives, i.e. the communal and provincial officials. The Instructions for the Provincial School Inspectors, issued by Sarafov in January, 1881, was an enormously detailed document, a trademark of Jireček, its principal author.[13] However, many of the most important ideas

---

[12]Tsonkov, Razvitie, p. 59. The fourteen provinces were: Sofia, Tŭrnovo, Varna, Vratsa, Kiustendil, Ruse, Razgrad, Lom, Silistra, Vidin, Sevliev, Svishtov, and Pleven. See also Teokharev, "Zapiska," p. 18.

[13]The Instructions for Provincial School Inspectors were published in Dŭrzhaven vestnik, III, 13, 14, 15, 16, 17 (1881).

and innovations came from a man who had long crusaded for an efficient system of school inspection, Iliia Blŭskov, school inspector in Shumen.

The work on the reform legislation had begun in January, 1881, when Jireček wrote to the Shumen inspector, asking his opinion on the proposed new division of school districts.[14] It was not the first contact between the two. Blŭskov had sent Jireček a warm letter on the latter's appointment to a job in the Ministry, calling him "our magnanimous benefactor" and assuring Jireček that he held him in high esteem.[15] Jireček on his part was aware of Blŭskov's reputation as the most successful thus far of all inspectors and turned often to him for advice. His queries were always answered with long valuable lists of suggestions, many of which ended up in the final version of the Instructions. Blŭskov suggested dividing the larger provinces into districts and appointing aides to the inspectors. Some important ideas for encouraging public support of the schools also came from Blŭskov, such as the idea of

---

[14]Jireček, letter to Iliia Blŭskov, January 16, 1881, ABAN, F. 3 (Jireček), op. 1, ae. 63, p. 4.

[15]Iliia Blŭskov, letter to Jireček, January 21, 1880, ABAN, F. 3 (Jireček), op. 1, ae. 63, p. 2.

making it a custom to donate to the schools the wine ordinarily consumed on Ivanovden.[16]

Jireček and his aides gathered all the items of information they could about matters that should occupy the attention of school inspectors and fashioned them into a very detailed list of Instructions for the Provincial School Inspectors which was finally issued in January, 1881.

Even before its publication, the reform work was hailed in the press. For example, an editorial in Nezavisimost commented on the anticipation surrounding the "great plans" of the Ministry of Public Instruction for reform of the inspectorate, among other projects. The editorial vigorously endorsed rumored plans for a comprehensive law on school inspectors, citing the absence of detailed regulations as the chief reason that the inspection of the schools had met such resistance and had proved so useless until now.[17]

---

[16] Iliia Blŭskov, letter to Jireček, February 13, 1881, ABAN, F. 3 (Jireček), op. 1, ae. 63, p. 11. My statement that Jireček used many of Blŭskov's suggestions is based on my examination of correspondence between the two and the drafts and final version of the Instructions for the Provincial School Inspectors. The material on the Instructions is in Jireček's archives, ABAN, F. 3 (Jireček), op. 1, ae. 1125.

[17] Nezavisimost, February 11, 1881, p. 1.

The editors of <u>Nezavisimost</u> and those who may have supported this view were not disappointed for the final instructions went a long way toward making the inspectorate extremely useful.

The Instructions began with a summary of thirteen points of the inspectors' major duties, and this job description differed remarkably from the vague definitions in Drinov's measure. Several important new elements were added. One immediate difference was that the new inspectors were given authority to supervise all schools in the Principality, whether communal, state, or private. This no doubt was in response to pressure from church and patriotic organizations which were upset about the activity of foreign religious groups. Another new emphasis was placed on financing. The inspectors were ordered to take special pains to see that the communes provided adequately for schools in their annual budgets and also that they could afford any new school openings before undertaking such activities.[18] This also was a response to post-Drinov developments, namely the flood of requests for aid from communities which had rushed to rebuild or repair schools

---

[18] Bulgaria, Ministry of Public Instruction, "Instruktsiia za Okrŭzhnite Uchilishtni Inspektori," <u>Dŭrzhaven vestnik</u>, III, 14 (1881), 108.

only to discover half-way through a project that funds were lacking.

The most important new item, however, was the emphasis on frequent visits to the schools and the careful reminders scattered throughout the Instructions that the inspectors represented the Ministry and must act accordingly in this new public relations role. The principal author of the Instructions, Jireček, was well aware of the suspicion and hostility especially among rural residents to any government officials, including those of the Ministry of Public Instruction. Thus, the carefully worded article 11 tersely reminded the inspectors:

> In relations with all people, the inspector must behave with utmost circumspection and courteous prudence because the success of his mission depends very often on the good will of the people. Despite the fact that in many places the populace shuns good work and looks suspiciously on all that is done for its education, more can often be accomplished with friendly advice and persuasion than with violent threats.[19]

The principal means for ensuring a good rapport was through maintaining a high profile, and thus the inspectors were ordered into the countryside at least once a month. (Drinov's decree in 1877 had said nothing about inspection trips, monthly or otherwise.)

---

[19] Ibid., p. 101.

The Instructions spelled out in meticulous detail exactly what the inspectors were to do on these monthly reviews. This again was a departure from the vague descriptions of Drinov's time, yet many of the duties were the same. Essentially, the inspectors had to make certain that students attended classes regularly, that teachers were qualified for their jobs, that local officials fulfilled their obligations to the schools, and that the programs and policies of the Ministry were enforced.[20] But the actual descriptions under each of these categories left little to the imagination. For example, in the section on the physical condition of the schools, Jireček gave precise measurements for desks and blackboards, as well as insisting that new schools be designed so that light fell over the left shoulders of the students and that curtains of suitable density be placed on windows to shield students from direct sunlight.[21] Such precision was, no doubt, probably intended as a future goal rather than a present requirement.

In two significant areas of inspectors' duties, Jireček's precision was to have important and fruitful

---

[20] Ibid., p. 108.

[21] Ibid., no. 17, p. 132.

results. One area concerned the functioning of school boards, the other the relationship of school boards and teachers.

The Instructions for the Provincial School Inspectors was a continuation of the unconstitutional activities of the Ministry, to use Karolev's phrase. That is, since the tangled state of government made it impossible to pass legislation through the Parliament, the Ministry had to issue decrees and instructions, taking the place of regular laws. In this regard, the Instructions for the Provincial School Inspectors served as an important tool for gaining more control over the activities of local institutions involved with school affairs such as the communal school boards. The school boards frequently clashed with teachers councils and directors over authority in school matters. The Instructions designated the inspectors as arbitrators in such disputes.[22] (This entire important subject will be discussed in a later chapter.)

These major tasks of the school inspectors were supplemented by numerous minor ones, such as ensuring that the education of females received as much attention as that of males and encouraging teachers to set up

---

[22] Ibid., p. 131.

reading clubs for students not able to continue their education in middle or secondary schools. This, it was hoped, would keep education alive in the minds of the students.[23]

The actual implementation of this remarkable set of instructions realized definite successes in some areas and disappointing failures in other aspects. One item (Section I, paragraph 17) of the new instructions almost immediately yielded unequivocably important results. That section of the Instructions had carefully spelled out how many reports had to be filed annually by the inspectors, as well as listing precisely what must be included. Although monthly reports had to be submitted, the most important by far was the report to be submitted at the end of each academic year. These reports had to give complete statistics on teachers, students, buildings, etc., as well as to offer comments on everything from the material condition of the schools to how regular was attendance and how well the teachers conveyed lessons. The reports began to flow in soon after the Instructions were issued.[24]

---

[23] Ibid., no. 18, p. 149.

[24] Many of these reports were analyzed before the fire that destroyed much of these archives of the Ministry of Public Instruction. See Vankov, Iz Arkhivite na Ministvototo.

These annual reports of the provincial school inspectors supplied an incredible wealth of information not only on school affairs but on many other aspects of life in the provinces of the Principality. Tales of clashes with peasants over school openings in Shop areas alternated with accounts of equally dramatic gestures of support for the work of teachers and inspectors. Information on local attitudes towards the Ministry of Public Instruction and the government in general, reports on population figures and economic conditions, as well as accounts of relations between local government officials and of peculiar local problems all found their way into these reports. Of course, the inspectors also wrote at length about educational affairs. All of this information helped the Ministry to formulate better decisions on local needs as well as to shape plans for future reforms or programs.[25]

Furthermore, judging by the information contained in the reports, the inspectors were now touring their districts with some regularity and visiting places that had never before seen a school inspector. The inspectors' reports helped the Ministry decide more wisely how to allocate aid to struggling communities since the

---

[25]Ibid., especially pp. 9-39.

inspectors could better supply data as to a community's resources and whether aid was even needed. The Ministers of Public Instruction frequently cited these annual and monthly reports in appearances before the Ministerial Council, the State Council, and the Parliament.[26]

Besides such important information, these reports also often contained amusing anecdotes. One inspector with a high opinion of himself ruefully reported that the peasants in his district (Ruse) had never heard of him but were familiar with Jireček. According to the inspector, the peasants argued constantly about whether their Czech minister was of the Orthodox faith. Opinion at the time was that Jireček could not have written so wisely about Bulgaria unless he were indeed Orthodox.[27]

The influence of the strengthened corps of inspectors, armed with their new instructions, was also evident in the area of school expansion. This had been perhaps the only area in which school inspectors under Drinov had had any real impact. Schools had blossomed

---

[26] This was especially the case in requests by the Ministry of Public Instruction for emergency aid for particular communities, as outlined in Chapter Three of this thesis.

[27] Vasil Stoianov, letter to Jireček, March 26, 1881, ABAN, F. 3 (Jireček), op. 1, ae. 79, p. 41.

quickly but erratically and often in such a way as to creat severe financial difficulties for the communities. While the "Instructions" recognized that the encouragement of school openings was an important task of the provincial school inspectorate, Sarafov and Jireček also cautioned the inspectors to ascertain as well as possible just how much the individual community could afford before embarking on school expansion of even repair projects.[28]

The inspectors took this task seriously and while constantly urging communities that could afford expansion to undertake it, these same inspectors began to file background reports to accompany a community's request for aid from the central government. Often the inspectors would suggest a lower amount than that requested by the community. This was in line with another mandate of the Instructions which explained to the inspectors the Ministry's desire to curb what Jireček perceived as the growing habit of depending too much on the central government for funding in school affairs. Now grants would be given only in the event that the commune suffered unforeseen misfortune such as fire,

---

[28] Bulgaria, Ministry of Public Instruction, "Instruktsiia za Okrŭzhnite Uchilishtni Inspektori," Dŭrzhaven vestnik, III, 14 (1881), 108ff.

earthquake, or famine. In these cases, moreover, application for financial assistance had to be made through the school inspector.[29] One immediate result of this was that school expansion tended to be undertaken on a more solid financial basis.[30]

Needless to say, such increased authority on the part of the inspectors in financial matters carried over into other spheres as well. This was especially true in the realm of relations between communal officials and teachers. Inspectors played increasingly important roles as mediators between mayors, school boards, and teachers. This role was perceived by the Ministry and by others as perhaps the most critical of all. In a debate in the Sŭbranie over the pay scales of school inspectors, Stefan Stambulov pointed out that the inspectors must be well-paid considering the arduous work expected of them. But more importantly, better pay would attract more qualified people to the jobs. This

---

[29] Ibid., no. 15, p. 116.

[30] In appearances before the Ministerial Council for budget requests, the Ministers began with increasing frequency to attach copies of the inspectors' reports to communal requests for aid. Such reports usually cast a better light on the resources of the community in question. For typical examples of this, see Bulgaria, Ministerial Council, sessions of May 4, 1882; April 3, 1883; May 2, 1883; TsDIA, F. 708 (Ministerial Council), op. 1, ae. 251, p. 3; ae. 382, pp. 1-3; ae. 416, p. 1.

was significant said Stambulov since:

> they /the inspectors/ must be able to relate to simple people who do not yet appreciate what can be had from schools, and they must urge them to build a school where none exists. The work of an inspector is the work of an apostle because he works for the people's enlightenment.31

Many of the "simple people" mentioned by Stambulov were communal leaders who, in some areas, frequently considered their responsibilities towards the schools as unwanted burdens. This then resulted in poor pay for teachers or outright strife. In such cases, the school inspector could intervene and bring the matter to the attention of higher authorities. For example, the school inspector for Sofia province discovered in the course of an inspection tour that the mayors of several villages did not even know the location of schools in the vicinity and did little to encourage the populace to support schools. When the inspector informed the district officials of the situation, the result was a stern lecture on legal duties to the mayors of the villages in question. The same lecture outlined the fines and punishments provided for communal officials who neglected to see that teachers were paid on time.32

---

[31] Stenograficheski dnevnitsi na II ONS, pŭrva redovna sesiia, session of May 31, 1880, p. 617.

[32] Samokov, City Communal Administration, "Prepiska sŭs Samokovsko uchilistno nastoiatelstvo, Sofiiski

Provincial school inspectors also took direct action themselves at times. It was not at all unusual for them to attend meetings of school boards and teachers councils in their assigned areas. Some teachers councils specifically invited provincial inspectors on a regular basis.[33] Also, the provincial inspectors had increased powers in relation to seeing that school boards honored the provisions of their contracts with teachers. (This same article gave teachers the right to sue local officials for breach of contract.)

The provincial inspectors often took a direct part in planning of school improvements or new school construction, mostly to ensure that the new strictures on physical specifications were met. An extreme example of this was the case of Tsani Ginchev, inspector for Rakhovsko province. The communal officials of Bela Slatina ignored his suggestions to build a new four-room school and instructed the contractors to lay out

---

okrŭzhen upravitel i drugi otnosno izbor na uchilishtni nastoiateli, sŭstoianie na uchilishtata v niakoi Samokovski sela, i dr.," SGODA, F. 41K (Samokov City Administration), op. 1, ae. 525, pp. 8-11.

[33]Sofia, Sofia School Board, "Protokolna kniga na zasedaniiata na uchitelski sŭvet pri Sofiiski osnovni narodni uchilishta, 1880-1885," SGODA, F. 5K (Sofia School Board), op. 1, ae. 87, pp. 41-42.

plans for a two-room building instead. Ginchev and his aides went out at night and repositioned the surveyor's pegs. The construction workers did not discover the change until it was too late,[34] and the village of Bela Slatina got a four-room school, in keeping with Jireček's instructions. Such forceful actions, however amusing, did not make the inspectors very popular. But the Ministry supported its inspectors in times of difficulty. One inspector, D. Kotsov (Belogradchik province), had several clashes with school and local officials over attempts to enforce new provisions, yet had a record of building 40 schools in his three-year tenure of office. In a letter to Jireček, he pointed out that he could not have survived without the consistent and firm support of the Ministry in his struggle to improve conditions.[35] Such actions won high praise in many circles for the work of the inspectors. An editorial in *Nezavisimost* on the inspectorate concluded:

---

[34] Bulgaria, Ministry of Public Instruction, report to State Council, May 4, 1882, TsDIA, F. 708 (State Council), op. 1, ae. 251; Minev, "Tsani Ginchev," p. 54; Minev, *Tsani Ginchev, Nikola Kozlev*, p. 46.

[35] D. Kotsov, letter to Jireček, October 10, 1881, ABAN, F. 3 (Jireček), op. 1, ae. 128, p. 2.

For our part, we have no doubts whatsoever about the need of its existence and of its success, while being intimately aware of the capability and intense patriotism of the people who administer our public instruction.[36]

Praise also came for the inspectors on the floor of the Sŭbranie, where the name of Blŭskov in Shumen was singled out for special mention. Brushlianov, a frequent critic of the Ministry, noted the great efforts of the inspectors for the uplifting of the people in school affairs.[37]

If the Ministry and its provincial school inspectorate received a good deal of praise, they also received a similar measure of criticism. Despite the successes and advances, problems persisted, and failures were not uncommon.

The problem of communities overextending themselves to build new schools at the instigation of school inspectors has been discussed earlier in the chapter of this thesis dealing with community school finances. This tended to ease somewhat after the new instructions to school inspectors since specific limits were put on requests from communities for aid.

---

[36]*Nezavisimost*, February 11, 1881, p. 2.

[37]*Stenograficheski dnevnitsi na II ONS, pŭrva redovna sesiia*, session of May 31, 1880, p. 671.

The really important problems, however, originated in the ranks of the inspectorate itself and in the system of their selection. As always in this early period of Bulgarian national existence, experienced and highly qualified people were in short supply. Inevitably, the Minister of Public Instruction had to fill a vacancy with someone not quite prepared for the critical tasks ahead of him. This resulted in unevenness of performance. Minister Dimitŭr Agura addressed this question in a speech to the School Council in 1883. Agura noted that as specific and detailed as the instructions issued by Jireček and Sarafov were, they had no force of law, and, in fact, the local officials and the inspectors were not legally bound to follow them. Therefore, implementation depended entirely on the presence of conscientious people in office and, even then, they met great difficulties in fulfilling their tasks.[38]

Jireček, in a letter to one such conscientious inspector, complained that inexperience and youth were causing problems for some inspectors, and these same factors still caused Parliament to look askance at the

---

[38] Dimitŭr Agura, "Otkrivanieto na uchebniia sŭvet pri Ministerstvoto na Narodno Prosveshtenie," Ucheben vestnik, I, 1-4 (1883), 107-110.

work of the inspectors.[39] Within Parliament, voices were often raised to complain that a school inspector had never been seen in this or that district within the deputies' jurisdiction.[40]

Unfortunately, many of these charges were indeed true and resulted from the still too unwieldy size of the provinces. Efforts to persuade the Sŭbranie to fund assistants met with little success. Also, many positions went begging for long periods of time. Indeed, after the positions became elective in 1884, irregularities sometimes voided an entire province's election.[41] This latter circumstance, however, mostly occurred because the government had never explained in sufficiently clear terms when a government employee could run for political office. Often when a government servant such as a clerk or a teacher decided to run for office,

---

[39]Jireček, letter to Iliia Blŭskov, January 16, 1881, ABAN, F. 3 (Jireček), op. 1, ae. 63, p. 4.

[40]*Stenograficheski dnevnitsi na II ONS, pŭrva redovna sesiia*, session of May 31, 1880, p. 671.

[41]Bulgaria, Ministry of Public Instruction, "Prepis okrŭzhno do gg. okrŭzhnite upraviteli v Kniazhestvo," in Samokov School Board, "Prepiska sŭs Samokovsko okoliisko upravlenie, Ministerstvo na Prosveta i dr. osnosno naznachenie na okrŭzhni uchilishtni inspektori," January-November, 1885, SGODA, F. 41K (Samokov City-Communal Administration), op. 1, ae. 526.

his election was challenged by his opponents and declared void because the bid was considered illegal. This confusion persisted throughout the period 1878-1885.[42]

Another source of confusion was the poor communications network then existent in the country. When this was coupled with the all too frequent changes of government, the result was uncertainty on the part of many inspectors as to whether they still had a job, and if they did, where exactly was their assignment. For example, in April, 1881, the Minister at the time, Jireček, received a letter from the inspector of Ruse, inquiring as to whether or not he had been fired. His suspicions were based on several facts: first, a reference to him by Ruse provincial officials as the "former chief inspector"; and second, the fact that he alone of all bureaucrats employed by the Ministry in the area had not received his pay for the month of April.[43]

---

[42] Ibid.; see also, Bulgaria, Ministerial Council, sessions dealing with this issue after spring elections in 1885, TsDIA, F. 284 (Ministerial Council), op. 1, ae. 371-380.

[43] Vasil Stoianov, letter to Jireček, April 20, 1881, ABAN, F. 3 (Jireček), op. 1, ae. 179, p. 44; also letter to Minister of Public Instruction Mikhail Sarafov, April 23, 1881, ABAN, F. 3 (Jireček), op. 1, ae. 179, p. 46.

In that same year, Iliia Blŭskov wrote to Jireček, asking for information as to which province he was supposed to take charge of as inspector.[44]

This confusion, as well as other problems connected with the inspectorate, hurt the efforts to reform the system. Minister Karolev, looking back on this period, claimed that the while inspection system came to naught, mostly because of the frequent changes and also because many of the provinces went for long periods of time without an inspector. Such a judgment was too harsh because the system was not without notable achievements. Perhaps the most useful of all was the fact that the inspectors helped establish closer contact with the people and thus made it easier to assess the needs of the various regions. One need only look at the inspectors' reports to realize how much vital information was recorded therein. And, the Ministry used these reports effectively, frequently citing them or attaching them to its own reports before the Sŭbranie and the Ministerial Council.

The inspectorate represented the Ministry before the people, an important and critical task considering the nature of the Ministry's work. Favorable public

---

[44] Iliia Blŭskov, letter to Jireček, April 22, 1881, ABAN, F. 3 (Jireček), op. 1, ae. 63, p. 14.

relations were absolutely vital to the success of the government's efforts to improve the quality of the country's educational system. Another significant area of the Ministry's relations with the Bulgarian people, of course, was its relation to the guardian of the country's culture and civilization for 500 years, the Church.

CHAPTER SEVEN

THE MINISTRY OF PUBLIC INSTRUCTION

AND THE BULGARIAN ORTHODOX CHURCH

    The pervasive role of the Orthodox Church in Bulgarian education has been discussed in Chapter One of this thesis and in other preceding sections. To repeat, up until the late eighteenth century hardly a school existed that was not dependent in some way on the Church. Even the secular schools established during the Renascence period depended heavily on church support. Thus, it would seem that a sudden transition from church control and supervision of education to supervision by a secular Ministry of Public Instruction would be fraught with clashes, disagreements, and misunderstandings. Such, however, was not the case, at least in the period of 1878-1885. The reasons for the lack of disharmony throw important light on the fundamental changes occurring in this critical transition period.

    The remarkable smoothness of relations between the Ministry of Public Instruction and the Church was even more important considering that church relations with the State in general were not always cordial. Serious clashes occurred in this period, for example, between the government of the Principality and the leaders of the Exarchate (still located in Istanbul). Such clashes revolved around the Exarchate's control of church affairs within the Principality. Church leaders as well as civic leaders within the new state were uneasy over the fact that the Exarchate was still too closely tied to the Ottoman government.[1] This, of course, was because the Ottoman sultan had issued the decree establishing the Bulgarian Exarchate (in 1870) and maintained the Turkish government's right to supervise the affairs of this Bulgarian religious institution.[2] In later periods, church and state leaders within the Principality would quarrel over the election of a Catholic dynasty to the throne in the 1890s. However, as far as the Ministry of Public Instruction itself was concerned, relations with Bulgarian church officials inside and outside the Principality remained cordial throughout the period 1878-1885. The relations between

---

[1] Black, Establishment of Constitutional Government, pp. 84, 89-90; Cyril, Patriarch of Bulgaria, Bŭlgarskata Ekzarkhiia v Odrinsko i Makedoniia sled Osvoboditelna voina, 1877-1878 (Sofia: 1970), pp. 170-183.

[2] Meininger, Ignatiev, pp. 129-131; A discussion of the provisions of the firman of 1870 is in Richard von Mach, The Bulgarian Exarchate: Its History and the Extent of Its Authority in Turkey (London: 1907), pp. 12-13.

the two institutions of Church and Ministry, one very old and the other very new, illustrate the prevailing attitudes and concordance at the time in the country as a whole towards the subject of education.

There was general recognition at the time of the important role of the Church in preserving the country's identity during the period of Turkish rule. Justifiably or not, Bulgarians saw the Church in this role as conservator, and church officials fostered this attitude. Exarch Steven writing in the 1890s, for example, detailed at great length that role of the Church, which reached its zenith with the calling of countrywide teachers congresses in the early 1870s. Without the Church, claimed Exarch Steven, there would be no Bulgarian history.[3] He also pointed out, perhaps superfluously, the role of the Church had played in the schools.

That role was severely diminished by the establishment for the first time in 500 years of a civil government. The nature of that civil government itself was

---

[3] Steven, Exarch of Bulgaria, Bŭlgarskata tsŭrkva (Sofia: 1932), pp. 10-14; a concise discussion of the problems that prompted Exarch Steven to write this may be found in Mikhail Madzharov, "Bŭlgarskata tsŭrkva i svetskata vlast'," Dukhovna kultura, I, 5-6 (1921), 386-415

an important reason for the lack of rancor between the new state and the Church. However, it must be noted that the birth pangs of that same state, namely the Russo-Turkish War, caused enormous destruction of church real estate and thus diminished the most important element of the Church's influence over education, its financial resources. Prince Alexander Dondukov-Korsakov detailed the losses in his reports to the Russian government and despaired of any quick regeneration of the lost resources.[4] This diminution of church resources, of course, would have made it difficult for church leaders, so disposed, to criticize the government's assumption of control over the schools. But that eventuality never came to pass because many church officials saw the establishment of a Bulgarian state not as an interruption but rather as a continuation on a higher plane of the Church's own work.

The reason such an attitude was possible lay in the Tŭrnovo Constitution itself which guaranteed a leading role for the Bulgarian Orthodox Church in the country's affairs. Chapter nine, article thirty-seven

---

[4] Prince Alexander Dondukov-Korsakov, "Otchet," July,16, 1878, and "Otchet ego siatel'stvu Grafu D. A. Miliutinu," September 18, 1878, in Muratov, Dokumenti, pp. 106-132, 133-169.

of the Tŭrnovo Constitution made Orthodoxy the state religion of the new country and proclaimed that the Prince of Bulgaria, as well as his descendants, should be of that faith. The Principality, in ecclesiastical matters, was under the jurisdiction of the Holy Synod of the Principality, and this same Synod, in turn, remained united to the Exarchate in matters of dogma and faith.[5] When this statement came up for debate in the Tŭrnovo Constituent Assembly in 1879, several bishops protested the original wording. The original version had ignored the Holy Synod in Sofia and proclaimed the country as being under the direct authority of the Exarch in Istanbul. This again was due to suspicion of the location of the Exarch since supposedly he was too far removed from actual affairs within the country itself. Thus, a compromise cited both Synod and Exarchate.[6] The same Tŭrnovo Consitution also removed religious affairs from the realm of the Ministry dealing with education.

---

[5] Bulgaria, Ministry of Justice, Godishen sbornik, pp. 21-22.

[6] Black, Establishment of Constitutional Government, pp. 89-90. See also the debates in Bulgaria, Narodno Sŭbranie, Protokolite na uchreditelno sŭbranie, pp. 1-9.

During the Russian occupation, the Department of Public Instruction also administered matters involving religious affairs. But that situation changed with the Tŭrnovo Constitution which transferred such authority to a new ministry called the Ministry of Foreign Affairs and Religions (sometimes called "cults" in English). The Constitution left unexplained exactly what duties this Ministry would have in regard to religious affairs. However, an earlier section of the Tŭrnovo Constitution had specified that all non-Orthodox and non-Christian subjects would manage their own church affairs by their own ecclesiastical administration. However, these ecclesiastical administrations were subject to the superintendence of "the responsible Ministry" according to the special laws the responsible Ministry might promulgate. Presumably this was the Ministry of Foreign Affairs and Religions, but the language suggested more than one ministry could become involved.[7]

To these constitutional assurances must then be added the fact that the leading figures of the Bulgarian Church at the time were not only themselves well-versed

---

[7] The relevant article of the Tŭrnovo Constitution was Chapter IX, Bulgaria, Ministry of Justice, Godishen sbornik, pp. 16-17; Khristo Giaurov, "Tsŭrkva i dŭrzhavata," Dukhovna kultura, I, 13-14 (1922), 89.

in secular education, but strongly endorsed it. Metropolitan Simeon of Varna, for example, crusaded in the 1870s for more secular subjects in the schools as well as for greater participation of secular authorities in school affairs. This did not mean an elimination or diminution of religious education, however, since that was ensured by the Constitution. Most inflential of all in this respect was Metropolitan Clement of Tŭrnovo, who himself was Minister of Public Instruction in this period (holding office from November, 1879, to March, 1880). His secular name was Vasil Drumev, but he was already Metropolitan of Tŭrnovo when he became Minister of Public Instruction. While working in Brăila, he was disturbed by how far removed Bulgarians were from educated Europeans and was convinced that only a deep commitment to "enlightenment" could help the Bulgarian people take their place among cultured peoples. He saw no conflict whatsoever between secular learning and religion. "Faith gives to us the higher truths of morality, while science elucidates these truths and more clearly instills them in us,"[8] he explained. Clement

---

[8] Vasil Drumev, "Zhivotopisanie," Periodichesko spisanie na Bŭlgarskoto knizhovno druzhestvo, III (1870), 24; M. Stoianov, "Mladiiat Vasil Drumev," Prosveta, III, 4 (1941), 426.

also believed that exploration of the wonders of science led to faith in God. His vision of a national and spiritual unity of the country symbolized by the Tŭrnovo Constitution and manifested in an independent state was shared not only by many other religious figures, but also by many of the rulers of the country at the time.[9]

Most important for good relations between Church and State was the fact that most of the Ministers of Public Instruction, but especially Jireček and Drinov, strongly endorsed an active role by the Church in the country's educational affairs.

This, for reasons of financial loss, was not as easily attained as before. Another new factor entered the picture at this time. The creation of an independnet Bulgarian state created vast new opportunities that proved irresistible to educated, ambitious young men. While Bulgaria was in subject status to the Ottoman Empire, practically the only way young men could improve their lot in life was to become teachers and priests.

---

[9] Stoianov, "Mladiiat Drumev," pp. 422-427; Vasil Drumev, "Za Otkhranata," *Periodichesko spisanie na Bŭlgarsko knizhovno druzhestvo*, I (1870), 61-102; see also his article, "Namisvanieto na svetskata vlast' v cherkovnite raboti," *Periodichesko spisanie na Bŭlgarsko knizhovno druzhestvo*, I, 11-12 (1870), 19-73; similar ideas were also expressed in his autobiographical notes, BIA, F. 146 (Vasil Drumev), op. 1, ae. 1, pp. 1-36.

In fact, the two professions were often synonymous, although it is impossible to determine how many became priests and vice-versa.[10] After the Liberation, Bulgaria needed soldiers and statesmen in great numbers, and the rise of such new opportunities considerably reduced the numbers available for traditional occupations in teaching and the priesthood. The growing shortage of priests was a source of great frustration both to the Church and to the Ministers of Public Instruction. The Ministry and the Church had cooperated in setting up seminaries on the theory that these government-controlled schools would provide better-trained men to serve the priesthood and therefore attract more to the calling. This proved not to be the case. While the two seminaries did indeed attract students, most of them did not become ordained upon graduation. Instead, they became bureaucrats and military officers.[11]

---

[10] Atanas Shopov, Bŭlgariia v tsŭrkovno otnoshenie (Plovdiv: 1889), p. 6. Shopov was one of the most important historians of the Bulgarian Orthodox Church. While constantly bemoaning the lack of figures on the subject, he did manage to come up with statistics for 1888. At that time, the country was unified, but the figures still give a rough idea. Of a total of 2,350 servants of the Church (including deacons and monks), 1,951 were priests, and of these, 1,012 had been teachers before becoming priests. These figures were used as official statistics by the Exarchate.

[11] Jireček, letter to Metropolitan Clement, August 14, 1881, ABAN, F. 3 (Jireček), op. 1, ae. 125, p. 8; Shopov, Bŭlgariia, pp. 5-6.

Although church officials and the Ministry cooperated in attempting to find a solution, later observers of the situation complained that not enough had been done by the government in the first years after the Liberation to assure the status and financial well-being of the priests. This negligence thus assured that the priesthood would not become a career desired by educated young men. Also, the critics noted that the Ministry of Defense purposely wooed young men away from theological schools into the highly prestigious new schools for military officers.[12]

The Ministers of Public Instruction consulted church officials on this problem and on many others affecting the country's education. They also provided for church participation in educational affairs. The spirit of this cooperation was exemplified in a remark sent by Jireček in 1880 to Metropolitan Clement of Tŭrnovo, who was also Minister of Public Instruction at the time. At the end of a long memorandum dealing with

---

[12]Shopov, Bŭlgariia, pp. 5-6; D. Mishev, letter to Stoian Kostov, February 7, 1900, SSTsIO, F. Kostov, ae. 9830, p. 216; also confidential letter of Exarchate to Bulgarian Minister of Foreign Affairs, 1883, SSTsIO F. Kostov, ae. 9905, pp. 1-2. This last item was written by the Exarch to protest plans to amend the Constitution to allow a Catholic dynasty to come to the throne. It traces the history of Church and State relations.

various school affairs, Jireček noted that it would not be a bad idea for the teaching profession also to include the clergy, especially if education was going to develop along with general progress. "In such a way," he continued, "the clergy could fulfill the most beautiful aspects of its calling and could perform immortal tasks for the nation."[13]

Much of the Church's direct participation in school affairs occurred, naturally, in the theological seminaries that were state operated. While the curricula for such schools were set by the Ministry of Public Instruction, the actual operation was left in the hands of church officials appointed to run them. Especially important in this respect was the Saints Peter and Paul monastery in Liaskovets, which was plagued with a host of problems ranging from poor facilities and poor teachers to trouble between regular students and those transferring from the Samokov school.[14] In all these

---

[13] Jireček, "Zapiska," ABAN, F. 3 (Jireček), op. 1 ae. 1125, p. 10.

[14] Jireček, letter to Metropolitan Clement, March 31, 1881, ABAN, F. 3 (Jireček), op. 1, ae. 125, pp. 7-8; letter to Metroplitan Clement, July 4, 1880, F. 3 (Jireček), op. 1, ae. 125, p. 2.

matters, church officials worked closely with the Ministry to effect solutions.[15]

However, participation by clergy was not limited to the theological schools. They were also consulted at various times on different aspects of school affairs. For example, in a meeting with the country's leading bishops, Jireček discussed with them everything from the matter of which schools should become state controlled to the significant influence priests could have in encouraging good attitudes toward the schools among the populace. The bishops agreed to work closely with the provincial school inspectors to improve conditions in local schools. In fact, an outstanding example of such cooperation came between Inspector Iliia Blŭskov and the Metropolitan of Varna, Simeon.[16] Of course, church leaders could and did also voice their opinions in the

---

[15] Vasil Drumev, Curriculum for Liaskovets Seminary, BIA, F. 146 (Vasil Drumev), op. 1, ae. 8, p. 5; Stanimir Stanimirov, "Nashite dukhovni uchilishta: Iz istoriia na Tŭrnovskoto Eparkhialno Bogoslovsko uchilishte," Arkhiv na Ministerstvoto na Narodna Prosveta, I, 2 (1909), 80ff.; Arkhimandrite Theofilakt, letter to Stoian Kostov, Secretary of the Holy Synod, September 16, 1898, SSTsIO, F. Kostov, ae. 9389, pp. 1-4; V. D. Stoianov, letter to Minister of Public Instruction M. K. Sarafov, April 23, 1881, ABAN, F. 3 (Jireček), op. 1, ae. 179, p. 46.

[16] Jireček, Bŭlgarski dnevnik, II, p. 258.

Parliament, to which many of them belonged and attended regularly.

The Church did not obtain the right formally to help approve textbooks until 1898, and even then this was limited to books used for catechism instruction.[17] There were other ways of influencing policy, however, since the regulations dealing with the composition of local school boards specifically mentioned the desirability of including clergy as members.[18] In some districts such as Sofia and Samokov, priests became very influential on the school boards. It must be noted that some school boards served also as executive boards for local church affairs and thus carried the title Church-School Board.[19]

---

[17] Bulgaria, Ministry of Public Instruction, Circular letter of Minister Ivan Vazov, January 14, 1898, Uchilishten pregled, III, 2 (1898), 146.

[18] Bulgaria, Ministry of Public Instruction, "Instruktsiia za okrŭzhnite uchilishtni inspektori," Dŭrzhaven vestnik, III, 17 (1880), 131; III, 18 (1880) 139.

[19] The Sofia School Board for the city of Sofia was, in fact, officially called "Church-School Board" and included at least one priest, Ikonom pop Todor, as a very active member. Sofia, Sofia School Board, "Protokolna kniga ot zasedaniiata na Uchitelskiia Sŭvet pri Sofiiski osnovni uchilishta, 1880-1885," SGODA, F. 5K (Sofia School Board), op. 1, ae. 87, p. 22.

In addition to this, provisions in the "Instructions for the Provincial School Inspectors" spelled out the procedures for opening schools and the ceremonies to mark the new school year which included a significant number of church services and blessings. These same instructions advised the inspectors to invite local priests to help teachers in their own work.[20]

Despite the relative overall smoothness of relations, some problems did occur between the Church and the State in the realm of educational affairs. Many of the problems, however, did not involve, directly at least, the Ministry of Public Instruction. For example, in 1878, while the country was still under the Russian provisional government, a serious clash occurred in the Ruse area between civil and religious authorities over priestly duties involving marriages. Villagers in the Ruse area were upset that several marriages had been allowed to take place between blood relatives--a practice contrary to canon law. Since the priests of the area had been negligent in their attention to the matter, the local citizens petitioned Russian authorities to forbid another such marriage that was slated to occur.

---

[20] Bulgaria, Ministry of Public Instruction, "Instruktsiia za okrŭzhnite uchilishtni inspektori," Dŭrzhaven vestnik, III, 18 (1880), 112, 139.

The Russian Guard Captain Poloskov forbade the marriage, which action in turn angered church authorities. The latter appealed to Drinov to investigate the matter since the Department of Public Instruction was also responsible at the time for religious affairs.[21] Whatever action Drinov took was never recorded, but such occurrences ceased when the Russian occupation ended. The entire matter exemplified the kinds of problems the Ministry escaped after the promulgation of the Tŭrnovo Constitution. That Constitution had transferred religious affairs to the Ministry of Foreign Affairs.

The Ministry of Public Instruction had its own difficulties with priests when it tried to improve working conditions for teachers in rural areas. One special sore spot was that which these teachers perceived as abuse by local priests. Village priests often demanded that only teachers with good voices be hired so that they could participate in church choirs as cantors and directors. In fact, teachers were expected to spend quite a bit of time in various church

---

[21] Exarch Iosif, letter to Marin Drinov, Department of Public Instruction, August 2, 1878, TsDIA, F. 405 (Department of Public Instruction and Religious Affairs), op. 1, ae. 1, pp. 1-4.

activities.[22] However, ministerial attempts to remedy met with little opposition from church leaders. From time to time there would be complaints that teachers were atheists or at least agnostics. For instance, in 1884 some of the bishops complained to Minister of Public Instruction Karolev that the majority of public school teachers not only failed to encourage students to attend Church regularly, but themselves failed to attend regularly, which created a bad example for their students. This resulted in a formal circular to the provincial school inspectors, instructing them to order teachers, especially in villages, to attend church services regularly (at least on holidays) together with the students in their charge.[23]

Many squabbles also occurred from time to time over the plans to open new seminaries. In 1880, Minister Giuzelev proposed the closing of the Samokov seminary. Giuzelev arged that due to a shortage of experienced teachers and other shortages as well, it would be

---

[22] This question was discussed in Chapter Three. See Blŭskov, "Nuzhdata ot revis'or Inspektor," pp. 145-162; Ganvhev, Spomeni.

[23] Bulgaria, Ministry of Public Instruction, letter of Minister Raicho Karolev, December 4, 1884, in Balabanov and Manov, edds. Sbornik s otbrani okrŭzhni, p. 518.

best to consolidate the Samokov school with the one in Liaskovets.[24] This proposal met with stiff opposition from church leaders. Speaking on their behalf, Metropolitan Meletius pointed out the declining state of the clergy due to the war and new opportunities for youth. Closing the Samokov school would worsen the situation, he argued, and proposed instead the construction of a third seminary.[25] The clergy lost the battle then, although another school was opened later. A similar altercation over the Samokov school occurred in 1898.[26]

One bizarre exchange over the status of priests occurred during the tenure of Georgi Teokharev as Minister of Public Instruction. Teokharev, for reasons known only to himself, constantly blamed the Church for the backward state of Bulgarian educational affairs at the time. He stunned Parliament in February, 1883, by openly denouncing the clergy for abandoning its traditional role in school affairs. He sarcastically remarked that they seemed to be now involved in "more

---

[24] *Stenograficheski dnevnitsi na II ONS, purva redovna sesiia*, session of May 21, 1880, p. 537.

[25] Ibid., p. 539.

[26] Georgi Ivan Kertev (church official in Samokov), letter to Stoian Kostov, August 8, 1898, SSTsIO, F. Kostov, ae. 9446, pp. 1-2.

important work," which he left unspecified.[27] Not one deputy rose to support his charge, while many refuted it as completely unwarranted. He made the same statement, to the horror of Jireček, in a meeting between Ministry officials and the higher clergy, who shrugged off the remark as the ravings of a madman. Jireček, in his private diary, dismissed Teokharev as an idiot.[28]

The problems between the Ministry of Public Instruction and the Church described thus far were all solved by compromise or cooperation. Two other church-related issues also confronted the Ministry at this time, both were extremely delicate yet also potentially explosive in nature. One issue was that of the school affairs of the Bulgarian Exarchate, which involved the Ministry to only a very limited extent. The other issue concerned the schools founded by foreign or non-Orthodox religious groups. This issue generated considerable debate and excitement in the period 1878-1885. Yet the Ministers of Public Instruction managed to stay out of the controversy for a considerable time. When the Ministry finally became involved, it was only reluctantly.

---

[27] Stenograficheski dnevnitsi na III ONS, pŭrva redovna sesiia, session of February 9, 1883, p. 3.

[28] Jireček, Bŭlgarski dnevnik, II, pp. 299-302.

The Exarchate Schools

When the Great Powers imposed the Berlin Treaty on Bulgaria, Russia, and Turkey in July, 1878, a great portion of the state (Thrace and Macedonia) set up by the Russians returned to the administration of the Ottoman Empire. The Macedonian region became the object of intense efforts by Serbs, Greeks, and Bulgarians to claim the region as part of the national heritage of bygone days. Indeed, Macedonia had been an apple of discord for centuries. After 1878, it was the Exarchate, which remained headquartered in Istanbul, that maintained the claim of Bulgarians to this region. The Exarch took it upon himself to preserve, through schools, the identity of the region as Bulgarian in the event that the Berlin Treaty could be overturned and nullified.[29]

For this reason, the whole question of exarchial schools was fraught with complex diplomatic questions involving mostly Russia, France, Austria-Hungary, and the Ottoman Empire, as well as Serbia and Greece. The Tŭrnovo Constitution put this whole delicate question in the charge of the Ministry of Foreign Affairs and

---

[29] Cyril, Patriarch of Bulgaria, Bŭlgarskata Ekzarkhiia, pp. 9-81.

Religions, thus sparing the Ministry of Public Instruction from having to expend time and energy over such problems.[30] Yet the latter Ministry did not entirely escape contact with the exarchial schools.

Officials of the Exarchate had made several pleas to the Principality for aid in setting up schools in Macedonia. The appeals finally succeeded in 1881 [31] when the Ministry of Public Instruction opened negotiations on this question with Metropolitan Nathaniel of Okhrid and Plovdiv. Precisely how and why the Ministry of Public Instruction was expected to underwrite a portion of the school expenses of the Exarchate is unclear. The first formal request, however, came in a letter from Metropolitan Nathaniel to Minister Jireček in June, 1881. From then onward, the request was made and negotiated each year. Always, the negotiations and

---

[30] This assertion is based on detailed examination of available correspondence between the Ministry of Public Instruction and the Exarchate between 1878-1885. The archives of the Exarchate itself, which are closed to researchers, might reveal other areas of concern between the two institutions. On the other hand, the Archives of the Ministerial Council, TsDIA, F. 284, reveal that all other questions or problems were addressed to the Ministry of Foreign Affairs and Religions, as would be appropriate considering the title of the ministry.

[31] Cyril, Patriarch of Bulgaria, Bŭlgarskata Ekzarkhiia, pp. 180-181.

correspondence between the Exarchate and the Ministry of Public Instruction involved this matter of financial support.[32]

The requests for aid from the Exarch or his representatives always contained polite reminders that exarchial schools served to protect the identity of Thrace and Macedonia as Bulgarian. In other words, the schools countered the influence of Serbs (in Macedonia) and of Greeks (in Macedonia and Thrace).[33] The replies of the Ministers, almost always reducing the amount requested, contained equally polite reminders that the needs of the schools within the Principality always took precedence over schools outside.[34]

---

[32] It is possible that an earlier letter requested such help, but the letter from Metropolitan Nathaniel to Jireček is the earliest I was able to locate. In its content, it gives every indication of being a first request. See Metropolitan Nathaniel, letter to Ministry of Public Instruction, June 16, 1881, ABAN, F. 3 (Jireček), op. 1, ae. 1132, p. 1. From then on, the request was made and negotiated each year. See debate on this in Bulgaria, Ministerial Council, session of October 18, 1883, TsDIA, F. 284 (Ministerial Council), op. 1, ae. 203, p. 1.

[33] Metropolitan Nathaniel, letter to Minister of Public Instruction Jireček, June 16, 1881, ABAN, F. 3 (Jireček), op. 1, ae. 1132, p. 1

[34] See, for example, Bulgaria, Ministry of Public Instruction report to State Council, June 12, 1882, ABAN, F. 3 (Jireček), op. 1, ae. 1132, p. 3.

In 1881, the same year during which the monetary aid began, a terrible controversy broke out between the Exarch and the central government in Sofia (then in the hands of Prince Alexander's cronies). The root of the problem lay in the fact that before 1878 the Exarch had received from each diocese an annual contribution towards defraying the expenses of the Exarch's administrative offices. After 1878, however, bishops within the Principality (the Holy Synod in Sofia) discontinued sending the contribution and used it to replace churches and buildings destroyed in the war.[35] The Exarch failed to receive any assistance from the government of the Principality in recovering the former revenue. Therefore, when the Ministerial Council of the Principality of Bulgaria requested an accounting of the use of the funds it had given the Exarchate for its schools, the Exarch refused for two reasons. First, he claimed that since the government had not helped recover the lost revenue of the annual contribution, the Exarchate was desperately poor. Second, the Exarch pointed out that no matter how much money the Exarchate received from the Principality, the Exarchate itself was not an

---

[35] Cyril, Patriarch of Bulgaria, Bŭlgarskata Ekzarkhiia, pp. 170-231.

organ of the government in Sofia, and if it had to account to anyone, it was to the Ottoman imperial government. In retaliation for this refusal, the Ministerial Council ordered that all Exarchate property in the Principality be placed in trust with the Holy Synod in Sofia.[36] The Principality and the Exarchate eventually resolved these differences, but throughout the Ministry of Public Instruction managed to remain aloof from the disputes. It was not so successful, however, in avoiding entanglement in controversies over the activity of non-Orthodox missionaries in establishing schools in the Principality.

The Problem of School Openings by Foreign Missionaries

There were several kinds of schools in the Principality over which the Ministry of Public Instruction exercised little or no control. One such category of schools were those operated by Bulgarian citizens of faiths other than Orthodox and of ethnic identities other than Bulgarian. The other category of schools comprised those operated and established by foreign missionaries such as Catholics and Protestants (chiefly

---

[36] Ibid., pp. 170-211; Bulgaria, Ministerial Council, session of December 23, 1881, TsDIA, F. 284 (Ministerial Council), op. 1, ae. 74, pp. 1-3.

Methodists and Congregationalists).[37] The first category, that of Bulgarian citizens of minority nationalities or religions, included schools set up by Turks, Greeks, Armenians, and Jews. Despite the fact that the Ministry of Public Instruction occasionally helped one or more of the schools operated by these minorities, formal responsibility was technically in the hands of the Ministry of Foreign Affairs and Religions. The Tŭrnovo Constitution of 1879 had guaranteed non-Christian and non-Orthodox communities the right to administer their own ecclesiastical affairs with appropriate supervision by the responsible ministry (i.e. the Ministry of Foreign Affairs and Religions).[38] Nevertheless, the Ministry of Public Instruction, from time to time, did mention the existence of Turkish, Greek and other minority schools in its own reports and

---

[37] These categories are only for the purposes of discussion. Obviously, Catholic and Protestant native Bulgarians could fit in the first category (as non-Orthodox). Government officials often treated the Catholic and Protestant native Bulgarians separately because of the controversies surrounding the activities of these groups. However, at other times, government officials included these two groups in the "private schools" category of all non-Orthodox, non-ethnic Bulgarian schools, even though some ethnic Bulgarians were Catholics and Protestants.

[38] Bulgaria, Ministry of Justice, Godishen sbornik, pp. 21-22.

correspondence. But information always remained at a minimum. Jireček, in an otherwise very detailed report (the <u>Glavno izlozhenie</u>) gave a few facts and figures on "private schools."[39] The terms private or "non-Bulgarian" were consistently used by ministerial officials to describe schools other than the Bulgarian communal (<u>narodni</u>) schools. (These facts presented by Jireček are the only ones for this time period that have ever been available to historians of Bulgarian education.) In the year 1880-1881, there were 66 Turkish schools in Razgrad province, 63 in Tŭrnovo province, and 7 in Kiustendil.[40] Jireček claimed the government was unable to study properly the status of Turkish schools since the Turkish population itself had been migrating back and forth from Turkey to Bulgaria in the years between 1876-1881 because of the dislocation caused by the war for independence of the Bulgarians.

As far as Jewish schools were concerned, Jireček reported only that Jewish schools existed in several cities including Sofia, Kiustendil, Samokov, Vidin, Lom,

---

[39] Jireček, <u>Glavno izlozhenie</u>, p. 26.

[40] <u>Ibid</u>.

Ruse, Shumen, and Razgrad.[41] He also noted that Spanish-speaking Jews had better organized their schools than had the other Jewish groups. Jireček was even less informative when it came to Armenian or Greek schools. For the Armenians, he reported schools in Varna, Shumen, Silistra, and Ruse. For the Greeks, he reported the existence of schools in Varna, Balchik, several villages on the Black Sea coast, and Silistra.[42]

This report represented the extent of the Ministry's concern for such schools. However, occasionally schools operated by the minorities did receive money from the Ministry of Public Instruction. This was always on an *ad hoc* basis, and the funds were usually earmarked for purposes of hiring a teacher for the Bulgarian language.[43] In rarer cases, the Ministry of

---

[41] Ibid., p. 27.

[42] Ibid.; see also Tsonkov, Razvitie, pp. 161-163; Vankov, Iz Arkhivata, pp. 39-47 *et passim*.

[43] In 1884, for example: the Ministry gave a grant of 500 leva to a Pomak (Bulgarian Moslem) school in the village of Kamenitsa; a grant of 3,000 leva went to aid the Moslem schools in Sofia; but a plea from a Jewish school in Berkovsko village remain unfulfilled. All such actions by the Ministry had to be approved by the Ministerial Council, and the archives of the Ministerial Council, TsDIA, F. 284, for the years 1880-1885, is the source of all this information.

Public Instruction granted money for school repair or for teacher training. The amounts spent on non-Bulgarian schools did not begin to approach the amounts spent to aid the state or communal schools. Outside of these occasional grants of aid or brief references in ministerial reports, the Ministry of Public Instruction did not otherwise concern itself with the school affairs of these particular minorities.

Such was not the case, however, in matters regarding the other category of schools in the country. These were the schools run by the Protestants and Catholics, whether native Bulgarian citizens or foreign missionaries. The reason for this is that many Bulgarians perceived the activities of these religious groups as a threat to the Orthodox Church and to the Bulgarian nationality.[44] This was partly due to the fact that the

---

[44] When the Bulgarian intelligentsia was not attacking Greek clergy or Turkish officials, they often turned their attention to Catholic activity. One of the most eloquent pamphlets against the Jesuits, for example, is Marin Drinov's "Strashni li sa za narodnostŭta ni fanariotite i iezuitite?" Sŭchineniia, III, pp. 1-9. For an excellent discussion of other opinions in this regard, see B. Mintses, "Dŭrzhavno-politichnite i sotsialno-stopanskite idei v bŭlgarskata doosvoboditelna literatura. Kritikobibliografska studiia," Sbornik za narodni umotvoreniia, XVI-XVII (1900), 1-58. An excellent treatment of the views of the intelligentsia in this and other related issues is Thomas A. Meininger, "The Formation of a Nationalist Bulgarian Intelligentsia, 1835-1878" (unpublished Ph.D. dissertation, University of Wisconsin-Madison: 1974), especially pp. 323-392.

activities of both Protestants and Catholics were strongly connected with, and sometimes controlled by, outside forces (Rome in the case of the Catholics, England and America in the case of the Protestants). Also, both groups were far more active in the work of conversion than such groups as the Moslems or Jews. The activities of both Catholics and Protestants stirred some of the Bulgarian communities in which they were located to crisis levels for the entire government. The Ministry of Public Instruction tried desperately to remain out of the ensuing fray but was unsuccessful.

Catholicism had always existed in the Balkans to a limited extent, but the interest of the Catholic Church towards the area had waxed and waned throughout the centuries. In 1862, however, the Catholic Church established a special organization to work among the Orthodox peoples of the Ottoman Empire, but especially in the Balkans. This organization, the Society for Negotiation with the Oriental Rite, was attached to the larger organ of the Roman Curia, the Society for the Propagation of the Faith.[45] This event had significant

---

[45] Cyril, Patriarch of Bulgaria, Katolicheska propoganda sred Bŭlgarite prez vtorata polovina na XIX vek, 1859-1865 (Sofia: 1962), pp. 7-40; for an earlier history of the Catholic Church in Bulgaria, see Ivan Duichev, Il Cattolicesmo in Bulgaria nel sec. XVI, Vol.

repercussions in the Balkans, especially since the Church could offer the Orthodox peoples of the Balkans a "middle way." This middle way was the Uniate Rite, an outgrowth of several attempts at unification between Catholics and Orthodox, such as the Council of Florence in 1439, and the Union of Brest (in the Ukraine) in 1596. In this rite, the people retained the Slavonic language and ritual but swore allegiance to the Pope in Rome. Another such unification attempt occurred in Constantinople in 1860. Along with this new surge of Uniate activity came an influx into Bulgaria after the Crimean war of French missionary orders (such as the Capucins) and also the Jesuits, who established missionary centers in cities such as Plovdiv and Edirne.[46]

The efforts of the Uniates, especially, achieved enough success to alarm Russian diplomats, who tended to view the extension of any form of Catholicism as an extension of French and Austrian political influence in

CXI of *Orientalia Christiana Analecta* (Rome: 1937), pp. 1-200.

[46] Meininger, *Ignatiev*, pp. 22-23; Cyril, Patriarch of Bulgaria, *Katolicheska propaganda*, pp. 211-270; Emile Haumant, "Les Origines de la lutte pour la Macédoine," *Le Monde slav*, X (October, 1926), 55; Justin Amero, "Le Mouvement bulgare: ses causes et ses consequences," *Revue contemporaine*, XX (1861), 90; see also Cyril, Patriarch of Bulgaria, ed., *Prinos kŭm Bŭlgarskiia tsŭrkoven vŭpros; dokumenti ot Avstriiskoto konsulstvo v Solun* (Sofia: 1961), pp. 27-44.

the area. These fears were confirmed in 1860, when Bulgarian Uniates addressed a letter to the Pope, asking him to secure for them the political protection of the Emperor of France.[47]

Along with the renewed interest of the Catholic Church in the area, Protestant missionary groups also began to take a more serious interest in missionary work in Bulgarian regions. This work was carried on by two British and American missionary groups especially, the Congregationalists and the Methodists. Both of these groups had already worked extensively in the Turkish and Greek areas of the Ottoman Empire. It was in this matter that they came into contact with such Bulgarians as Neofit Rilski who, in fact, accepted a contract from the British and Foreign Bible Society to translate the New Testament into Bulgarian in 1835.[48] After several false starts and some hesitation as to

---

[47] Meininger, Ignatiev, p. 23; Count Nikolai P. Ignatiev was Russia's minister to Istanbul and a major figure in the Panslav movement. His impressions and reactions to these events are recorded in his "Zapiski grafa N. P. Ignat'eva, 1864-1874," Izvestiia Ministerstva inostrannykh del, I (1914), 93-135.

[48] James F. Clarke, Bible Societies, American Missionaries and the National Revival of Bulgaria (New York: 1971), pp. 225-239; Washburn, Fifty Years, pp. 1-50.

whether missionary effort would prove fruitful in
Bulgaria, a missionary effort finally began in the
1860s. After explorations of the region by missionaries
such as Theodore L. Byington, J. F. Clarke, and Albert
Long, the Congregationalists and Methodists came to an
agreement dividing their efforts in the Bulgarian territory. The Methodists were to concentrate their attention to the area north of the Stara Planina
Mountains, while the Congregationalists would work
primarily in the area to the south.[49] Less than ten
years after the start of the serious work in 1859, a
boys school had been established in Plovdiv and a girls
school in Stara Zagora. Missionary stations existed
from Varna in the eastern part of the country to Samokov
in the west. Meanwhile, Dr. Albert Long of the
Congregationalist Church began publishing a Bulgarian

---

[49] Clarke, Bible Societies, pp. 251-269; Washburn, Fifty Years, pp. 1-50 et passim. There are several other good accounts of this Protestant activity. See, for example, Floyd Black, The American College in Sofia: A Chapter in American-Bulgarian Relations (Boston: 1958), pp. 1-14; L. F. Ostrander, ed., Fifty Years in Bulgaria. Jubilee Publication of the American Board of Commissioners of Foreign Missions (Samokov: 1911), pp. 24-32; Edward Thomas, Our Oriental Missions: China and Bulgaria (New York: 1870), II, pp. 117-127. A very hostile but information-filled account is Man'o Stoianov, "Nachalo na protestanskata propaganda v Bulgariia," Izvestiia na institut za istoriia pri Bŭlgarskata akademiia na naukite, XIV-XV (1964), 45-67.

language newspaper in Istanbul with the title
Zornitsa.[50]

When the Principality of Bulgaria came into existence in 1879, the activities of both the Catholic and Protestant schools and churches came under the supervision of the Ministry of Foreign Affairs and Religions. Although statistics are practically non-existent for the Principality, schools operated by Protestant or Catholic religions were still few in number. From the scanty records that do exist, the Protestants had only one school, which was in Samokov. On the other hand, a Catholic school run by French priests existed in Sofia.[51] Since the affairs of these two religious groups were under the supervision of the Ministry of Foreign Affairs and Religions, the eventual controversy over Protestant efforts, especially, to expand their schools did not at first concern the Ministry of Public Instruction. However, despite its best efforts to remain aloof from the developing controversy, the Ministry eventually became enmeshed.

---

[50] Ostrander, Fifty Years, p. 25; Thomas, Our Missions, II, pp. 117-118.

[51] Tsonkov, Razvitie, pp. 161-162; Black, American College, pp. 7-8. There were 11 schools in Eastern Rumelia, reflecting the fact that the original Protestant effort had been in the southern territory.

Jireček, while still Executive Secretary of the Ministry of Public Instruction in 1880, had sensed that the activities of foreign missionaries would eventually cause extreme difficulties. At the time that he wrote a secret memo on the matter to the Minister of Public Instruction Metropolitan Clement in 1881, the crisis had not yet arisen. That would come in 1883. Jireček informed Minister Clement that it was his belief that problems were inevitable and would eventually involve the Ministry of Public Instruction.[52] He advised the Ministry should prepare itself for that eventuality by defining its position on the matter. He suggested the possibility of giving legal status to small religious communities consisting entirely of foreign subjects living in the country, such as the French and the Americans. This would allow them to open communal schools. The big problem, claimed Jireček, was to define to what extent Bulgarian children would be allowed to enroll in such schools. He also raised the possibility of establishing an international, interfaith school, perhaps in Varna.[53]

---

[52] Jireček, "Zapiska," ABAN, F. 3 (Jireček), op. 1, ae. 1125, p. 11.

[53] Ibid.

As far as government supervision over these schools was concerned, Jireček suggested a strict control based on the government's right to approve programs, texts, and teachers. He also advocated that administrators of such schools be responsible to the Ministry of Public Instruction which would have the right to check their accounts and enrollments. Also, the Bulgarian language would be a required subject, and the schools would have to conform, generally, to communal school laws.[54]

Jireček's prediction as to the inevitability of a crisis proved entirely correct. And many of his proposals were indeed adopted, but not without considerable reluctance on the part of the Ministers of Public Instruction, who evidently considered it a proper matter for the Ministry of Foreign Affairs and Religions. In fact, it was the latter ministry which bore the brunt of the controversy. The controversy was a long time in developing, but started with alarums by church officials, as well as local government officials, over renewed and growing activities of Catholic and Protestant missionaries. The Catholic problem at this time centered in Plovdiv, while the Protestant question arose mostly in Lovech, Samokov, and Svishtov. In April, 1882, the

---

[54] Ibid.

question of a proposed Protestant school in Lovech came before the Ministerial Council at the request of the then Minister of Public Instruction Jireček, the same individual who had predicted problems with such schools.[55] The documents considered included a petition ostensibly given to local officials by local inhabitants. The Ministerial Council decided: "not to allow Protestant missionaries to establish the school there, since with this school they proselytize, which cannot be allowed in Bulgaria, where the people have their own Christian religion."[56] This imbroglio was only one of several that dragged on through 1883 without solution. The Church, signatory to many of the petitions, strove to combat the foreign missions. An important reason why Church officials protested the closing of the Samokov Theological Seminary by Giuzelev in 1880 was the desire to control Protestant influence. (The school had closed because of disciplinary problems and poor management.) In a petition that highlighted the perceived dangers, the citizens of Samokov added their voices to that of the Church and in March, 1883, urged

---

[55] Bulgaria, Ministerial Council, session of April 16, 1882, TsDIA, F. 284 (Ministerial Council), op. 1, ae. 94, p. 3.

[56] Ibid.

the reopening of the Samokov seminary.[57] The petition (which triggered another full session of the Ministerial Council) pointed out that Protestant activity grew from day to day. The inhabitants, claimed the petition, could not open a school on their own which could successfully compete with that opened by Protestants, who were possessed of greater financial resources. Also, the Protestant schools were better organized and equipped even if they did teach not science but propaganda.[58]

The Ministerial Council and the Ministry of Public Instruction delayed action until a law on private schools could be drawn up. In the meantime, piecemeal solutions were effected, to the dissatisfaction of all parties concerned. Many of these measures directly involved the Ministry of Public Instruction.

In March, 1883, the Ministry of Public Instruction informed the Ministerial Council that Protestant missionaries wished to open new schools in Svishtov and Lovech. The Ministerial Council summarily forbade the

---

[57] Samokov, City-Communal Administration, Petition of Citizens of Samokov, "Zaiavlenieto na zhitelite na Samokov do Samokovskoto gradsko obshtinsko upravlenie," March 11, 1883, SGODA, F. 41K (Samokov City Communal Administration), op. 1, ae. 523, pp. 27-28.

[58] Ibid.

opening of such schools.[59] In April of 1883, the
Ministerial Council heard testimony from citizens of
Samokov in which they pleaded to the Ministry of Public
Instruction to open a good secondary school in Samokov
to counter the influence of the excellent Protestant
school there. The Russian General Kaulbars informed
the Council that on his last visit to Samokov, he had
received a delegation of citizens who complained to him
that the Protestants not only tried to convert children
in the school but also proselytized from house to
house.[60] Whether or not that was really the case is
difficult to determine. While official Protestant
sources mention frequently the distribution of New
Testaments in the Bulgarian language, it is not clear
exactly how such distribution was accomplished.[61] It
is conceivable, however, that this distribution of

---

[59] Bulgaria, Ministerial Council, session of March 30, 1883, TsDIA, F. 284 (Ministerial Council), op. 1, ae. 154, p. 2.

[60] Ibid., session of April 14, 1883, op. 1, ae. 58, p. 5.

[61] See Ostrander, Fifty Years, pp. 24-29; Black, American College, pp. 9-11; the best discussion, however, of Bible distribution is "Chapter XIV: The Distribution of the New Testament and Its Effects on American Missionary Interest," in Clarke, Bible Societies, pp. 269-290.

Bibles is what the Samokov citizens opposed. In any event, the Ministerial Council decided to take several steps to help the citizens of Samokov. First, it ordered the Ministry of Public Instruction to open negotiations with the Exarch as to the advisability of opening a theological school in Samokov. Second, the Council ordered that all Catholic and Protestant schools in the Principality must henceforth supply the Ministry of Public Instruction with information on how the schools were funded and how many children were enrolled and to submit copies of the programs of the schools. Finally, the Catholic and Protestant schools would be required to engage, as soon as possible, an Orthodox priest who would teach Orthodox catechism to children of that faith twice a week. The schools would have to pay the priest from their own budgets.[62]

Meanwhile, the issue was complicated by the protests of the American consultate in Istanbul over the

---

[62]Bulgaria, Ministerial Council, session of April 9, 1883, TsDIA, F. 284 (Ministerial Council), op. 1, ae. 157, p. 1; and session of June 9, 1883, TsDIA, F. 284 (Ministerial Council), op. 1, ae. 171, p. 2. Only one school made any real attempt to comply with the demand for information, and that was the American Protestant School in Samokov which sent statistics to Samokov's administration, "Statisticheski svedeniia za amerikanskoto uchilishte v Grad Samokov," F. 41K (Samokov City-Communal Administration), op. 1, ae. 523, pp. 1, 40, et passim.

harrassment of Protestant missionaries.[63] While the American protest was wholly unsolicited, the Ministry of Public Instruction begged the Foreign Minister to discuss the problem with the English diplomats in Sofia.[64]

While a draft law on private schools was being prepared, the Ministerial Council laid down two basic rules for the opening of "private foreign religious" schools. First, such schools would be allowed to open only where there was a corresponding religious community, i.e. a legal entity based on shared religious beliefs.[65] Second, if students of a religion different from that of the community enrolled in the school, then the school had to provide separate teachers of catechism of the corresponding religion for those pupils.[66]

While these ineffectual measures were in progress, the Ministry of Public Instruction submitted to the

---

[63] The protest was specifically directed at the Ministerial Council's decisions on the Lovech school, as well as against Protestant school plans in Svishtov, Bulgaria, Ministerial Council, session of March 30, 1883, TsDIA, F. 284 (Ministerial Council, op. 1, ae. 154, p.2.

[64] Ibid., session of January 18, 1884, op. 1, ae. 246, pp. 2-3.

[65] Ibid., session of October 10, 1883, op. 1, ae. 196, p. 1.

[66] Ibid.

Ministerial Council a draft proposal on private schools that would have sharply limited the opening of such schools. Immediately, the draft came under attack from the Liberals in the journal Maritsa. The editorial especially criticized the provision that private schools would have to obtain the consent of the local inhabitants before opening.[67] This, claimed the Maritsa editorial, would cripple to rights of such minorities as Armenians or Protestants to open schools since they were always in a minority, and their neighbors would prevent any such opening. Also criticized was the provision that such schools would receive no help whatsoever from local or central government. This, it was noted, would only encourage the increasing tendency of ethnic groups to complain to foreign consuls.[68]

Some of these measures were eliminated before the final version appeared in 1884. The Law on Private Schools, passed during the tenure of Raicho Karolev, included provisions which strictly controlled every phase and aspect of private school functioning. The new provisions divided private schools into those opened by

---

[67] Editorial (unsigned), Maritsa, September 2, 1883, p. 6.

[68] Ibid.

religious communities (of Bulgarian citizens) and those opened by private citizens or organizations. In any such school, teaching a child a religion other than his own was expressly forbidden.[69] The Ministry of Public Instruction was given extensive rights of supervision over textbooks, curricula, quality of teachers, and activities of the school boards. Furthermore, no private citizen or group could open a school without first obtaining permission from the Ministry of Public Instruction. The law prescribed stiff fines for disobeying these rules.[70] The law did not, however, rule out the possibility of Bulgarian students attending schools operated by foreign religious groups, although it did mention that if such did occur, the school had to conform to all details of the law concerning private schools.[71]

The Karolev law did not eliminate the problem of foreign missionaries. That problem continued in varying degrees throughout the passing decades. But the

---

[69] Bulgaria, Ministry of Public Instruction, "Zakon za obshtestvennite i chastnite uchilishta," Dŭrzhaven vestnik, VII, 13 (1885), 8.

[70] Ibid., p. 9.

[71] Ibid.

law did give the Ministry a legal lever to use if the matters got out of control. The question abated in let-·ters between church officials and the Ministry. However heated the discussion over the issue became, it did not ever damage or destroy the essentially cordial relations between the Church and the Ministry of Public Instruction, relations which remained that way until the crisis over the election of a Catholic dynasty to the throne in the 1890s. The Church remained influential, in a less direct way, but influential nonetheless in the progress of education in the new Bulgarian state.

CHAPTER EIGHT

CHARTING A COURSE OF ACTION: SUCCESS
AND FAILURE IN FORMING EDUCATIONAL POLICY

In the struggle to set a progressive course of action for Bulgarian education in the period 1878-1885, the Ministers of Public Instruction did not simply react to existing problems, but attempted to formulate and to plan educational policies for the future. Many of these initiatives came to naught; others were extremely useful. Few were totally successful because in its attempt to deal with problems or to formulate plans, the Ministry was hampered by a special problem. This involved the highest office in the structure of the institution, that of the Minister. Given the critical shortage of people equipped to organize and to direct an educational bureaucracy, the office of Minister took on enormous importance. Unfortunately, the position changed hands twelve times within the seven-year period of 1878-1885.[1] Also unfortunate was the incompetence

---

[1] The twelve men and their tenure of office is listed here once again for purposes of reference: Marin Drinov (June, 1878-July, 1879); Todor Burmov (July, 1879); Grigorii Atanasovich (July-October, 1879); Vasil Drumev (October, 1879-March, 1880); Ivan Giuzelev

or inexperience of many of the dozen men who held the position. At a time when uniformity and regularity were essential to the educational system, the background, training, and outlook of the individual Ministers varied widely. Some held office for as little as two days, while the longest terms of office were those of Marin Drinov (13 months), Josef K. Jireček (13 months), and Raicho Karolev (25 months). It was no coincidence that these three men were the most important figures in Bulgarian education at the time. Yet longevity of tenure did not assure either a successful or a significant administration. Georgi Teokharev's eight and a half months as Minister of Public Instruction were disastrous because of his fumbling, incompetence, and utter lack of diplomacy in dealing with Prince, Parliament, and Church. Yet Dimitŭr Agura, in his six-month term, achieved enough to make him one of the

---

(March-November, 1880); Mikhail K. Sarafov (November, 1880-April, 1881); Josef K. Jireček (April, 1881-June, 1882); Georgi Teokharev (June, 1882-March, 1883); Dimitŭr Agura (March-September, 1883); Dimitŭr Mollov (September, 1883-June, 1884); Raicho Karolev (June, 1884-August, 1886). All dates are Old Style. A good list of each change of ministerial position and cabinets is found in Boian Sekulov, Nashite pravitelstva i ministri ot Osvobozhdenieto do dnes (Sofia: 1911),

four most influential Ministers of the period in question.[2]

As stated, the role of the Minister was crucial because of the lack of qualified help. But his power was also increased by the political problems wracking the new country. When a crucial piece of legislation died in the Sŭbranie because of political squabbles, the Ministers of Public Instruction began issuing what in fact amounted to laws in the guise of "instructions" or "regulations." In effect, they ruled by fiat, which, of course, exaggerated the constitutional powers of the Minister. Ministers such as Jireček, who took criticism unkindly, did not improve the situation. Eventually, sources within and outside of the Ministry realized the inadequacy and even danger of such a concentration of power in the hands of one individual. This chapter focuses on the ramifications of this development, the role of the Ministers in policy formation, and the eventual establishment of affiliate institutions to provide greater diversity of opinion in the formulation of decisions affecting Bulgarian education.

---

[2] Based on the research and readings for this thesis, the four most important figures in my estimation for this period were Drinov, Jireček, Agura, and Karolev.

The overall goals and policies of the Ministry of Public Instruction fluctuated and changed greatly in the brief but crucial period of 1878-1885. It is possible to distinguish four different stages: (1) the Drinov-Giuzelev period (1878-1880), (2) the Jireček period (1880-1882), (3) the post-Jireček period (1882-1884), and (4) the Karolev era (1884-1885). Two of these periods were transitional in nature although the entire period of 1878-1885 was one of transition. The Drinov-Giuzelev epoch marked the transition from independent educational systems to government-controlled ones. The post-Jireček period marked a transition from one well-ordered period run by a foreigner to another well-ordered period run by a native Bulgarian. Each of these periods, however, shared several common themes. One was an unwavering dedication to improving the Bulgarian people through education. Another common characteristic was a clash between the educational philosophies of the Ministers and those of the people's representatives in the Sŭbranie. A third was the problem of formulating the goals of Bulgarian education in what was unquestionably a very decisive period.

Such was Jireček's influence on Bulgaria's education at the time, that even this first period of 1878-1880 could be called the "pre-Jireček era." However, that title would be misleading because the tone and character of this era were unique in and of themselves. The spirit of the Bulgarian Renascence colored this period more than it did any of the following ones. Drinov, especially, believed deeply in the ability of the people to carry out their own destiny if only shown the way.[3] That prevailing philosophy manifested itself in most of the goals and policies of that first era. This period also stands out as the only one in which Russian educational ideals had any significant influence.

Drinov's major goal had been mandatory primary education for all Bulgarian citizens regardless of sex. He succeeded in getting this precept enshrined in the nation's first constitution.[4] But his administration was too preoccupied by the enormous problem of reconstruction of war-damaged physical facilities to be able to set any but the broadest and vaguest of goals. His immediate concerns (as detailed in Chapter Two) were to stabilize the situation of the teachers and to

---

[3] See for example his "Pismo do Bŭlgarskata inteligentsiia," Sŭchineniia, III, pp. 13-16, and his article, "Bŭlgarsko literaturno druzhestvo," Sŭchineniia, III, p. 17ff.

[4] Bulgaria, Narodno Sŭbranie, Godishen sbornik, p. 13.

write the first national programs and regulations for the Bulgarian school system. In short, he sought to define the exact duties of the people and the State toward the schools. In searching for precise goals in Drinov's administration (as well as, perhaps, in that of Giuzelev), one must look hard for any overwhelming aim or target, other than the somewhat unrealistic one of universal primary education which was clearly unattainable for many years. There seems to have been confusion over both the direction in which efforts were to be made and where the first steps should be taken.[5] Drinov himself had received a classical education, mostly in Russian theological academies. It was not surprising then that he regarded an emphasis on this type of education appropriate for Bulgaria. This also reflected the philosophy prevailing in the repressive educational system of Russia, headed at the time by the notorious Count Dmitri Tolstoy.

This amorphous situation changed somewhat when Ivan Giuzelev assumed office in March, 1880, when the first Liberal government, headed by Dragan Tsankov, was installed after the election in March, 1880. Giuzelev, unlike Drinov, had received much of his education in

---

[5] Noikov, *Pogled ot Paisiia*, p. 57.

Bulgaria and, also unlike Drinov, had earned his living by teaching in his native country. Giuzelev (1844-1916) was born in Gabrovo and received his primary and secondary education there. He attended higher schools in Russia, graduating from the university in Novorossiia in 1871. He returned to Gabrovo in the same year and, along with Raicho Karolev, effected controversial reforms as a teacher in the Gabrovo schools.[6] Giuzelev was far better attuned to the educational needs and realities of the country than the expatriate Drinov. It was during Giuzelev's incumbency that Bulgarian educational leaders shed the naive assumption that the people would everywhere welcome and applaud educational advancement. The State now intervened more readily in school affairs, whether to regulate teachers' salaries or to mandate the responsibilities of the people to the local schools.[7]

Giuzelev, unlike Drinov, was intimately acquainted with the pedagogical writings of such important Western figures as Jean Jacques Rousseau and Johann Pestalozzi, whose idea of teaching reading and writing simultaneously

---

[6] Karolev, Istoriia na Gabrovoskoto uchilishte, pp. 89ff; Ivanov, "Ivan N. Giuzelev," pp. 156-160.

[7] Noikov, Pogled ot Paisiia, pp. 61-63.

caused much discussion in contemporary European circles. Giuzelev endorsed the new method for Bulgarian schools.[8]

Giuzelev also delineated several goals for Bulgarian education that had to be fulfilled without delay. He took a more realistic approach to the goal of universal mandatory primary education as one that should be striven for, but which would be a long time in achieving.[9] Yet he called the constitutional provision for mandatory primary education the cornerstone on which Bulgarian education would be built. Giuzelev's primary goal, rather, was to rationalize Bulgarian schools into a coherent, systematic network. He was disturbed by the existence of so many different kinds of schools, most of which had no connection with each other and led nowhere academically.[10] He wanted a tiered system, with each type of school leading on to a higher one. The key would be a three-grade middle

---

[8] Ivan N. Giuzelev, "Rŭkovodstvata po pŭrvonachalnoto obuchenie," Periodichesko spisanie na Bŭlgarskoto knizhovno druzhestvo, LVII (1898), 137.

[9] Stenograficheski dnevnitsi na II ONS, pŭrva redovna sesiia, session of May 21, 1881, p. 529.

[10] Jireček, letter to Marin Drinov, April 27, 1880, in Sis, Korespondentsiia, p. 201; Chakŭrov, Uchilishtno zakonodatelstvo, p. 41; Stenograficheski dnevnitsi na II ONS, pŭrva redovna sesiia, session of May 21, 1880, pp. 536, 539.

school (then non-existent) which would link primary schools to gymnasia and <u>Realschulen</u>. Besides the three-grade school, Giuzelev also wanted each school in the system to have more clearly defined aims and purposes for its existence than they had had until that moment.[11] These goals were in addition to the challenges remaining from Drinov's years. Of those, the worsening financial situation and, as always, the plight of the teachers were the most pressing.

Giuzelev fought hard in the <u>Sŭbranie</u> for the three-grade middle school and for the rationalization of programs. In a speech to the <u>Sŭbranie</u> in May, 1880, Giuzelev explained the problem with existing schools and why he wished to institute a new type of school. He pointed out that the country had primary schools consisting of three grades and gymnasia consisting of anywhere from two to six grades. In between were institutions called two-grade and four-grade schools. Giuzelev charged that the goals, purposes, and even the reasons for the existence of the two-grade and four-grade schools were entirely unclear. They seemed to

---

[11] Jireček, letter to Marin Drinov, April 27, 1880, in Sis, <u>Korespondentsiia</u>, p. 201; <u>Stenograficheski dnevnitsi na II ONS, pŭrva redovna sesiia</u>, session of May 21, 1880, p. 539.

have no relationship to each other, or even to primary and secondary schools. Furthermore, Giuzelev was upset by the opening of too many gymnasia which had only two grades. In other words, many of the communities that had opened gymnasia had failed to assess properly whether or not they would ever be able to open the four extra classes needed to make the gymnasium complete.[12] Therefore, Giuzelev proposed that the State closely moniter the opening of new gymnasia. He also proposed that all two-class and four-class schools be abolished. In their place, he proposed the establishment nationwide of a three-grade school and an extra year to be added to all primary schools. The three-grade school would serve a very definite purpose. It would serve as a continuation of primary education but would also serve as the lower courses of a full secondary school. For those who had no desire to attend a secondary school, the three-grade school when combined with the four years of primary education would give a student seven years of solid education. This, argued Giuzelev, would permit him to function as an adult and as a responsible citizen. On the other hand, those students who did

---

[12] Chakŭrov, *Uchilishtno zakonodatelstvo*, p. 41; *Stenograficheski dnevnitsi na II ONS, pŭrva redovna sesiia*, session of May 21, 1880, p. 539.

wish to attend a secondary institution would be well-prepared and could probably enter advanced classes in the gymnasium, whether technical or classical.[13]

Giuzelev encountered opposition from some deputies who argued that three years was not long enough to provide an effective intermediate education. Others took Giuzelev to mean that cities that had started to establish a gymnasium would have to eliminate it in favor of a three-grade middle school, which would in effect be a regressive action.[14]

Giuzelev assured the delegates that he did not plan to eliminate any gymnasia, only to discourage openings of such schools unless there was a definite possibility of them becoming full-fledged institutions (i.e. with all six grades). The Sŭbranie accepted his explanations as well as his entire plan, and the three-grade school became a reality. The progymnasium, as the three-grade school eventually was called by the Ministry, represented a major breakthrough in systematizing Bulgaria's educational structure.[15] Giuzelev

---

[13] Stenograficheski dnevnitsi na II ONS, pŭrva redovna sesiia, session of May 21, 1880, pp. 539-540.

[14] Ibid., pp. 542-543, et passim.

[15] Ibid., p. 543; Chakŭrov, Uchilishtno zakonodatelstvo, p. 42.

was not so fortunate with another major proposal which has been mentioned many times in the course of this work, the "Basic Law on Public Schools." This law would have made Bulgarian curriculum and school operation much more regular and uniform throughout the country. Despite this failure, however, Giuzelev did make some progress towards his goal of rationalization. His ministry ended when the government of Dragan Tsankov fell, and new elections were held.

The Ministers of Public Instruction between Giuzelev and Jireček did not hold office long enough to have any chance to formulate policy, let alone to carry it out. Petko R. Slaveikov was named Minister of Public Instruction in the Liberal cabinet of Petko Karavelov, which took office in November, 1880. One month later, Karavelov transferred Slaveikov to the Ministry of the Interior and appointed Mikhail K. Sarafov as Minister of Public Instruction. Sarafov, who would hold the office until April, 1881, had been a public school teacher for a brief period of time and was not ignorant of the school situation.[16] Despite the brevity of his

---

[16] Sarafov had taught for a brief period in Turnovo in the 1870s, but after his arrest for revolutionary activities and subsequent release, he returned to Zagreb to complete his education, Sarafov, "Spomeni," ABAN, F. 17 (Sarafov), op. 1, ae. 290, pp. 28-52. Further information on Sarafov was given in Chapter Six.

administration, however, he did manage a few noteworthy accomplishments with the help of his chief advisor, Jireček. In fact, it was Jireček who provided a continuum from the Drinov-Giuzelev era until his own period of office as Minister.

It was during Sarafov's brief term of office that the "Instructions for the Administration of State Educational Institutions" took effect.[17] This was also the period during which Jireček's handiwork, "The Instructions for the Provincial School Inspectors" was issued. Both of these items owed their origin and final shape to Jireček. Sarafov's importance was that, as a friend and confidant of Jireček, he did not obstruct the advancement of Jireček's ideas as had been the case with Giuzelev and his associates. Thus, Jireček had a freer hand in compiling these landmark decrees which went so far towards improving the caliber of Bulgarian education. This fact was recognized by an editorial in <u>Nezavisimost</u> concerning the instructions regulating much of the activity in the state schools. The article noted that even those who were given to complaining about money wasted to no effect on education would delight in the new instructions.

---

[17] Aleksiev, <u>Nashata uchilishtna politika</u>, p. 36.

Bulgarian education desperately lacked something present in almost every other European school system; "that is to say, a meticulous structure and order, a strict determination of duties of teachers and students, a completely systematic instruction and training."[18] The article praised the goals of the "Instructions":

> Now, however, all is arranged in one pattern and the schools have been given guidance on how to proceed in the various situations which they are likely to encounter. The spirit of the entire instruction strives for the upbringing of a generation eager for progress, learning, and patriotism, for an education obtained with a stimulation of noble feelings of love of work and of mankind.[19]

Most of the credit, of course, belonged to the principal author of both documents. Sarafov might have been important in his own right, however, had he held office longer. He was a highly disciplined and confident individual. While still a student at the University of Zagreb, for example, he had written a treatise entitled "How and to What Extent the Tasks of the Middle School Can Be Resolved with the Study of Only Mathematics and Physics." The article called for greater attention to these subjects at every level of

---

[18] *Nezavisimost*, February 11, 1881, p. 1.

[19] *Ibid*.

the educational system in order to prepare students for the realities of modern life. Sarafov, however, had no time to introduce these ideas into school curriculum.[20]

Sarafov lost the position of Minister of Public Instruction when Prince Alexander I executed his coup d'état of April 29, 1881. The non-elected government installed by Alexander did not have a Prime Minister, although the Russian General Ernrot was unquestionably in charge. This same coup d'état put the Ministry of Public Instruction in the hands of Josef K. Jireček. Jireček had been travelling in the western provinces of Bulgaria when word reached him of the coup and of his appointment, without having been consulted. He reluctantly accepted the appointment because of his contractual obligations but worried about the ill effect such a responsibility would have on his freedom to travel and to do his own research.[21]

Without any doubt, the single most significant individual in Bulgarian education in this seven-year

---

[20] Mikhail Sarafov, "Kak i do kolko mozhe da se reshi zadazhata na srednite uchilishta s uchenieto samo matematikata i fizikata," ABAN, F. 17 (Sarafov), op. 1, ae. 8, pp. 1-10.

[21] Josef K. Jireček, Das Fürstenthum Bulgarien (Prague: 1891), p. 328.

period was Josef Konstantin Jireček, although he was most effective when he was Minister. In fact, he was probably the most influential figure in Bulgarian education in the whole second half of the nineteenth century. He brought to his position an incredible capacity for work, an almost fanatical zeal for organization and discipline, and keen insight into the needs and conditions of Bulgarian education. Unfortunately, his hard-driving personality and arrogance caused many uncomfortable episodes between him and his professional colleagues, but especially those who dared to criticize his ideas. The achievement of his profuse but well-defined goals was hindered by his martyr complex, his jealousy, and his perfectionism. On the other hand, his success in attaining most of his objectives was aided by his energy, his genuine dedication, and his creative genius.

In both setting and implementing goals and policies, Jireček brought with him an enormous store of experience and knowledge. His family had been influential in the educational affairs of the Austrian Empire. He had attended or visited educational systems throughout Western Europe.[22] What he did not know in

---

[22] Jireček's background was discussed in Chapter

detail about a particular country's system of education, he solicited from an impressive network of friends and colleagues, from England to Russia. His reading proficiency in at least a dozen languages allowed him to read foreign educational materials in their original form. He quizzed students of Robert College for information about American ideas on curriculum and Drinov about Russian policies on credits for auditors.[23]

Also, in formulating the goals and policies of his administration, he was careful to solicit the advice and opinions of native Bulgarians who usually responded with enthusiasm to his request for information. He made a practice as well of selecting his staff on the basis of merit or the possession of specialized

---

Two. Some good discussion of Jireček's general background include Bozho Tsvetkovich and Iosif Nagi, Trudovete na Profesora Dr. Konstantin J. Irecheka, 1854-1904 (Sofia: 1905), pp. 1-28; K. Dramaliev, "Doktor Konstantin Irechek, pŭrv organizator na uchebnoto delo u nas," Narod, April 14, 1948, p. 4; Ioto Nitov, "Zaslugite na Dr. K. Irechek za nasheto prosvetno delo," Uchitelsko delo, July 25, 1954, p. 4; Ioto Nitov, "Konstantin Irechek," Trud, December 17, 1954, p. 2; D. Boshniakov, "Bŭlgarskiiat dnevnik na Irechek," Sila, November 4, 1930.

[23] For examples of this correspondence, see Jireček's exchange of letters with S. Panaretov, a student at Robert College, ABAN, F. 3 (Jirecek), op. 1, ae. 152, pp. 10-11. Other sources of his correspondence include Petŭr Miiatev, Iz Arkhivata na K. Irechek (Sofia: 1953-1963), 3 vol.

knowledge. Mikhail Sarafov and Iliia Blŭskov were two outstanding examples of this approach.

Of all the school systems with which he was acquainted, Jireček most admired those of England and America. On the other hand, he detested the German system, under which he himself had been educated.[24] He definitely favored the more humanistic approach of other systems. He was intrigued by the relative independence and orderliness of the American and English systems of education, seeking a model for Bulgaria in them. In contrast, the German system, in his view, was overly dependent upon rote learning and harsh discipline. Serbia's school system he considered an example of good intentions gone astray, a definite example for Bulgaria of what not to do.[25]

Jireček's era did not lack ideals or goals, concrete or abstract. Jireček dreamed of, and planned for, universities and technical colleges in the future, but knew that without adequately prepared candidates and

---

[24] Jireček, letter to Marin Drinov, December 13, 1878, in Sis, Korespondentsiia, p. 195. Jireček completed most of his education in Vienna, spending 1864-1872 at the Theresianum in Vienna. He attended the university, however, in Prague.

[25] Ibid.; his views on Serbian education were discussed more fully in Chapter Three of this thesis.

teachers such ideas could not be fulfilled. Jireček never lost sight of the fact that while it was necessary to look ahead, all activity and planning had to be based on present realities--which were not very promising. In looking at the school situation when he assumed office, he coldly concluded that most of the schools in the country still could not meet the demands placed on any public school at the time in the enlightened countries of Western Europe. "But we must remember," he cautioned, "that its [the Ministry's] work is still in the beginning stages, and the beginning is always rough."[26]

Much of the activity of Jireček's own administration was foreshadowed in a memorandum which he wrote while Executive Secretary of the Ministry in 1880. In calling for primary education as the number one priority of the Ministry, he wrote:

> The entire progress of any people or state depends on the measure to which it has known how to extend and to introduce primary education into its country. Education must penetrate down to the last cottage, into the most farflung and inaccessible corners and valleys.[27]

---

[26] Jireček, Glavno izlozhenie, p. 12.

[27] Jireček, "Zapiska, " ABAN, F. 3 (Jireček), op. 1, ae. 1125, p. 3.

With that in mind, he posited the basic goals for primary education which he maintained throughout his own period of office. The first goal was to achieve the broadest expansion of literacy and basic knowledge. A second basic goal of the public primary schools was "the development of the mind and will along with the formation of character, the beginning of the moral training of the person to enable him to serve his nation as an able and useful member." An equally important goal would be the development of the body. Finally in some cases, a fourth goal was to give students a foundation for future perfection in higher schools.[28]

Not content with defining goals for education, Jireček also outlined secondary aims, the attainment of which would promote the achievement of the primary goals. First, reflecting his basic attitude on primary education, schools would have to be established everywhere. Also, it was important to assure that no one be excluded from the opportunity to study.[29] Implicit in this statement was a recognition that factors such as poverty, location of the schools, and shortages of

---

[28] Ibid.

[29] Ibid.

agricultural labor often worked against people who wished to take advantage of the "free" educational facilities established for them. He also argued that the schools must be materially secure. Finally, he urged that the schools be guided by competent people and be arranged and furnished in a practical and progressive manner.[30]

Jireček worked extremely hard in the time allotted to him to accomplish as many of the goals as possible. He was so intent on ensuring that these goals be advanced that he personally wrote almost every major regulations and statute, and many of the minor ones, issued between 1880-1883. Jireček's ability to do this points out the susceptibility of the Ministry at the time to the overwhelming control and influence of one man. While Jireček was certainly enlightened in his policies, it was possible that future Executive Secretaries or Ministers might not be as competent. There was too little provision for obtaining a balance of opinion. Jireček's own personality caused problems in this respect. While he did consult a few trusted colleagues such as Iliia Blŭskov and Spas Vatsov, Jireček's refusal to delegate responsibility caused jealousy and

---
[30] Ibid.

resentment. His own inability to tolerate those who, for whatever reason, crossed him often generated public scandal (as illustrated in Chapter Four). This, by Jireček's own admission, badly hurt the public image of the Ministry. Nevertheless, he accomplished a great deal.

Included among the formidable list of decress which Jireček personally authored were the critically important "Instructions for the Provincial School Inspectors" (March, 1881); "The Regulations on Stipendists Abroad" (February, 1881); "The Regulations on Stipends for State Secondary Schools" (February, 1881); "The Temporary Statute for Pedagogical Schools" (July, 1881); and "The Instructions for the Administration of State Educational Establishments" (January, 1881). He compiled as well most of the "Law on Public Schools" which Giuzelev had failed to have passed in the Sŭbranie in November, 1880.[31] (All of these decrees have been discussed at length in previous chapters.)

---

[31] These items have been cited throughout this dissertation. All of them exist in original form in Jireček's own handwriting in his archival fond at the Archival Institute of the Bulgarian Academy of Sciences, Fond 3. The arkhivni edinitsi which contain his official papers are numbered 116 to 1125. A good list of Jireček's laws and regulations as well as other projects is in Zlatarski, "Deinostůta," pp. 7-10.

Jireček was also the author of several very important memoranda and reports that influenced educational affairs. His "Memorandum for the Arrangement of Public Schools" submitted to Minister Clement in March, 1880, was subsequently used by Giuzelev to plan educational affairs. His memorandum regarding the arrangement of pedagogical schools (June, 1880) likewise influenced the location and nature of those schools.[32] Most important of all was his "Principal Account to his Royal Highness the Prince on the Postion of School Affairs in the Principality of Bulgaria," submitted in December, 1881. This "Principal Account" was based on detailed research and consultations with school inspectors and presented the first comprehensive picture of the school situation in the country. It became an invaluable tool for planning, as well as an important source for historians of education in Bulgaria.

Outside of school affairs proper, Jireček also helped plan the projects in 1880 and in 1882-1883 for a School Council to assist the Minister in forming policy. (This will be discussed in the latter part of this chapter.) He wrote the new constitution for the

---

[32]See preceding footnote. Zlatarski, "Deinostŭta," pp. 8-10.

Bulgarian Literary Society (1881), as well as a statute for the National Library, which he headed in 1883-1884. In addition, he helped compile a system of weights and measures and the "Law for Municipalities" and served on a variety of special commissions and councils dealing with items as diverse as providing a livelihood for landless peasants and preserving the ancient frescoes of the Boyana Church in Dragalevtsi.[33]

Despite these achievements, Jireček did not consider his work in Bulgaria a success. Even while Executive Secretary (1881), he was disheartened by opposition to his ideas and considered leaving Bulgaria. Stung by accusations that he demanded a contract because of greed, he exclaimed, "I have no need for Bulgaria, and I serve here for personal honor and for the achievement of a high idealistic task, not for money."[34] After giving up the Ministry, he confided to Drinov that only his travels, his occasional teaching in

---

[33] Ibid. Also, Miiatev, Iz Arkhiva, I, pp. 6-11. Jireček's correspondence dealing with the Bulgarian Literary Society is also in ABAN, F. 3 (Jireček), op. 1, ae. 1133. His correspondence and papers on the National Library is in the same Fond 3, and numbered ae. 1134.

[34] Ibid.

gymnasia, and his work for the Bulgarian Literary Society had given him any happy moments. The rest of his five years were "all too much a kind of exile filled with unaccomplished and abandoned plans and soured by the neglect of my various literary and scientific dreams and projects."[35] In a letter to a young admirer, S. Panaretov, he confessed that as the end of his contract as Minister of Public Instruction approached, he could think of little else but the end of his service. He concluded that: "I have no doubt that most of the 'notables' will greet my departure with sincere joy, and for me it will be a true liberation and the beginning of a more peaceful and more fortunate time."[36]

Many of Jireček's contemporaries and all of those who later wrote about educational affairs in that time completely disagreed with his pessimistic evaluation. Citizen groups sent him letters of appreciation and hailed his efforts for the uplifting of their countrymen. Teachers rejoiced in the mitigation of chaotic situations in schools. Newspaper editorials saluted his efforts to build solid foundations for Bulgarian

---

[35] Jireček, letter to Marin Drinov, April 26, 1884 (N.S.), in Sis, Korespondentsiia, p. 235.

[36] Jireček, letter to S. Panaretov, October 10, 1882, ABAN, F. 3 (Jireček), op. 1, ae. 152, p. 26.

education.[37] Finally, government officials of both parties urged him to stay on in an advisory capacity. When a reorganization of the government of General Ernrot saw Jireček replaced as Minister of Public Instruction by Georgi Teokharev in June, 1882,[38] Jireček accepted the proposals and became head of the National Library from 1883 to 1884. More importantly, his ideas for goals and policies again found a forum when he was named head of the School Council of the Ministry, which was established in 1883.

Jireček's continuation in an advisory role could not prevent the severe crisis for the Ministry caused by his immediate successor Georgi Teokharev. Teokharev, by his own admission to an angry Parliament, did virtually nothing in the first six months of his nine-month

---

[37] A beautiful letter (printed in gold) to Jireček from the people of Sliven sxpressing gratitude for his efforts, dated June 12, 1884, is in ABAN, F. 3 (Jireček), op. 1, ae. 1147, p. 26; Nezavisimost, February 11, 1881, p. 1. This article reported the elation of the teachers at the issuance of the "Instructions."

[38] Jireček, letter to Ministry of Public Instruction, February 5, 1883, ABAN, F. 3 (Jireček), op. 1, ae. 1114, pp. 23-24; Jireček, letters to Marin Drinov, July 6, 1882 (N.S.), and August 15, 1882 (N.S.), in Sis, Korespondentsiia, pp. 218, 227; Maritsa, August 30, 1883, p. 3; Boshniakov, "Bŭlgarskiiat dnevnik," p. 4.

term of office.[39] Fortunately, the momentum of Jireček's programs and policies carried Bulgarian education through this confused period until Dimitŭr Agura's accession helped stabilize affairs. But things remained stagnant until the coming to power of Raicho Karolev in June of 1884. Virtually no new goals were set or policies framed in this two-year hiatus. Two of the three men serving at the helm of the Ministry did nothing by way of policy formation. The remaining person, Agura, did set a few new goals and framed a few new policies, but only with controversial consequences.

When Teokharev was called to account in the Sŭbranie for failure to advise that body of the course of his stewardship of the Ministry, Teokharev tapped Jireček to help save the situation. Teokharev lamely excused his own maladministration by claiming that for the first six months in office, he had been obliged to follow programs already enacted by previous Ministers.[40] When Sŭbranie deputies demanded a report on his plans for the future, the result was a strange admixture,

---

[39]Stenograficheski dnevnitsi na III ONS, pŭrva redovna sesiia, session of January 18, 1883, p. 342, and session of February 9, 1883, p. 1.

[40]Ibid.

containing at least one idea resembling projects favored by Jireček. (It was Jireček, ironically, who successfully defended the budget against attempts to freeze all funds for the Ministry until an account was presented.) Teokharev, finally appearing in person, suggested that his major priorities would be to improve school furnishings and to establish a government pedagogical journal to publish various archives of the Ministry. Teokharev also called for the establishment of a School Council to provide a wider range of advice from pedagogical experts in the formation of policy affecting the schools.[41] The budget he submitted contained a request for the funding of these projects.

The hand of Jireček was apparent in this report by Teokharev. Jireček had confided to Drinov before departing the Ministry that he dreamed of a cure for Bulgaria's educational ills, and that cure would be a journal. Jireček claimed that "in serious literary endeavors, one finds a natural cure for the present charlatanism and follies in Bulgaria."[42] He had also suggested such a journal in his "Principal Account."

---

[41] Teokharev, "Zapiska," p. 30.

[42] Jireček, letter to Marin Drinov, December 2, 1880 (N.S.), in Sis, *Korespondentsiia*, p. 209.

The idea of an advisory body such as a School Council
permanently attached to the highest level of the
Ministry was, similarly, an old Jireček idea dating
from his tenure as Executive Secretary under Sarafov.
The two had managed to construct a prototype of such an
organ, but because it was ill-defined and unsupported
financially, nothing ever came of it.[43] Teokharev's
plan came to the same end. The proposed pedagogical
journal materialized only several decades later.

In the same report to the Sŭbranie, Teokharev
suggested that he would introduce bills dealing with
the regulation of stipends, temporary help to public
schools, and the regulation of dormitories. He also
promised a comprehensive bill on public primary education. When Teokharev's term ended three months later,
the Sŭbranie had seen none of the promised projects.
The humiliating situation improved somewhat under the
new Minister of Public Instruction, Dimitŭr Agura. His
accession to the office came about as a result of a
cabinet shuffle that made Teokharev Minister of Justice.
Agura, Executive Secretary of the Ministry of Public
Instruction at the time, became Acting Minister of that

---

[43] The history of the School Council will be discussed in the second half of this chapter.

same institution. (This was in the period that Prince Alexander's suspension of the Constitution was still in effect. Cabinet offices changed hands frequently but not as a result of parliamentary elections.)[44]

Dimitŭr Agura (1849-1911) was born in Bessarabia and attended the seminary and the university at Iași. He received a degree in history in 1872, after which he taught in Bulgarian gymnasia in Romania. In 1878 he came to Bulgaria to serve as a section chief in the Ministry of Internal Affairs.[45] Agura's administration as Minister of Public Instruction, like that of Teokharev, was marked more by failure than success. However, unlike his predecessor, Agura did have some definite goals and did take important initiatives in setting educational policies. His only real success

---

[44] Sekulov, *Nashite pravitelstva*, pp. 9-12; Radev, *Stroitelite*, I, pp. 347-366.

[45] After leaving the Ministry of Public Instruction in 1883, Agura held a succession of teaching and administrative positions at the university in Sofia, eventually becoming rector in 1907. His most important historical work dealt with the French Revolution and was published in 1892. See Sofia, University of, *Almanakh na Sofiiskii universitet Sv. Kliment Okhridski: zhivotopisni i knigopisni svedeniia za prepodavatelite*, 2nd ed., (Sofia: 1940), p. 3; Bulgaria, Ministry of Foreign Affairs, *Kabineti na Ministrite*, unpublished guide compiled in 1948, held in Central State Historical Archives reference collection, p. 85.

came in writing and promulgating a detailed statute on school discipline--a subject of great concern to him. Also, he was the Minister responsible for securing final approval for a School Council added to the Ministry of Public Instruction. In fact, his speech to the first session of that body gave indication of some of his priorities for Bulgarian education.

Agura told the assembled members that a comprehensive law on primary education was still the major goal of the Ministry, as it had been since Giuzelev. This item would ultimately further the systematization of all existing and future schools.[46] But other pressing needs, as cited by Agura, included a better arrangement of Turkish primary schools, reform of classical gymnasia curricula, and the adequate supplying of textbooks. Agura noted that the Ministry had totally ignored Turkish schools up to this point, preferring to leave such schools to the good will of the Turkish communities. The classical school curriculum issue revolved around the fact that not enough attention had been paid to the teaching of classical languages, which

---

[46]Dimitŭr Agura, speech on opening the first session of the School Council, April 10, 1883, "Otkrivanieto na Uchebniia Sŭvet pri Ministerstvoto na Narodnata prosveta," Ucheben vestnik, I, 1-4 (1883), 109.

was the very basis of such educational institutions. Where such instruction did exist, all too often it came from Russian textbooks which presented added difficulties for the Bulgarian students. In the same context, textbooks in general for all subjects in all the schools existed in short supply, making the transmittal of information a laborious, time-consuming process; students had to spend time copying a lesson before they could begin to learn it.[47]

Agura, in his brief, six-month term of office, addressed himself to at least one of these goals, the comprehensive primary school law. However, he also devoted considerable energy and attention to goals not mentioned in his speech before the School Council, such as disciplinary measures and the problem of students being promoted to higher grades or graduated before they were ready.

The comprehensive law on primary schools which Agura and his staff prepared generated controversy even before it was submitted to the Sŭbranie for consideration. The two most controversial sections dealt with teachers and private schools. Rigorous standards

---

[47] Ibid., pp. 107-110.

were suggested to assure that only proficient, qualified teachers would be hired to teach in the public schools.[48] In order to do this, however, the Ministry would strip the communities of most of their prerogatives in the hiring and firing of teachers. For example, the primary school teachers would be appointed by the provincial school inspectors, while teachers in higher schools would be appointed by the Ministry. Also, the Ministry would have more say in the composition of local school boards and the selection of school textbooks. Critics of these provisions saw all of this as an unwarranted usurpation of power by the Ministry.[49]

In the matter of private schools, the bill would have placed greater restrictions on the opening of private schools--a provision which critics regarded as an infringement upon the rights of minorities in the country. The law failed to win approval in the

---

[48] Raicho Karolev, "Podgotovka na uchiteli i pedagogicheski uchilishta sled osvobozhdenieto, 1878-1881," ABAN, F. 62K (Karolev), op. 1, ae. 8, p. 13; Aleksiev, Nashata uchilishtna politika, p. 46.

[49] Maritsa, August 16, 1883, p. 1; Aleksiev, Nashata uchilishtna politika, p. 46.

Sŭbranie, but many of these ideas were used by later Ministers.[50]

Agura never made much effort to achieve the other items on his list of priorities to the School Council. Rather, he devoted attention to writing a statute on discipline. Actually, it was the director of the Gabrovo gymnasium the future Minister of Public Instruction Raicho Karolev who first raised alarums about the decline of discipline in the schools. In a meeting of the Gabrovo Teachers Council in 1883, Karolev argued that discipline was declining precipitously in the schools of Gabrovo. He offered as examples of poor student behavior the drinking and smoking in dormitories, the snowballs with stones which students threw at each other, and student absence and tardiness in classes. He also mentioned the students' habit of roaming the streets late at night, association with "outsiders" (not explained), and general lack of respectful behavior towards teachers. Karolev decided to appoint a four-member commission to write a project for sterner

---

[50] Aleksiev, Nashata uchilishtna politika, pp. 30, 46; Karolev, "Podgotovka na uchiteli," ABAN, F. 62K (Karolev), op. 1, ae. 8, p. 13. This was discussed in another context in Chapter Six of this thesis.

punishment for students and send it to the Minister of Public Instruction in Sofia.[51] Almost certainly this project influenced the disciplinary statute that Agura issued two months later in April, 1883.

Whether or not the discipline problem of Gabrovo was characteristic of the country's schools as a whole is difficult to assess. Certainly no Minister before Agura in 1883 had ever addressed the problem so thoroughly, and Agura himself did not ever indicate that he personally was concerned over the issue. Two unusual discipline problems had attracted attention previous to this. One was caused by the closing of the Samokov Theological Seminary in 1881. The school was closed, as mentioned in a previous chapter, for lack of discipline among the seminarians. When these same students transferred to the Saints Peter and Paul Seminary in Liaskovets, they caused headaches for the rector of that school.[52] Another unusual situation concerning discipline had come during the turmoil over the

---

[51] Gabrovo, Realgymnasium, "Protokolna kniga na Gabrovska realna gimnaziia," ODA, F. 150K (Gabrovo City-Communal Administration), op. 1, ae. 1, p. 25.

[52] Jireček, letter to Metropolitan Clement of Tŭrnovo, Rector of Saints Peter and Paul Theological Seminary, March 31, 1881, ABAN, F. 3 (Jireček), op. 1, ae. 125, pp. 7-8.

suspension of the Tŭrnovo Constitution when teachers and students had taken to the streets to protest against Prince Alexander's coup d'état.[53] Outside of these incidents, no serious crisis of discipline rampant in all the schools would seem to be indicated by the records of the Ministry itself. Also, some of the poor behavior cited by Karolev seems rather normal. Nevertheless, it was certainly true that the country had no thorough statutes matching specific instances of misbehavior with specific punishments.

The disciplinary statute of April, 1883, established, for the first time, precise and uniform guidelines to be followed by directors and teachers councils in dealing with undesirable behavior on the part of students. It set forth rigorous procedures, including the ultimate punishment of exclusion from all schools in the Principality for severe cases of recalcitrance. Agura's special circular letter explaining the statute to school directors and provincial school inspectors left no doubt that his administration was devoted to enforcing the new regulations.[54]

―――――――――

[53] The problem of students and politics was discussed in Chapter Six.

[54] Dimitŭr Agura, "Distsiplinaren pravilnik za uchenitsite v Dŭrzhavnite gimnazii i triklasni

Another significant problem, according to Agura, was that of students being promoted to higher classes or even graduating without being fully prepared for the next level of instruction. The Ministry was receiving too many complaints from higher schools that entering students performed far below expected capacity. The only attention this problem received from Agura, however, was a general recommendation that final examinations be made more difficult.[55]

Given his hard work and near success in achieving the long-sought comprehensive law on public schools, Agura might have achieved very significant results had he remained in office longer. But his administration gave way to a new one in September, 1883, when Dimitŭr Mollov assumed the position of Minister of Public Instruction.

Mollov was appointed to the Ministry of Public Instruction in September, 1883. He was part of the

---

uchilishta," April 28, 1883, Ucheben vestnik, I, 1-4 (1883), 141-146; and Circular letter no. 94, January 11, 1883, in Balabanov and Manov, eds., Sbornik s otbrani, I, pp. 679-680.

[55]Agura, Circular letter no. 1203, May 14, 1883, Ucheben vestnik, I, 1-4 (1883), 92.

compromise that saw Dragan Tsankov assume the office of Prime Minister after moderate Liberals and Conservatives agreed to end the quarrels over the Tŭrnovo Constitution that were tearing the country apart. Although the Constitution was not fully restored, Prince Alexander did agree to allow the formation of a cabinet including leading Liberals such as Tsankov. (Mollov was not closely aligned to either Liberals or Conservatives.) Dimitŭr Mollov (1845-1914) was born in Elena (near Tŭrnovo) where he received his primary education. He taught in local schools for a while before his selection to study in Russia (c. 1862). He studied at the Kiev Theological Academy, but eventually studied medicine at Moscow University. In 1879, during the war, he attracted attention for his work to establish sanitary conditions. He was a member of the Tŭrnovo Constitutional Assembly. Aside from positions dealing with medical affairs, the Ministry of Public Instruction was his first public office. A doctor, with little understanding of educational matters, Mollov's most noteworthy activity as Minister was to write a long pedantic circular letter to teachers on the fundamentals of thesis writing. His tenure of office represents a blank page in the annals of the

Ministry.[56] His term ended when a new government was formed by the Liberals after the elections of June, 1884. Petko Karavelov became Prime Minister and appointed Raicho Karolev to the Ministry of Public Instruction.

Raicho Karolev was the first Minister of Public Instruction to work without the advice and support of Josef K. Jireček. He proved that a native Bulgarian was quite capable of skillfully directing the educational affairs of the country. He brought with him a thorough acquaintance with Bulgarian educational needs as well as a keen sense of professionalism. Both had been earned in his long years as a gymnasium teacher and director in his native land, mostly in Gabrovo.[57] He also proved a much more aggressive and active leader than his immediate predecessors, with the exception of Jireček.

---

[56] Dimitŭr Mollov, Circular letter no. 4595, December 31, 1883, in Balabanov and Manov, eds., Sbornik s otbrani, p. 341. For biographical information on Mollov, see his archival collection in BIA, F. 160 (D. Mollov), op. 1, ae. 5, pp. 1-7; B. Beron, "Pomenik na Dr. D. Mollov," Letopis na Bŭlgarsko knizhovno druzhestvo (Sofia: 1915); Bulgaria, Ministry of Foreign Affairs, Kabineti na Ministrite, pp. 96, 170.

[57] N. Nachov, "Raicho M. Karolev (1846-1928)," Letopis na Bŭlgarska Akademiia na Naukite, XI (1927-1928), 65-73. Karolev's own account of his years at Gabrovo is told in in his Istoriia na Gabrovskoto uchilishte.

From the beginning of his relatively long stay in office (25 months), he showed a firm belief in extensive research and consultation with experts in forming the goals and policies of his administration. This was especially true in the matter of improving the training and working conditions of teachers. This, along with the passage and implementation of a comprehensive law for schools, was the primary goal of Karolev.

He began his service by taking a long, hard look at the whole problem of teacher training, which resulted in a private memorandum entitled "The Preparation of Teachers and Pedagogical Schools after the Liberation, 1878-1884."[58] While he was mostly concerned with tracing the origins and developmental stages of the teacher question, he also examined many other aspects of the educational situation from Drinov's time to his own administration. Karolev was thus able to plan more thoroughly the reforms he wished to undertake. His look at the past had convinced him that:

> The biggest difficulty encountered by the government then was in the staffing and replacement of teachers' positions with people suited to the

---

[58] Raicho Karolev, "Podgotovka na uchiteli," ABAN, F. 62K (Karolev), op. 1, ae. 8,

calling; its greatest task was how to locate trained teachers for the public schools, a question which even today is not satisfactorily resolved.[59]

In fact, to improve the situation, Karolev attempted to enforce already existing legislation on teachers' salaries and also to alleviate certain conditions that held teachers back from improvement of their status. These included the problem of side work and summer unemployment. He also believed that the high turnover of teachers in the schools had to be ended.

Many of these problems he tackled in the "Law on Public and Private Schools" which gave the government greater authority over the hiring and firing of teachers, as well as greater control of local school boards. Karolev had blamed local officials for the existence of many of these unsavory conditions and now could act to remove those who stood in the way of reform. According to Karolev, many school boards dismissed teachers at the end of each school year without sufficient reason. This led to an undesirable situation for both teachers and students. The latter suffered by constantly having to adjust to new teaching personnel.[60]

---

[59] Ibid., p. 2.

[60] Raicho Karolev, Circular letter no. 1622, June 22, 1885, in Balabanov and Manov, eds., *Sbornik s otbrani*, I, p. 157.

According to inspectors, new teachers who could not compete with popular predecessors would punish students with poor marks or by not allowing them to progress to higher grades. The result was, understandably, the disenchantment of the victimized students. The teachers, meanwhile, suffered from the insecurity of their status. Karolev worried that the displaced teachers could not rest or read or even plan their teaching for the next year, but instead had to go from one community to another looking for new positions.[61] To this circumstance must be added the problem of teachers and outside work. Many teachers either voluntarily or involuntarily took jobs unrelated to their profession. Karolev deplored this no matter what its origins, which usually was low or irregular pay.

The problem of high turnover of personnel proved easier to resolve than that of outside work. The "Law on Private and Public Schools" gave Karolev more control over the disposition of teachers even in community-operated (i.e. public) schools.[62] Karolev attempted to

---

[61] Ibid.

[62] Aleksiev, *Nashata uchilishtna politika*, p. 49; Chakurov, *Uchilishtno zakonodatelstvo*, p. 42; Noikov, *Pogled ot Paisiia*, p. 63; Nikolov, "Poiava i razvitie," p. 52.

tackle the outside work issue in various ways, all with mixed results. One step was to resist vigorously any attempt to lower teachers' salaries. This he did with a fair amount of success. In a blistering speech triggered by such an attempt, he observed: "Ever since I became Minister, I have tried to find more teachers and cannot do it in face of present pay scales; what will I do if you lower them?"[63] He took further action in 1885 by outlawing any such work. But merely outlawing the practice did not erase the fact that teachers were often forced to supplement their low or often-delayed pay with odd jobs.[64]

Another item on Karolev's list of reforms was curriculum, specifically that of the higher schools. The lack of clarity in the tasks and programs of the middle and secondary schools bothered Karolev. He wanted to effect a compromise between the very general education then offered in such schools and a more professional orientation.[65] The "Law on Public and Private

---

[63]Aleksiev, Nashata uchilishtna politika, p. 56; Stenograficheski dnevnitsi na IV ONS, pŭrva sesiia, session of December, 1884-January, 1885, pp. 362-429.

[64]Nikolov, "Poiava i razvitieto," p. 52.

[65]Chakŭrov, Uchilishtno zakonodatelstvo, p. 43.

Schools" mandated in broad outlines the inclusion of such subjects as agriculture in the curriculum of middle schools. But Karolev had greater plans for curriculum reform which he managed to combine with another major goal, the inclusion of teachers in the formation of the goals and policies affecting the country's education. (His attempt to accomplish both of these will be discussed later in this chapter.)

Karolev was one of the most effective Ministers of Public Instruction in the second half of the nineteenth century. This was mostly due to his success in achieving a comprehensive law on public and private schools; the importance of which was recognized in his own time as well as by later historians of education.[66] The significance of his Ministry must also be attributed to his vigorous efforts to open even further the channels of communication in the Ministry to those who best knew the hard realities of Bulgarian schools--the teachers.

This opening of channels came in the form of a Teachers Congress which Karolev convoked in August, 1885. The Teachers Congress of 1885 cannot be discussed,

---

[66] Ibid.; Aleksiev, Nashata uchilishtna politika, p. 49; Noikov, Pogled ot Paisiia, p. 63; Nachov, "Raicho M. Karolev (1846-1928), pp. 65-73.

however, without first examining another institution, the School Council, which came into existence in 1883 since it was the School Council which officially arranged and organized the first Teachers Congress in the Principality of Bulgaria.

<u>School Councils and Teachers Congresses:</u>
<u>The Expansion of Educational Bureaucracy</u>

<u>The School Council</u>

Both the School Council and the Teachers Congress which came after it were concrete expressions of a growing realization within the Ministry of Public Instruction that one man or one small group of men could not and should not entirely control the future of Bulgarian education. The School Council, which only existed from April, 1883, to September, 1884, was the first successful attempt to expand educational policy making beyond the control of a professional oligarchy surrounding the Minister. The history of the School Council illustrates the process of opening up channels that eventually culminated in the Teachers Congress of 1885.

The first attempt to establish an advisory body to assist the Minister in devising school policy came

in the administration of Minister of Public Instruction
Mikhail Sarafov (from December, 1880-April, 1881).
Much of the credit almost certainly belonged to the
Executive Secretary at the time, Jireček, although the
facts are not entirely clear as to whose ideas it
originally was. A "School Council" was established as
part of a law covering random items on December 18,
1880. This was only one day after Sarafov became
Minister of Public Instruction. Sarafov's predecessor,
the poet and publicist Petko R. Slaveikov, had held
office only for 19 days. Therefore, Jireček emerges
as the likely prime figure behind this first attempt
since he was Executive Secretary throughout this
period of rapid turnover within the government of Petko
Karavelov.[67] (Slaveikov resigned as Minister of Public
Instruction to become Minister of Foreign Affairs.)
Actually, as far back as December of 1879, Jireček
had noted in his diary that he had attended a meeting

---

[67] These deductions were first made by Vasilev in his excellent study, Ucheben sŭvet, p. 6. I see no reason to disagree with this line of reasoning, given the fact that Jireček initiated almost every other major project in this period. See Bulgaria, Ministry of Public Instruction, "Zakon za sŭstavian'e ucheben sŭvet pri M.N.P., za preustroistvoto na pravitelstvenite uchilishta, etc." Dŭrzhaven vestnik, II, 96 (1880), 1. See also following footnote.

with Metropolitan Clement in which the idea of a School Council was discussed. According to Jireček, he and Metropolitan Clement discussed Ivan Giuzelev, Petko R. Slaveikov, and Jireček himself as potential members of such a council. "Plans and textbooks" were the words Jireček used after the diary entry to summarize the duties of the council.[68]

Whoever was ultimately responsible for its creation, the School Council of 1880 swiftly faded into extinction without accomplishing anything. The decree setting up the Council was extremely vague about goals, purpose, operating funds, meetings, composition, and legal duties. The only thing it did specify was that the Council would consist of an Executive Secretary, Section Chiefs, and two advisors (not named).[69]

According to the decree, the School Council "will occupy itself with school questions relating to textbooks and the instructional aspect of the schools, the development of programs, the reviewing of textbooks, evaluation of teacher credentials, and, in general with

---

[68] Jireček, *Bulgarski dnevnik*, I, p. 70.

[69] Bulgaria, Ministry of Public Instruction, "Zakon za sŭstavian'e ucheben sŭvet," p. 1.

everything which relates to the organization of the schools."[70] The idea was to assign a group of professionals to examine aspects of education such as textbook selection, teacher credentials, and curriculum, leaving the Ministry more time for administrative and financial affairs. But the precepts of the actual law were so vague that it was no wonder that this Council never amounted to anything. Also, since the Council was composed entirely of bureaucrats already in the employ of the Ministry, there was no attempt to bring in outside opinions. Evidently, the Council never bothered to meet and vanished without a trace.

When a second and eventually successful attempt was made to establish a School Council, the motives, as well as the intended scope of the institution, had changed. In the interval between attempts, several factors had helped ensure the success of the second effort made by Georgi Teokharev and Dimitŭr Agura in 1882 to 1883.

The more effective organization of a system of school inspectors certainly contributed to renewed plans to establish a School Council in the Ministry by

---

[70] *Ibid.*

demonstrating clearly the value of "outside" opinion. The provincial school inspectors had become experts in the field and provided much valuable information to the central organization. This information was utilized by every Minister from Jireček onward to formulate policy. Eventually, however, the Ministers began openly to solicit not just facts but also the opinions of the provincial school inspectors, as in the long-running correspondence between Minister Jireček and Inspector Iliia Blŭskov. After a while, this solicitation of ideas spread as well to the directors of various institutions under the control of the Ministry. Thus, the groundwork was laid for eliciting discussion of ideas or suggestions for programs from sources outside of the central offices of the Ministry in Sofia.

Coupled with this must be the occasional but important criticisms of overcentralization of the decision-making process regarding educational affairs in general, but especially in relation to communal schools. Most of this criticism emanated from the press or the Sŭbranie. This was especially true in times of weak leadership at the ministerial level. Occasionally, as in an 1883 article in Maritsa, the critics ridiculed the Ministry's unwillingness to give teachers a greater voice in matters of direct concern to them, such as the choice of textbooks for their courses.[71]

The campaign to establish a School Council, as well as the resulting legislation, reflected these new needs and developments. The struggle to set up a School Council was a long one, but the goal had a high priority for all the Ministers from Jireček to Agura, who finally succeeded. The law went through several stages, from formation in the Ministry to discussion in the <u>Sŭbranie</u> and the State Council, to its final promulgation.

The proposed legislation for the creation of the second School Council was written by Jireček, but sustained several changes before finally becoming law. Jireček, however, never introduced the plan while Minister. Instead, it was his successor Teokharev who formally submitted the proposal to the <u>Sŭbranie</u>, which had to approve the funding for the project.[72] Most of the debate and subsequent changes in the plan, however, were made in sessions of the State Council, where the

---

[71] <u>Maritsa</u>, September 2, 1883, p. 5.

[72] Bulgaria, State Council, sessions of June 20 and June 25, 1882, TsDIA, F. 708 (State Council), op. 1, ae. 275, pp. 2,5.

bill was introduced in 1882, but sat in committee. Teokharev, in urging the Sŭbranie to expedite the establishment of the Council, mentioned that the Ministry urgently needed a gathering of experienced, knowledgable forces to deliberate questions of educational organization and policy.[73] Thus, in a few years, the idea of a Council had changed from one of a casual, advisory board composed of insiders to one of active participation with at least some members from outside of the Ministry. The State Council actually strengthened Jireček's original plan so that the Council would meet more often and have some right of initiative.[74]

The School Council finally came into existence in April, 1883. The first session was convened on Sunday, April 10, 1883, with a solemn blessing by Ikonom pop Todorov (one of the members). The Council consisted of twelve members as prescribed by law. Josef K. Jireček was president of the new Council, and his fellow members were: Spas Vatsov, Pavel Genchev, Ivan Giuzelev, Georgi Kirkov, Iosif Kovachev, Ikonom pop Todorov,

---

[73]Ibid., p. 5; Teokharev, "Zapiska," p. 29.

[74]Bulgaria, State Council, sessions of June 25, July 27, August 4, August 7, 1882, TsDIA, F. 708 (State Council), op. 1, ae. 275, pp. 2-5, 3-10, 13, 15.

N. Mikhailovski, Vasil Popovich, Mikhail K. Sarafov, Vasil D. Stoianov, and Doctor Iordan Bradel. With the exception of Bradel, all of these men had been very active in Bulgarian education before or after 1878 and were well qualified to serve on such a panel.[75] Dr. Iordan Bradel (1847-1899) was a graduate of the Medical Faculty of Moscow University and a member of the country's Supreme Medical Council. He had taught a few years in his native Elena in the 1840s.[76] The chief reason for his being named was no doubt his enthusiastic support for Bulgarian cultural affairs and also to provide opinion from outside the ranks of professional educators.

The Minister of Public Instruction at the time, Dimitŭr Agura, opened the new session by reminding the

---

[75] Bulgaria, Ministry of Public Instruction, School Council, "Otkrivanieto na Uchebniia Sŭvet pri M. na N. Pr.," Ucheben vestnik, I, 1-4 (1883), 107. In a memorandum to himself, Jireček had listed his preferences for the members of the Council, and of these, only Iliia Blŭskov, Vasil Drumev, and Raicho Karolev were not actually named, ABAN, F. 3 (Jireček), op. 1, ae. 114, p. 15. For an explanation of how the School Council functioned in a much later time (1900-1921), see Aleksandŭr Girginov, Dŭrzhavnoto ustroistvo na Bŭlgariia (Sofia: 1921), p. 28.

[76] Bradel later became a docent at the University of Sofia, teaching forensic medicine. See his obituary in Periodichesko spisanie na Bŭlgarskoto knizhovno druzhestvo, LVIII (1899), 694; also Jireček, Bŭlgarski dnevnik, I, pp. 58, 100-107, 205-207, et passim.

members of what would be expected of them. (This has been discussed in previous sections.) Agura cautioned the Council that, in addition to the performance of its specific duties, he would expect its aid on every important question in the area of educational affairs.[77]

The President of the new Council also addressed the assembled members on the first day. Jireček noted that the School Council would serve as a vanguard for the future progress of instruction in the Principality and in the development of Bulgarian education. He advised that the real purpose of the Council was one of organization and that this involved two tasks. The first concerned the external structure of education, i.e. the legal statutes and regulations. The other task revolved around the internal maintenance of educational affairs, which depended on such things as selection and distribution of textbooks, curricula, and teacher credentials.[78] Finally, he reminded the members that "all educational affairs must be moved by

---

[77] Dimitŭr Agura, speech to the opening session of the School Council, in "Otkrivanieto na Uchebniia sŭvet pri M. na N. Pr.," p. 107.

[78] Jireček, speech to the opening session of the School Council, "Izvlechenie iz dnevnitsite na Uchebnii sŭvet," April 10, 1883, Ucheben vestnik, I, 5-6 (1883), 39.

a spirit, the spirit of system and order which gives to all work(s) the proper strenth and thoroughness that ensures appropriate success."[79] In private letters to friends, Jireček confided that he expected great things from the new institution, especially in the realm of systematization and school organization.[80] Unfortunately, those high hopes were never quite realized.

The law which set up the School Council designated basic rules of operation, as well as the duties of the Council. Internal regulation was left for the Council members to determine. The members, named by special decree of the Prince, were to serve for two years and would meet at least three times each month. A precise list of their duties included such things as textbook selection, development of curricula, selection of books for the National Library, and final selection of candidates for stipends.[81] The Council was also supposed to give its opinion on the opening of new state educational

---

[79] Ibid.

[80] Jireček, letter to Marin Drinov, April 14, 1883, in Sis, Korespondentsiia, p. 225; Jireček, letter to Iliia Blŭskov, April 14, 1883, ABAN, F. 3 (Jireček), op. 1, ae. 63, p. 21.

[81] Bulgaria, Ministry of Public Instruction, "Zakon za Uchebniia sŭvet pri Ministerstvoto na N. Pr.," Ucheben vestnik, I, 1-4 (1883), 135-137.

institutions or the reform of older ones. Also, the
Council, acting with the Minister, had the privilege of
deciding on the convocation of special "Educational
Congresses." The Council was charged with elaborating
a special statute to govern these new gatherings, but
the basic outlines were decreed in the law establishing
the School Council itself. These educational congresses
would take place in the summer and were to include, at
the discretion of the Minister, school inspectors,
directors of state schools, members of the School
Council, and some of the more experienced teachers.[82]

The educational congresses, according to these
provisions, would be convoked to debate pressing questions of education as defined by the Minister. The
law was unclear as to the exact role of the School
Council in the formation of agenda for such congresses.
In any event, all the activities prescribed for the
School Council itself were always at the initiative of
the Minister.[83] In other words, the Council was supposed to discuss only those items submitted by the
Minister. In actual practice, the School Council in

---

[82] Ibid., pp. 136-137.

[83] Ibid., p. 137.

its brief existence displayed a will of its own on several occasions.

The first business undertaken by the School Council was the establishment of its own internal rules of operation. These were of no great importance except for the interesting debate they engendered on whether the Minister should be free to sit in on sessions of the Council. After a surprising number of objections to free attendance, the Council decided, no doubt wisely, that since the Minister had the right to revise or to repudiate decisions of the Council, he could attend any session he desired, but could not take part in the formal decision of any questions.[84]

This attempt to limit the voice of the Minister in the affairs of the Council had no negative repercussions. It would not be the last time the newest branch of the Ministry of Public Instruction would assert itself. Its first tasks were to devise a better law on foreign stipends, as well as to decide on the proper textbooks for the approaching academic year. In the first case, the Council informed Minister Agura that, rather than work just on foreign stipends, the

---

[84] Bulgaria, Ministry of Public Instruction, "Izvlechenia iz dnevnitsite na Uchebnii sŭvet," Ucheben vestnik, I, 5-6 (1883), 39-45.

Council would prepare a law on stipends in general. In the second case, the Council informed the Ministry that it would not begin the consideration of textbooks until he (Agura) submitted for discussion the programs of the schools in the Principality.[85]

Agura, evidently, was not offended by the active role of the Council and made effective use of it. He even submitted many items that need not have been introduced for discussion in the Council, such as whether to turn a school in Dobrich into an agriculturally-oriented school.[86] The agenda of the Council was filled with special requests for opinions from the Minister alongside its regular duties. The Council, in its lifetime of 20 months, made useful decisions on everything from a new comprehensive law on public schools, to when, where, and how the body of Vasil Aprilov, the great benefactor of Bulgarian education, should be brought to Bulgaria from Romania.[87]

---

[85] Ibid., session of May 4, 1883 and session of July 9, 1883, I, 7 (1883), 44, 51-52.

[86] Ibid., session of May 12, 1883, I, 5-6 (1883), 45.

[87] Ibid., sessions of May 25, June 1, June 8, June 15, June 22, I, 5-6 (1883), 47-49 ;July 2, I, 7 (1883), 46-51; July 20, August 30, 1883, I, 8 (1883), 40-43.

Unfortunately for Bulgarian education, the School Council came to a very untimely end mostly for financial reasons, but also, no doubt, because of the departure of its chief architect and inspiration, Jireček. The immediate cause of the School Council's collapse was the Subranie's refusal to renew funding for it in the budget of 1885.[88] But in August, 1884, Jireček resigned his position as President and left Bulgaria permanently in that September. The presidency fell to the elderly Nikola Mikhailovski for the remaining months of the Council's existence.[89]

The collapse of the School Council was nothing less than tragic for the progress of Bulgarian education because the Council, in only a very short time, had accomplished an enormous amount of work, lessening the burden of details on the Minister and his top assistants. Its existence had proved the need for, and potential effectiveness of, such an institution. Its failure was caused by the poor financial situation of the time, but also by the inactivity of Dimitŭr Mollov, who served as Minister after Agura.

---

[88] Vasilev, Ucheben sŭvet, p. 15; Stenograficheski dnevnitsi na IV ONS, vtora sesiia, pp. 362-429.

[89] Vasilev, Ucheben sŭvet, pp. 13-15.

The existence of a School Council, however brief, did set the stage for another important gathering, the Teachers Congress of 1885. That event was also part of the same process that had resulted in the establishment of the defunct School Council, a need for more influence on the formulation of policies and goals by the Ministry of Public Instruction

The Teachers Congress of August, 1885

When the teachers of the Principality gathered together in Sofia in August, 1885, for the Congress convoked by Karolev, it marked the first time that teachers had assembled for a general conference since the 1870s in Shumen. Yet even that meeting had been a regional affair. The historic significance of the Sofia Congress suggested the meeting would be a useful and productive one. Unfortunately, despite its relatively long duration of several weeks, it accomplished little. But it was an important step in the recognition of the potential role of teachers in deciding important questions of Bulgarian education.

Before Bulgaria's liberation and national existence, the liberal revolutionaries and church officials had endorsed the concept of such meetings. It was not until 1885, however, that such a congress was convoked

in the newly independent state. The reasons for the
delay included the existence of more pressing needs demanding attention, the low caliber and scarcity of
teachers, and the political turmoil of the first five
years of the nation's existence. A large gathering of
teachers, notoriously anti-Prince and anti-Conservative
in orientation, in 1882 or 1883 could have had embarras-
sing and unpleasant political overtones. By 1885,
however, the political situation had calmed, and some
order had been created in the educational sphere. Thus,
then Raicho Karolev submitted his budget for the Ministry to Parliament, it included a request of 10,000 leva
for the purpose of summoning a Teachers Congress.[90]
Karolev also wrote a provision for such congresses into
his "Law on Communal and Private Schools" and into the
law establishing the School Council, which received the
privilege of helping to arrange the congresses. All
of these provisions were approved by the Sŭbranie and
the Ministerial Council. Yet when Karolev informed the
Ministerial Council that he intended to convoke a
teachers congress in August, the Council decided that
one should not be called because "almost all the

---

[90] Ibid., p. 24; Stenograficheski dnevnitsi na IV ONS, vtora sesiia, sessions of December, 1884-January, 1885, pp. 362-429.

provincial school inspectors were new and had not had sufficient time to determine the educational needs of their provinces."[91] The Ministerial Council's reasoning was valid only to a certain degree since the school inspectors were not the only ones who would attend such a congress. Karolev's persistence prevailed, however, and a congress was scheduled for August, 1885.

The law which established the School Council in 1883 had noted that the purpose of a teachers congress was to help create unity in the arrangement of the programs and regulations of primary and secondary schools.[92] This theme was echoed in Karolev's opening remarks to the Congress on August 1, 1885. Karolev advised the assembled delegates that their mission was both difficult and painstaking. On the basis of their knowledge and experience, they would be asked to give their opinions on ways to reform and to improve Bulgarian schools.

Karolev informed them that as Minister, he recognized that teachers would best be aware of the good and

---

[91] Bulgaria, Ministerial Council, session of June 7, 1885, TsDIA, F. 284 (Ministerial Council), op. 1, ae. 387, pp. 2-3.

[92] Vasilev, Ucheben Sŭvet, p. 16; Bulgaria, Ministry of Public Instruction, "Zakon za Uchebniia sŭvet pri Ministerstvoto na N. Pr.;" Ucheben vestnik, I, 1-4 (1883), 135-137.

bad aspects of current rules and programs.[93] By this, he presumably meant that teachers had to work from day to day with the rules, regulations, and instructions of the Ministry and had the best opportunity to observe any flaws or loopholes. Several projects involving both the programs and the management of primary and secondary schools, he promised, would be submitted to them for discussion. He especially urged them to consider making final examinations public so as not to divorce school affairs from the people. In a statement recalling his interest in the subject while he was Director of the Gabrovo Technical Gymnasium in 1883, Karolev urged the teachers to give some attention to the question of discipline in the schools.[94]

Unfortunately, due to the poor planning by Karolev and his associates, the most important projects were not submitted to the assembled delegates until August 13 and 14. Meanwhile, the funds designated for the entire affair proved insufficient, and the Congress was forced to close on August 20 without completing any of the designated tasks, an ignominious end for an

---

[93]Vasilev, Ucheben sŭvet, p. 25.

[94]Ibid.

auspicious beginning.[95] The protocols of the Congress were never published. Nevertheless, this first Congress was a catalyst for later attempts to organize Bulgaria's teachers on a more stable basis. The war for unification of the Principality and Eastern Rumelia in 1885 temporarily disrupted the lives of teachers because of conscription and made such congresses impossible. But soon after, the teachers congress became a permanent part of the educational life of the country.

While the first teachers congress and its attempt to elevate the role of teachers in educational affairs came to naught, other attempts to secure a greater role for teachers were far more successful. In fact, the role of teachers grew steadily through this entire period by means of the institution of teachers councils.

Teachers, School Boards, and the Problem of Cooperation on Local Levels

The idea of teachers meeting regularly to discuss affairs in their own school was hardly new to Bulgarian education. Such events had occurred in the early part of the nineteenth century when schools accommodating more than one teacher began to appear.

---

[95] Ibid., p. 26.

However, until the establishment of special regulations by the Ministry of Public Instruction, such arrangements were extremely informal and irregular in nature and often without any clear purpose.[96] This general situation changed radically with the introduction, in stages, of very precise guidelines for the purpose, activity, and responsibilities of teachers councils. As these teachers councils grew and developed, so too did problems between these new organizations and older ones, such as the school boards. Many of these problems surrounded the interpretation of legal rights and duties, which in turn invited ministerial intercession and mediation.

The first attempts to organize and to regulate the existence of teachers councils after 1878 came with the

---

[96] Of all the questions in Bulgarian education, the subjects of teachers councils and school boards are still the least known and documented. Of these two, almost nothing is known about the role, function, rise, and development of teachers councils (as opposed to congresses) before 1878. The lack of records make the tracing of such organs difficult, which might account for the paucity of information on teachers councils. In any event, much remains to be done in the study of this institution, as well as in the study of all other local organs that had anything to do with the administration of schools before and even after 1878. Vasilev's study on school councils and school committees mentions teachers councils only in passing, and that is about the extent of the discussion on the subject in Bulgarian literature.

"Instructions for the Administration of State Educational Establishments," issued in 1881.[97] Nothing had been mentioned on the subject during Drinov's time, yet some teachers councils existed in very organized form since at least 1875 in Gabrovo and 1880 in Sofia. Raicho Karolev, in his history of the schools in Gabrovo, mentions that in February, 1875, the school board of Gabrovo permitted the teachers of Gabrovo to form a teachers council complete with a written statute. According to Karolev, the statute approved by the school board granted the teachers council the right to define the methods and standards of teaching in all the schools of Gabrovo and left the "instructional part" of all schools in the hands of the teachers council. The financial affairs of the school would remain the prerogative of the school board. Conceivably financial affairs meant such things as pay scales for teachers, purchasing of equipment, administration of income and expenditures, approval of remodeling and construction of buildings, etc. The teachers council also received the right to decide on such things as which students should be

---

[97] Bulgaria, Ministry of Public Instruction, "Instruktsiia za Upravlenieto na dŭrzhavnite uchebni zavedeniia v Kniazhestvo Bŭlgariia," Dŭrzhaven vestnik, III, 4 (1881), 27-29.

accepted into the schools, the number of students to be admitted, grading, and who should be permitted to graduate or pass to the next class. All the teachers of Gabrovo schools were members and could elect their own president of the council.[98]

In September, 1880, a group called the Sofia Teachers Council adopted a "Statute" which suggested a high level of development. As defined by the "Statute," the purpose of the Sofia Teachers Council was "pedagogical--to concern itself with the success of the Sofia communal schools in educational and moral relations."[99] The Council was composed of teachers in Sofia communal schools, thus making it larger than other teachers councils centered on one school. Attendance was obligatory, and meetings were scheduled every Wednesday.[100] Yet even this rather specific set of rules did not indicate exactly what the Council was expected to do or by what authority it would act.

---

[98] Karolev, *Istoriia na Gabrovoskoto uchilishte*, pp. 121-122.

[99] Sofia Teachers Council, "Protokolna kniga ot zasedaniiata na Uchitelskiia Sŭvet pri Sofiiski osnovni narodni uchilishta," session of September 5, 1880, SGODA, F. 5K (Sofia School Board), op. 1, ae. 86, pp. 1-3.

[100] *Ibid.*

It was not long before teachers councils received formal definition of their duties and privileges. One year later, the same Sofia Teachers Council had to select a commission to revise its rules to bring them into line with those laid down by the "Instructions on the Administration of State Educational Establishments."[101] The provisions in that law, issued by Sarafov and written by Jireček, were not as thorough as later ones, but they did invest the councils with specific authority as well as specific functions. The purpose of the teachers council was defined by article 23, which stated:

> A teachers council will be set up /to provide/ for the collective supervision of instructional and disciplinary progress in the school; the director /of the school/ or his representative is president, and all of the teachers are members.[102]

The council would meet twice a month regularly and whenever at least two teachers requested an additional meeting. The teachers councils would now serve as the setting in which directors would read instructions from the Ministry and also as the scene of official inquiry

---

[101]Ibid., session of September 28, 1881, p. 21.

[102]Bulgaria, Ministry of Public Instruction," "Instruktsiia za upravlenieto na dŭrzhavnite uchebni zavedeniia v Kniazhestvo Bŭlgariia," Dŭrzhaven vestnik, III, 4 (1881), 29.

by the directors into teaching and disciplinary conditions in the school. One unusual provision called for the teachers to praise several of the best students and to excoriate several of the worst on the second day after the meeting, evidently to present an example to their schoolmates.[103] The teachers council gained the right to decide on the acceptance or expulsion of students when the director requested assistance. But the teachers alone, in council, designated candidates for government stipends, compiled credentials for students, and divided class subjects and hours among teachers at the beginning of each semester.[104]

Further orders from the Ministry elaborated on these duties. The most important of these were the "Instructions for the Provincial School Inspectors" and the disciplinary statutes of Agura. The first had tried to define the relations of teachers councils, provincial school inspectors, and local school organs such as the school boards.[105] The disciplinary

---

[103]*Ibid.*

[104]*Ibid.*

[105]Actually, the "Instructions" defined the rights of the provincial inspectors in relation to each of these organs, and the inspectors served as intermediaries for the groups. This was discussed in Chapter

statute spelled out in detail exactly what punishments could be administered by the teachers councils and under what circumstances.[106] Both helped strengthen the position of teacher participation by giving confirmation of the right of teachers to participate in matters of school administration. Such strengthening and clarification was, in fact, much needed by the fledgling teacher organizations because disputes soon arose between the councils and other school organizations.

For the most part, the activity of the teachers councils was fairly routine. Most of the topics on the agendas of the Sofia and Gabrovo teachers councils, for example, involved the duties described in various ministerial precepts. Most often, this included disciplinary measures, decisions on stipends, division of subjects and class hours among teachers, selection of textbooks and other furnishings for the school. Less often, the councils revised school codes of behavior

---

Six of this thesis. For the relevant section of the "Instructions," see Dŭrzhaven vestnik, III, 14 (1881), 108ff.

[106] Bulgaria, Ministry of Public Instruction, "Distsiplinaren pravilnik za uchenitsite v Dŭrzhavnite gimnazii i triklasni uchilishta," Ucheben vestnik, I, 1-4 (1883), 141-146.

412

or discussed new construction plans.[107] Occasionally, the councils would gather to discuss a proposal of the Minister of Public Instruction regarding a new policy. For example, in May, 1883, the Ministry submitted to the Gabrovo Teachers Council for its opinion, a regulation on entrance examinations for the Technical Gymnasium in Gabrovo.[108] This kind of activity was a departure from all the duties specified in the codes governing teachers councils, but it was in line with the trend in the Ministry to seek advice from teachers on policies directly affecting them.

The minutes of the teachers councils show ample evidence that they followed diligently the relevant mandates of the Ministry in making decisions on various problems. Discussions and decisions on topics as

---

[107]This is based on a detailed examination of sessions of the teachers councils of Gabrovo, Samokov, and Sofia for the period 1880-1885; Sofia Teachers Council,"Protokolna kniga ot zasedaniiata na Uchitelskiia Sŭvet pri Sofiiski osnovni narodni uchilishta," SGODA, F. 5K (Sofia School Board), op. 1, ae. 85-88; Gabrovo, "Protokolna kniga na Gabrovska realna gimnaziia," ODA, F. 150K (Gabrovo City-Communal Administration), op. 1, ae. 1; Samokov, City Provincial Administration, SGODA, F. 41K (Samokov City Administration), op. 1, ae. 521-526.

[108]Gabrovo, City-Communal Administration, "Protokolna kniga na Gabrovska realna gimnaziia," session of Teachers Council for May 27, 1883, ODA, F. 150K (Gabrovo City-Communal Administration), op. 1, ae. 1, pp. 32-33.

diverse as stipends and construction of school buildings invariably cited one or more laws on the subject.[109] This was especially true, however, in decisions on disciplining students, which closely followed the required procedures as outlined by Agura and Karolev. In these matters as well as others, the teachers councils frequently received assistance from the provincial school inspectors, who acted as official liaisons between teachers councils and the central Ministry.

Unfortunately, things were not so clear cut in the one area that caused the most difficulty for teachers councils, namely, the absence of clear regulations governing relations between teachers councils and school boards. The absence of such regulations contributed to the friction that arose between them. While such problems were also a common feature on the agendas of teachers councils, they were seldom resolved in routine fashion.

Animosity between teachers and the school boards was traditional in Bulgaria, if "traditional" can be used to describe a situation that had existed for less than one hundred years. Most of the problems between

---

[109] Ibid., session of November 10, 1882, and April 7, 1883, pp. 11, 29.

school boards and teachers had their roots in the pre-1878 period when the school boards had wielded great powers in matters of school affairs. The institution of the school board or church-school board was largely a product of the increased privileges the Bulgaria communities had received by means of the Hatti-Hümayun of 1856.[110] (This decree of reform had recognized the right of non-Turkish subjects of the Ottoman Empire to manage their own affairs through organized institutions.) Although the exact duties differed from one community to the next, most school boards had significant control over both the financial and the instructional aspects of the local schools. Financial duties included the management of school income and expenditures, the purchasing of equipment, the collection of special school taxes, and negotiating contracts with teachers (this last item applying only to the larger communities). Another important duty of the school boards was to administer special bequests to communal schools. Some or all of these financial duties were often shared with communal councils. However, in areas where Greeks

---

[110] Khristov, Bŭlgarskite obshtini, pp. 115-120; Vankov, Razvoi, pp. 74-77; I. Prosenichkov, ed., Iubileina kniga na Rusenskata narodna mŭzhka gimnaziia "Kniaz Boris" po sluchai 50 godishninata i (Ruse: 1934), pp. 51-52.

still controlled the affairs of the towns, the Bulgarians usually set up separate school boards for their own schools.[111]

Before 1878, the school boards also took care of a substantial amount of the actual instructional part of the schools. The school boards set the dates opening and closing the school year, helped fashion curricula, and hired and fired teachers.[112] These duties did not go unchallenged, especially by the guilds (esnafi) and the teachers. Both groups resented the fact that many school boards were in the hands of the wealthy, conservative merchant class (chorbadzhi). The chorbadzhi were not only Hellenified but also had close ties with Turkish officialdom. This was especially true in such well-developed school systems as those of Gabrovo, Shumen, and Tŭrnovo, where the guilds attempted to place guild representatives on school boards and teachers fought with the chorbadzhi over control of teaching

---

[111] Vankov, Razvoi, pp. 27-28; V. D. Zlatarski, ed., Iubilena kniga na V. Tŭrnovskata narodna mŭzhka gimnaziia "Sv. Kiril" po sluchai 50 godishninata i (Tŭrnovo: 1933), pp. 32-33, 111-112; Khristov, Bŭlgarskite obshtini, pp. 118-120; Blunt, "Educational Movement," pp. 804-805.

[112] Gandev, Faktori, pp. 169-170; Karolev, Istoriia na Gabrovoskoto uchilishte, pp. 125-133; Khristov, Bŭlgarskite obshtini, pp. 111-112.

methods and reform of curriculum.[113] Eventually, in Gabrovo, the school board relinquished some of its authority over the instructional aspect of the schools to a teachers council in 1875. It is significant, however, that it was the school board which granted a statute to the teachers to organize a formal council.

The Ottoman firman of 1870 setting up an autocephalous Bulgarian Exarchate reduced the role of the school boards somewhat since the decree recognized that the Church would have the right to regulate the educational affairs of the Bulgarian people.[114] At least in Shumen, church leaders did begin to assert their right to supervise school affairs. But before that movement could have much effect, the events of 1876 to 1878 caused the establishment of the independent state and its concomitant governmental agencies.

Two institutions in particular caused a significant diminution of the range of activities for the school boards after 1878. One of course was the Department, later Ministry, of Public Instruction. The

---

[113] Zlatarski, Iubileina kniga, p. 111; Zhechev, "Uchitelskiiat sŭvet," pp. 80-81; Khristov, Bŭlgarskite obshtini, pp. 118ff.

[114] Nikov, Vŭzrazhdane na Bŭlgarskiiat narod, pp. 307-311; von Mach, Bulgarian Exarchate, pp. 13-15.

other was the institution (or institutions) of local government--chiefly the city-provincial administration (<u>gradsko-obshtinsko upravlenie</u>). This institution took on many of the former tasks of the school boards, especially in the matter of setting annual budgets for the communal schools.[115] The Ministry of Public Instruction and the communal governments often assumed powers and privileges over school affairs without ever defining what exactly would be left to the school boards. Some attempts were made, however, to define who was responsible for what. The first such attempt was made by Marin Drinov.

Despite his firm belief in letting the people continue to manage their own school affairs, Drinov's Department of Public Instruction reserved the right to set curricula, teaching standards, and other important matters affecting the communal schools. Drinov did, however, endorse the formation of school boards "to collect school revenues and to spend them as necessary."[116] But, aware that many school boards misused

---

[115] Bulgaria, Ministry of Justice, "Zakon za obshtinite," pp. 924-930.

[116] Bulgaria, Department of Public Instruction and Religious Affairs, "Privremenen Ustav za narodnite uchilishta," <u>Uchilishten sbornik</u>, p. 9.

funds and were negligent in paying teachers, he sharply curbed their duties. According to Drinov's "Temporary Statute for the Public Schools" (1879), temporary provincial school councils would be set up to manage the setting and paying of teachers' salaries. He envisioned this situation as lasting one year until the whole matter of irregular pay for teachers could be studied.[117]

The school boards, according to Drinov's definition, would be primarily organs to supervise financial affairs (with the exception of teachers' wages). Further provisions of the Temporary Statute ordered that school boards would discuss ways to improve the material aspects of the schools and would seek ways to help poor students succeed in their studies. Unfortunately, Drinov was rather vague in defining what exact role school boards would have in the instructional aspect of the schools. On that matter the Temporary Statute stated: "The school board, although it does not interfere in the instructional part of the schools, all the same gives moral support to the teachers in their efforts to improve this part."[118] This remark was

---

[117] Ibid.

[118] Ibid., p. 10.

unclear as to what exactly constituted moral support or how such support could be given without adequate knowledge of what was going on in the instructional part of the communal schools. Perhaps foreseeing trouble, Drinov stated that the special provincial school councils he had set up for one year would also serve to arbitrate disputes between school boards and teachers.[119]

Trouble was not long in coming, as teachers councils and school boards clashed over what each believed to be the other's interference in its work. A particularly virulent conflict occurred in 1880 between the Sofia Teachers Council and the Sofia Church-School Board, illustrating well the need for stricter delineation of responsibilities. The problem started when the School Board in September, 1880, sent two letters to the Sofia Teachers Council, demanding information on the internal arrangements of the Teachers Council and the schools. The teachers resented not only what they considered to be the imperious tone of the letters, but also the intrusion into "instructional" matters.[120]

---

[119]Ibid.

[120]Sofia, Teachers Council, "Protokolna kniga," sessions of September 26, October 8, October 9, 1880, SGODA, F. 5K (Sofia School Board), op. 1, ae. 86, pp. 12-17.

After a heated debate on the powers of the school boards over teachers and schools, the Teachers Council decided to turn over only that information which the School Board might legitimately need. To this, the Council appended an explanation of the voluntary nature of its action. The Council stated clearly that pedagogical affairs of the schools were the prerogative of the teachers and not of the school board. It refused to turn over any information, for example, regarding the performance or behavior of teachers.[121]

This one incident alone pointed out that despite some regulations on the subject, the situation was still extremely fluid. The conflicts, when they occurred, were sometimes uneven because the school boards often held the purse strings, although this power could not be abused without escaping the attention of the Minister of Public Instruction and local officials. Given the potential for further disagreements, the Ministry wisely attempted to define more precisely the duties of school boards, even as it encouraged and strengthened the teachers councils.

That explanation and elucidation came in the form of "The Instructions for the Provincial School

---

[121] *Ibid.*, p. 17.

Inspectors" of March, 1881. The provisions in these Instructions which dealt with school boards (as well as teachers councils) gave a much more satisfactory and specific description of school board powers. The Instructions, authored chiefly by Jireček, began with detailed provisions on the election of board members and emphasized the need of finding "honorable and education-loving people who are distinguished by their zeal towards schools."[122] Jireček, in a long memorandum on school affairs (March, 1880), had fumed over the fact that in rural areas many school board members were poorly educated or even illiterate.[123] In a statement reflecting the continuation of such conditions, the Ministry advised the inspectors to nominate for the job "people who enjoyed general respect, who were able to travel to different locales and had seen something of the world, who knew the value and utility of education." But the same article cautioned the inspectors that they would encounter many people who, despite their own lack of education, greatly admired learning and

---

[122] Bulgaria, Ministry of Public Instruction, "Instruktsiia za Okrŭzhnite uchilishtni inspektori," Dŭrzhaven vestnik, III, 17 (1881), 131.

[123] Jireček, "Zapiska," ABAN, F. 3 (Jireček), op. 1, ae. 1125, p. 8.

would work very hard to ensure that the younger generation had a chance to study on a regular basis.[124] Thus, the Instructions urged the provincial inspectors to remember that board members might include such diverse types as young, hard-working people, respected elderly people, and village priests.

By far the most important tasks of the school boards remained the same as in Drinov's time: to administer school assets, to collect revenue, to maintain school buildings in good condition, and to locate support for poor students. The Instructions did not return the control of teachers' salaries to the school boards. That duty remained permanently entrusted to the new municipal authorities. The school boards received additional duties, however, in the realm of recordkeeping. This included keeping lists of teachers, students, and school board members, as well as of individuals who had paid any special school levies (which the board determined as well). Of course, lists of all income and expenditures connected with the schools had to be kept by the boards. The provincial school

---

[124]Bulgaria, Ministry of Public Instruction, "Instruktsiia za Okrŭzhnite uchilishtni inspektori," Dŭrzhaven vestnik, III, 17 (1881), 131.

inspectors had the right and the duty to examine such records at any time.[125]

On the subject of the rights of the school boards to participate in other aspects of the schools (besides finances), the Instructions were quite emphatic. The decree forbade any involvement whatsoever by school boards in the educational or school part (*uchebnata chast*) of the schools. On the other hand, the boards were to support the teachers in their school activity and help the teachers spread a respect and a desire for education among the people.[126] While the Instructions did not state it, the implication was clear that the pedagogical affairs of the local schools were matters for teachers councils, provincial inspectors (representing the Ministry), and school directors. However, the authors of the Instructions did recognize that the school board members might have cause to express an opinion on matters regarding teaching or curriculum. In such cases, the school board members were to communicate their opinions to the provincial inspectors.[127]

---

[125]*Ibid.*

[126]*Ibid.*

[127]*Ibid.*

These provisions definitely helped ease the difficulties, and further *ad* *hoc* decrees touched on issues still in question. The end of the period 1878-1885 clearly saw a slow but sure coordination of all the various units charged with different aspects of school functions on the local level. The lines of authority became somewhat more distinct even though problems still occurred. Much of the credit without question goes to the provincial school inspectors who acted as middlemen between teachers councils, school boards, municipal authorities, directors of schools, and ultimately the Ministry. While snags and obstacles still existed, the basic framework of the educational bureaucracy had taken its final form. As always, lack of funds and trained personnel remained critical problems. But the day-to-day transactions assumed a smoother, more regular pattern. This basic structure of school boards, teachers councils, and provincial school inspectors reflected, in a sense, a broader participation in the school affairs of the nation. But always, the Ministry of Public Instruction continued in its leading role as supervisor and ultimate decision-maker on national educational policy. This state of affairs remained largely the same until after the unification of the two parts of the country in 1885. When the country finally settled down after the turbulence of unification and war with Serbia, it was faced once again with wholesale reform of education, but always from the starting point of the structure so laboriously fashioned from 1878 to 1885.

CONCLUSION

In 1870, the British diplomat, Sir John Elijah Blunt, wrote a detailed report on the state of educational affairs in Bulgaria (cited in the second chapter of this dissertation). Blunt came to the conclusion that the Bulgarian people had erected the groundwork for a national system of education. He also claimed that the only things needed to improve upon that foundation were uniformity in the course of instruction and government control and support. If the situation described by Blunt had remained unchanged, the Ministry of Public Instruction would have had a relatively clear cut and easy task. However, between the time that Blunt filed his report and the establishment of the Department of Public Instruction in 1878, events in Bulgaria changed drastically the basic status of educational affairs in that country. The war for independence, as well as the subsequent emergence of an independent national state, completely changed the nature of Bulgarian education.

These same events also determined the ultimate goals and tasks of the nascent Ministry of Public Instruction.

When war and its destruction wiped away most of the gains of the previous decades, the Ministers of Public Instruction faced the formidable challenges of rebuilding the basic foundations of the local school systems while also striving to create a uniform system of education with a national character. The first part of this dual challenge occupied, by far, the greater amount of attention in the formative period of 1878-1885. In fact, so many problems, obstacles, and difficulties confronted the leaders of Bulgarian education at this juncture in the country's history, that it is difficult to evaluate the work of the Ministry of Public Instruction. In other words, it is not easy to determine where the successes and failures occurred.

One of the best ways to judge the performance of any institution is to compare its actual performance against the goals postulated by the institution itself. In the case of the Bulgarian Ministry of Public Instruction from 1878-1885, this standard cannot be applied so readily. As might be expected in a period of newness and formation, basic goals and tasks were either non-existent or confused. Uncertainty over the proper course of action in each instance requiring a decision was a characteristic of the entire period. In fact, the inability to make definite long-range decisions and to determine definite long-range goals were two of the chief shortcomings of the Ministers of Public Instruction at this time. True, the basic goal, as enshrined in the Turnovo Constitution, was to give all Bulgarian citizens a basic primary education. But no one really expected to achieve that goal for a very long time. Another broad goal was to create good Bulgarian citizens. But precisely what would constitute a good Bulgarian citizen never received further definition by any of those in charge of educational affairs.

Given the efforts of the intelligentsia during the Renascence to define and to create a Bulgarian national identity, one might have expected this work to assume major importance in the work of the Ministry of Public Instruction. It did not. There are several reasons why the Ministers of Public Instruction did not and in fact could not pay more attention to this type of task. One reason, of course, was the flight of so many of the intelligentsia into other fields of endeavor after the creation of an independent state. Many of those who had concerned themselves with intellectual and cultural work before 1878 now occupied themselves with administering the political and bureaucratic affairs of the new state. This had serious repercussions on the work of the Ministry in shaping the course of the country's school system because many of the members of the intelligentsia had previously been educators. When they abandoned teaching for the more lucrative and prestigious jobs in government, this reduced the pool of experienced and creative individuals available for cultural work. On top of the financial problems arising from the destruction of the schools, the Ministers now had to devote precious time and energy to replacing the teachers lost to political and bureaucratic work. In other words, basic components of a modern efficient and unified educational system had to be supplied before anything more ambitious could be attempted, let alone achieved.

Other factors also inhibited any attempt to form a Bulgarian national character through the schools. These included the need to attend to the basic work of rebuilding, which has already been mentioned. The schools lacked the basic supplies and conditions necessary to anything other than imparting the most basic of educations. Even textbooks were in very short supply, and many of those that did exist were written by foreigners (many Russian) and used by the teachers alone rather than by all of the students. Also, many of the leaders of the Ministry of Public Instruction at this time had been educated abroad and were imbued with foreign ideas of education. Drinov, though intimately aware of Bulgaria's history, language, and literature, had lived all of his adult life in Russia. He was impatient to return to Kharkov and saw his role as strictly temporary. While he accomplished a great deal in setting up basic foundations, he never really addressed himself to larger issues, at least not in a thorough or decisive manner.

Jirecek, so important in this period, devoted much effort to creating uniformity in instruction and did campaign to convince the public of the need to support schools. He never addressed, however, the question of creating a national self-awareness. He also backed away from such issues as whether or not the schools should be centralized, preferring to leave that matter for resolution in the future.

Intimately connected with the problem of defining goals was the problem of determining priorities. Here again, events and circumstances in the newly created state hampered efforts on the part of the Ministers of Public Instruction to be decisive. In many ways, the priority questions revolved around many of the same issues as those involving goals. But in many cases, they were different. One area in which Ministers had to establish priority lay in what kind of education should be most emphasized in the first decade of the country's statehood. This brought on the clash between those who favored immediate establishment of higher educational or technical institutions and those who favored a basic general education. Connected with this was the controversy over whether or not Bulgarians should be sent abroad for higher education. Another important priority problem was whether or not more time, money, and energy should be invested in educating a few quickly or all at a slower pace. This was no insignificant matter, since the new state desperately needed people with good technical educations to help operate railroads, banks, national defense, etc., in which the country had few trained personnel. In short, the country needed experts to help smooth the transition from subject status of an independent, modern, self-sufficient European state in the latter part of the nineteenth century. Despite its agricultural fertility and a well-developed middle class, Bulgaria remained economically backward in comparison to its more advanced European neighbors. It needed a supply of well-trained people if it was to advance on a course of modernization. Yet it also needed, if it was to progress as a democratic nation, a literate people who could partake in the process of managing the nation's political affairs. The Ministry of Public Instruction was called upon, time and again in the <u>Subranie</u>, to fulfill both tasks: that is, to train as quickly as possible a corps of professionals to govern the country while raising the level of education of all the citizens of the nation. The Ministry never succeeded in determining which should be given higher priority and attempted to do both, with mixed results. The Ministers certainly helped expand and strengthen the basic network of primary schools but at the cost of quality and financial security for the communal schools. On the other hand, by investing large sums of money in state schools of higher education with a general character, it attempted to supply the country with a pool of bureaucrats. The Ministers also invested considerable amounts of money in sending students abroad. This netted low returns when few students returned to serve their country. It also helped stir resentment on the part of those who disliked having to rely on foreign training for young Bulgarians, the future leaders of the country.

One of the most important issues in the matter of determining priorities involved the question of how much centralized government control should be imposed on the nation's school affairs. The officials of the Ministry of Public Instruction had to face the painful fact that the school system so proudly and carefully nurtured in the Renascence period might no longer answer the needs in the totally new situation Bulgaria faced after 1878. On the one hand, Bulgarians valued highly the traditions of local self-rule which had existed throughout the Ottoman period. Indeed, the Liberal Party used this tradition as the basis for claiming that the people were ready for full-fledged democratic government. On the other hand, the country's leaders were aware that the local organs of government often mishandled their responsibilities, especially in the realm of educational affairs. After considerable debate, the country chose to attempt to preserve as much as possible the independence of the communities in determining their school affairs. While this independence was lost in the 1890s, the course of action chosen in the first years of the country's existence was probably the best since it allowed further time to consider the impact and consequences of centralization.

Despite the hesitations and uncertainties and failures, the Ministry of Public Instruction accomplished a good deal in the period 1878-1885. It succeeded in devising standards and regulations to give the country some uniformity and direction in its educational system. It also succeeded in identifying the most pressing needs and weaknesses of the country's school system, even though the Ministry did not effectively eliminate such problems at this time.

One of the most significant achievements in this period was the preservation of educational affairs from damage that might have occurred given the political situation in the country. The political atmosphere was such that the schools were often blamed for any failures or setbacks in the political realm. The country was extremely fortunate to have in charge of the Ministry of Public Instruction men of outstanding character, training, and experience. They were also politically astute in defending the work of the Ministry from its detractors and from those who would have politicized educational affairs. Especially remarkable was that throughout the entire constitutional crisis, school affairs proceeded apace, despite the involvement of teachers and students in the struggle to restore the Turnovo Constitution.

Two other important factors also facilitated the work of the Ministry at this time. One was the absence of any serious Kulturkampf between Church and State in the realm of cultural affairs. The Church not only welcomed, but in fact, endorsed the activity of the secular institution of the Ministry of Public Instruction. Another significant factor was the general support for the work of education displayed by the representatives of the people in the <u>Subranie</u>. Many of the country's political elite had themselves been educated as a result of the locally-supported schools of the Renascence period and thus were favorably disposed, with some exceptions, to the work of the Ministry. In connection with this, the same political elite displayed a very favorable attitude to the idea of educating the masses; in contrast, the absence of such a positive attitude held back the advancement of more powerful countries such as Russia.

The emphasis on popular instruction served the country well. It accounted, unquestionably, for the smooth and unbroken advancement in the economic sphere as well as in the political one, at least until World War I. The exposure of every segment of the population to the rudiments of education certainly contributed to the successful working of a full-fledged parliamentary system where none had existed before. Universal mandatory education, which was achieved in practice as well as in theory several decades into independent existence, assured in turn the participation of all segments of the population in the democratic process. That advance was interrupted only by World War I and the rise of irredentist movements aimed at recapturing the provinces lost through the peace treaties ending the war.

In order to achieve what progress they did, the leaders of Bulgarian educational affairs built upon and utilized the traditions and accomplishments of the Bulgarian Renascence of the eighteenth and nineteenth centuries. Even though much of that heritage was outdated or destroyed by the process of independence, its significance cannot be discounted. The existence of so many schools within the country helped provide a larger pool of literate people than other countries have had on the eve of independence.

Despite the setbacks, obstacles, and difficulties, the Ministers of Public Instruction in seven years managed to fashion a comprehensive and fairly unified educational program designed to launch the country into modern development. The nation and people of Bulgaria reaped a rich harvest of the time and money invested in the institutions responsible for the development of its educational affairs in the very first years of its national existence. In this and many other respects, the spirit and heritage of the Renascence continued secure and unbroken.

SOURCES CONSULTED

PRIMARY SOURCES

I. **ARCHIVES** (all used in Sofia, Bulgaria)

    A. ARKHIVEN INSTITUT PRI BŬLGARSKATA AKADEMIIA NA NAUKITE

Fond 3   Josef K. Jireček

Fond 62K   Racho Karolev

Fond 17   Mikhail K. Sarafov

Fond 43   Dragan K. Tsankov

Fond 69K   Spas Vatsov

    B. ARKHIV NA INSTITUT ZA ISTORIIA PRI BŬLGARSKATA AKADEMIIA NA NAUKITE

Fond 4   British Foreign Office (photocopies of British consular reports from the collections of the British Museum in London)

    C. BŬLGARSKI ISTORICHESKI ARKHIV PRI NARODNATA BIBLIOTEKA "KIRIL I METODII"

Fond 10   Iliia R. Blŭskov

Fond 47   Nesho Bonchev

Fond 16   Todor S. Burmov

Fond 111   Marin S. Drinov

Fond 146   Vasil Drumev

Fond 66   Aleksandŭr Ekzarkh

Fond 69   Gabrovskoto uchilishte

Fond 19   Todor Ikonomov

Fond 156   Georgi Kirkov

D. DŬRZHAVEN OKRŬZHEN ARKHIV

Fond 5   Gabrovskoto gradsko-obshtinsko upravlenie

Fond 150K Gabrovska realna gimnaziia

E. SOFIISKI GRADSKI OKRŬZHEN DŬRZHAVEN ARKHIV

Fond 1   Sofiiski gradsko-obshtinski sŭvet

Fond 5   Sofiisko uchilishtno nastoiatelstvo

Fond 5K   Sofiisko uchilishtno nastoiatelstvo

Fond 41K   Samokovsko gradsko-obshtinsko upravlenie

F. TSENTRALEN DŬRZHAVEN ISTORICHESKI ARKHIV

Fond 708   Dŭrzhaven sŭvet

Fond 284   Ministerski sŭvet

Fond 173   Narodno Sŭbranie

Fond 405   Otdel narodnoto prosveshtenie i dukhovni dela pri Kantselariia na Ruskiia Imperatorski Komisar

Fond 104   Georgi Zhivkov

G. TSENTRALEN TSŬRKOVEN ISTORIKO-ARKHEOLO-LOGICHESKI MUSEI PRI SVETI SINOD: TSŬR-KOVNO-ISTORICHESKI OTDEL

Arkhiv na Stoian Kostov, Sekretar na Sveti Sinod

II. PUBLISHED SOURCES

A. PARLIAMENTARY PROCEEDINGS

Bulgaria. Ministerstvoto na pravosŭdieto. <u>Godishen sbornik ot zakoni na Bŭlgarskoto Kniazhestvo prieti ot Tŭrnovskoto Uchreditelno Narodno Sŭbranie prez 1879 god.</u> Sofia: 1887.

Bulgaria. Narodno Sŭbranie. <u>Protokolite na uchreditelno Bŭlgarsko Narodno Sŭbranie v Tŭrnovo.</u> Plovdiv: 1879.

_____. Stenograficheski dnevnitsi na chetvŭrtoto Obiknoveno Narodno Sŭbranie. Pŭrva redovna sesiia. Sofia: 1885-1886.

_____. Stenograficheski dnevnitsi na chetvŭrtoto Obiknoveno Narodno Sŭbranie. Sesiia izvŭnredna. Sofia: 1885.

_____. Stenograficheski dnevnitsi na chetvŭrtoto Obiknoveno Narodno Sŭbranie. Treta izvŭnredna sesiia. Sofia: 1885.

_____. Stenograficheski dnevnitsi na chetvŭrtoto Obiknoveno Narodno Sŭbranie. Vtorata redovna sesiia. Sofia: 1884.

_____. Stenograficheski dnevnitsi na pŭrvoto Obiknoveno Narodno Sŭbranie. Sofia: 1879.

_____. Stenograficheski dnevnitsi na tretoto Obiknoveno Narodno Sŭbranie. Pŭrva redovna sesiia. Sofia: 1883.

_____. Stenograficheski dnevnitsi na tretoto Obiknoveno Narodno Sŭbranie. Vtorata redovna sesiia. Sofia: 1883.

_____. Stenograficheski dnevnitsi na vtoroto Obiknoveno Narodno Sŭbranie. Sofia: 1880.

B. OFFICIAL PUBLICATIONS OF THE MINISTRY OF PUBLIC INSTRUCTION

Atanasov, V. ed. Otchet na dŭrzhavnata zanaiatchiinitsa za uchebnata 1883-84 do 1886-87 god. Sofia: 1887.

Balabanov, Nikola, and Manov, Andrei. Sbornik s otbrani okrŭzhni ot Osvobozhdenieto do kraia na 1942g. Sofia: 1943.

Blŭskov, Iliia R. "Izlozhenie do Ministra na Narodnata Prosveta za Shumenskiia ucheben okrug. 1885 god." Uchitelski vestnik, I (1885), 182.

/Bogdanov,K./ Otchet na Kiustendilskoto dŭrzhavno pedagogichesko triklasno i obraztsovo uchilishte za uchebnata 1899-1900 god. Sofia: 1901.

Brŭshlianov, Iacho. Otchet na Shumenskoto dŭrzhavno pedagogichesko i triklasno uchilishte za uchebnata 1897-1898 godina. Shumen: 1898.

Buchvarov, N., and Sharov, K., et.al. Otchet za sŭstoianieto na uchebnoto delo i fermata na dŭrzhavnoto zemledelchesko uchilishte pri grad Russe prez 1896-1897 uchebnata godina. Ruse: 1898.

Bulgaria. Ministerstvo na Narodnata Prosveta. Dokumenti za deinostŭta na Rusite po uredbata na grazhdanskoto upravlenie v Bŭlgariia ot 1877-1879 god. Edited by Muratov. Sofia: 1905.

_____. Dŭrzhaven Vestnik. 1879-1885.
 This was the official gazette for all the laws of the Principality of Bulgaria. For the greater part of the period 1879-1885, the publication of this gazette was the responsibility of the Ministry of Public Instruction. This work has been frequently cited since most of the laws and regulations of the Ministry appeared in the Dŭrzhaven Vestnik. Those that did not were listed in the Ucheben Vestnik listed below.

_____. "Kratki vesti ot nauchni i knizhovni sviat." Periodichesko spisanie na Bŭlgarskoto knizhovno druzhestvo, IV (1883), 165.

_____. Ucheben Vestnik. 1880-1885.
 This is the official gazette of the Ministry of Public Instruction and contains many laws, regulations, statutes, special instructions, etc. In conjunction with the Dŭrzhaven Vestnik (see above entry), it is an invaluable tool for locating the chief documents of the Ministry for this period. It has been cited extensively in this dissertation.

_____. Uchilishten sbornik koito sŭderzhava ustavi, pravila, instruktsiia, naredbi, razporezhdaniia, po uchebnoto delo v Kniazhestvo Bŭlgariia ot vreme na okupatsiiata do kraia na 1882 g. Sofia: 1883.
 This publication served for the Drinov period what the Ucheben Vestnik did for the 1880-1885 period. Selective rather than comprehensive.

Gorna-Oriakhovitsa. Godishen otchet na obshtinskoto triklasno i pedagogichesko uchilishte v grad Gorna-Oriakhovitsa za 1896-97 godina. Tŭrnovo: 1897.

Jireček, Josef Konstantin. Glavno izlozhenie do Negovo Visochestvo Kniaza vŭrkhu polozhenieto na uchebnoto delo v Kniazhestvo Bŭlgariia. Sofia: 1882.
    Compiled from early reports of the provincial school inspectors and from Jireček's own research, this source is unquestionably one of the most vital for this period of 1878-1885.

Kiustendil. Otchet za Kiustendilskoto dŭrzhavno pedagogichesko triklasno i obraztsovo uchilishte za 1896-97 uchebna godina. Sofia: 1891.

Mitev, T.P. ed. Lomsko dŭrzhavno pedagogichesko i triklasno uchilishte: vtori godishen otchet za uchebna 1897-98 godina. Lom: 1898.

Ruse. Otchet za prakticheskoto zemledelchesko uchilishte pri obraztsovi chiflik krai grad Ruse za 1886-1887 g. Ruse: 1887.

Silistra. Pŭrvi godishen otchet za sŭstoianieto na uchebnoto delo na Silistrenskoto dŭrzhavno triklasno pedagogichesko i pŭrvonachalno uchilishte za 1896-97 godina. Sofia: 1897.

Strezov, S.K. Godishen otchet na obshtinskoto triklasno i pedagogichesko uchilishte v grad Gorna-Oriakhovitsa za 1896-97 uchebna godina. Tŭrnovo: 1897.

Vankov, Nikola Ivan. Iz Arkhivata na Ministerstvoto na Narodnata Prosveta. Sofia: 1905.
    An extremely valuable compilation from the reports of the provincial school inspectors discussing conditions of education in the country.

C. COLLECTED DOCUMENTS

Arnaudov, Mikhail. ed. Kliment Tŭrnovski, Vasil Drumev, za 25 godishninata ot smŭrtata mu; izsledvaniia, spomeni, i dokumenti. Sofia: 1927.

Blŭskov, Iliia R. ed. Materiali po istoriiata na nasheto vŭzrazhdane: grad Shumen. Shumen: 1907.

Bulgaria. Ministerstvo na Vŭnshnite Raboti i Izpovedaniiata. Korespondentsiia po Ministerstvoto na vŭnshnite raboti i na ispovedaniiata (ot 26 marta do 15 oktomvriia 1880). Sofia: 1880.

Bŭlgarska akademiia na naukite. Dokumenti za novata istoriia na Bŭlgarskiia narod, iz vienskite dŭrzhavni arkhivi (1830-1877). Edited by Petŭr Noikov. 2 vols. Sofia: 1948-1951.

_____. Materiali za istoriiata na Sofiia. Sofia: 1910.

Dimov, Georgi. ed. Bŭlgarsko knizhovno druzhestvo. Dokumenti za istoriiata na Bŭlgarsko knizhovno druzhestvo v Brăila 1876-1878. Sofia: 1958.

Georgiev, Iordan. "Dokumenti po uchebnoto delo v Vratsa, Gradets, Elena, Gabrovo, Razgrad, Sofiia, Sliven, i Shumen." Uchilishten pregled, XII (April, 1907), 370-397.

_____. "Materiali po uchebnoto delo v grada Vidin prez 1870-1872 god." Uchilishten pregled, XII (1908), 1-47.

Ivanov, Vicho. Nesho Bonchev, pŭrviiat Bŭlgarski kritik, 1839-1878-1939: Pisma i dokumenti. Plovdiv: 1939.

Khristov, Khristo. ed. Dokumenti za istoriia na Bŭlgarskoto knizhovno druzhestvo (1878-1911). Sofia: 1966.

Kirov, G. "Materiali za istoriiata na Kotlenskoto uchilishte." Sbornik za narodni umotvoreniia, XXII-XXIII (1906-1907), 1-64.

"Materiali za istoriiata na uchebnoto delo v Ruse i Silistra." Uchilishten pregled, XII (1907), 562-578.

Mikhov, Nikola V. Naselenieto na Turtsiia i Bŭlgariia prez XVIII i XIX; bibliografsko-statistichni izsledvaniia. Sofia: 1958.

Nikitin, S.A., Konoveeva, V.D., and Gandeva, K. eds. Osvobozhdenie Bolgarii ot turetskogo iga. Dokumenti v trekh tomakh. 3 vols. Moscow: 1967.

Palauzov, Nikolai. "Dokumenti ot vremeto na Bŭlgarskoto vŭzrazhdane." <u>Periodichesko spisanie na Bŭlgarsko knizhovno druzhestvo</u>, LVIII (1899), 619-629.

_____. "Tri pisma ot Odeski Bulgarii." <u>Periodichesko spisanie na Bŭlgarskoto knizhovno druzhestvo,</u> LX (1899), 987-989.

Paskaleva, Virzhiniia. ed. <u>Dokumenti za Bŭlgarskata istoriia iz germanski arkhivi, 1829-1877</u>. Sofia: 1963.

Russia, Glavnyi Ustav. <u>Sbornik materialov po grazhdanskomy upravlenii i okupatsii v Bolgariia v 1877-1879 g.</u> Edited by N. Ovsianyi. St. Petersburg: 1903-1907.

Veleva, Darina. <u>Dokumenti za Bŭlgarskoto vŭzrazhdane ot arkhiva na Stefan I. Verkovich, 1860-1893.</u> Sofia: 1969.

Vŭzvŭzova-Karateodorova, K. "Nepublikuvani pisma na Konstantin Irechek, sŭkhraniavani v Bŭlgarski istoricheski arkhiv, do nashi obshtestvenitsi i knizhovnitsi." <u>Izvestiia na narodnata biblioteka "Kiril i Metodii,"</u> VII (1967), 169-221.

Zlatarski, Vasil. ed. "Materiali po tsŭrkovnata borba." <u>Sbornik za narodni umotvoreniia</u>, XXII-XXIII (1906-1907), 1-80.

_____. "Materiali za istoriiata na Bŭlgarskoto vŭzrazhdane." <u>Sbornik za narodni umotvoreniia</u>, XV (1898), 1-32.

D. COLLECTED WORKS AND CONTEMPORARY LITERATURE

Aprilov, Vasil E. <u>Sŭbrani sŭchineniia</u>. Edited by Mikhail Arnaudov. Sofia: 1940.

Balabanov, Marko. "Pismo (ot doktora P. Beron) za urezhdane Bŭlgarskite uchilishta predi 5-60 godini." <u>Periodichesko spisanie na Bŭlgarskoto knizhovno druzhestvo</u>, XXXI (1889), 131.

Beron /Berovich/, Petŭr. <u>Sbornik Dr. Petŭr Beron po sluchai stogodishninata na Ribniia bukvar, 1824-1924.</u> Edited by Khristo Negentsov. Sofia: 1926.

Blagoev, Dimitŭr. *Izbranni proizvedeniia.* Sofia: 1950.

Blŭskov, Iliia R. "Nuzhdata ot revis'or Inspektor nad selskite uchilishte." *Uchilishte* (Bucharest and Ruse), III (1873), 145, 153, 162.

Bonchev, Nesho. "Za uchilishte." *Periodichesko spisanie na Bŭlgarskoto knizhovno druzhestvo (Brăila)*, I (1871), 3-16, 26-51.

Bulgaria. Glavna Direktsiia na Statistikata. *Annuaire statistique du Royaume de Bulgarie année 1909.* Sofia: 1910.

──────. *Résultats définitifs du recensement de la population le 1er janvier 1881.* Sofia: 1890.

──────. *Spisŭk naselenite mesta v Kniazhestvo Bŭlgariia. 1 ianuari 1883.* Sofia: 1894.

──────. *Statistikata na vsichki detsa v Bŭlgariia, podlezhashti na zadŭlzhitelno uchenie kakto i na oniia koito sa uspulniavali tova zadŭlzhenie prez 1888-1889 uchebna godina.* Sofia: 1889.

──────. *Uchilishtna statistika na Kniazhestvo Bŭlgariia prez 1883, 1889, 1890, i 1891 uchebna godina.* Sofia: 1890-1891.

Drinov, Marin. *Istoricheski pregled na Bŭlgarskata tsurkva ot samoto i nachalo i do dnes.* Vienna: 1869.

──────. *Sŭchineniia.* Edited by Vasil N. Zlatarski. 3 vols. Sofia: 1909-1915.

──────. *Zapiska za deiatelnostŭta na privremennoto Rusko pravitelstvo v Bŭlgariia.* Tŭrnovo: 1879.

Drumev, Vasil. (Metropolitan Clement of Tŭrnovo). "Namestvaneto na svetskata vlast' v cherkovnite raboti." *Periodichesko spisanie na Bŭlgarskoto Knizhovno druzhestvo*, XI-XII (1876), 19-73.

──────. *Sŭchinenie.* Edited by Docho Lekov and Ivan Sestrimski. 2 vols. Sofia: 1968.

———. "Zhivotopisanie." *Periodichesko spisanie na Bŭlgarskoto knizhovno druzhestvo (Braila)*, I (1870), 17-36; II (1871), 30-52; III (1872), 17-41.

Geshov, Ivan E. "Chinovnicheskiiat proletariiat (kritika vŭrkhu srednoto obrazovanie)." *Periodichesko spisanie na Bŭlgarskoto knizhnovno druzhestvo*, XIX (1886), 118-133.

Giuzelev, Ivan. "Rŭkovodstvata po pŭrvonachalnoto obuchenie." *Periodichesko spisanie na Bŭlgarskoto knizhovno druzhestvo*, XI (1898), 136-147.

Gruev, Ivan. "Vzaimnoto uchilishte v Koprivshtitsa prez 1837-1838 i 1838-1839 godini." *Periodichesko spisanie na Bŭlgarskoto knizhovno druzhestvo*, XIX (1896), 688.

Jireček, Josef K. *Korespondentsiia s Marin Drinov*. Edited by Vladimir Sis. Sofia: 1924.

Ivanchev, T. "Gramotnostŭta na naselenieto v Bŭlgariia." *Uchilishten pregled*, I (1896), 27-66.

Karavelov, Liuben. *Sŭbrani sŭchineniia*. Edited by Mikhail Arnaudov. 10 vols. Sofia: 1966-1968.

Lekov, Docho. ed. *Iz Arkhiva na Vasil Drumev, Kliment Tŭrnovski*. Sofia: 1973.

Miiatev, Petŭr. ed. *Iz Arkhiva na Konstantin Irechek. Dokumenti za obshtestvenno-politicheskata i kulturnata istoriia na Bŭlgariia ot 1871-1914 god.* 3 vols. Sofia: 1953-1963.

Ned'ov, Tsvetko. "Po istoriia na uchebnoto delo u nas (Razprostranenie na zvuchnata metoda." *Sbornik za narodni umotvoreniia*, XIV (1897), 726-732.

Thomson, Edward. *Our Oriental Missions. Bulgaria and China*. New York: 1870.

Uspenskii, F. *Obrazovanie vtorago bolgarskago tsarstva*. St. Petersburg: 1879.

Usta-Genchov, D. ed. *Statisticheski sbornik na Kniazhestvo Bŭlgariia*. Sofia: 1897.

E. MEMOIRS AND TRAVEL ACCOUNTS

Balabanov, Marko. Stranitsi ot politicheskoto ni vŭzrazhdane. Sofia: 1904.

Black, Floyd. The American College of Sofia: A Chapter in American Bulgarian Relations. Boston: 1958.

Blŭskov, Iliia R. Spomeni iz uchenicheskiia, uchitelskiia, i pisatelskiia mi zhivot. Sofia: 1907.

Brakalov, Ivan T. Spomeni i belezhki po uchebnoto delo. Sofia: 1927.

Drumev, Vasil. "Avtobiografichni belezhki." Dukhovna kultura, XXXI (November-December, 1951), 2-10.

Enicherev, N.G. "Spomeni ot moeto uchitelstvo v Prilep." Sbornik za narodni umotvoreniia, XIX (1903),

Ganchev, Dobre. Spomeni, 1864-1887. Edited by Stoian Argirov. Sofia: 1939.

Ignat'ev, Nikolai P., Count. "Zapiski grafa N.P. Ignat'eva, 1864-1874." Izvestiia Ministerstva inostrannykh del, I (1914), 93-135.

Iurukov, Daniil. Spomeni iz politicheskiia zhivot na Bŭlgariia. 2nd. ed. Sofia: 1932.

Jireček, Josef K. Bŭlgarski dnevnik, 1879-1884. Edited by K. Zlatarski. Translated from the Czech by Stoian Argirov. 2 vols. Sofia: 1930.

_____. Pŭtuvanie po Bŭlgariia. Edited by Evlogii Buzhashki and Velizar Velkov. Sofia: 1974.

Kanitz, Felix P. Donau-Bulgarien und der Balkan. Historish-geographish-etnographishe Reisestudien aus den Jahren 1860-1875. Leipzig: 1875-1879.

Mitev, N. "Bŭlgarskiiat periodichen pechat v Makedoniia ot 1878 do 1913 g. Spomeni." Slaviane, II (1966), 32-33.

Ostrander, L.F. Fifty Years in Bulgaria. Jubilee Publication of the Collegiate and Theological Institute of the American Board of Commissioners of

Foreign Missions. Samokov: 1911.

Vasil'ov, Toma. Spomeni za litsa i sŭbitiia prez XIX-XX vek. Sofia: 1934.

Washburn, George. Fifty Years in Constantinople and Recollections of Robert College. Boston: 1909.

F. CONTEMPORARY MAGAZINES

Bratski trud. Moscow. 1860-1862.

Chitalishte. Istanbul. 1870-1875.

Rŭkovoditel za osnovnoto uchenie. Istanbul. 1874.

Slavianski sbornik. St. Petersburg. 1877.

Uchilishte. Bucharest and Ruse. 1870-1876.

G. CONTEMPORARY NEWSPAPERS

Bŭlgarski glas. Sofia. 1880-1883.

Dunavska zora. Brăila. 1867-1871.

Izgrev. Kiustendil. 1900-1903.

Maritsa. Plovdiv. 1878-1885.

Nezavisimost. Bucharest. 1872-1874.

Nezavisimost. Sofia. 1880-1883.

Svoboda. Bucharest. 1869-1873.

Sŭvetnik. Istanbul. 1863-1865.

Tselokŭpna Bŭlgariia. Sofia. 1879.

SECONDARY SOURCES

I. BOOKS, PAMPHLETS, AND DISSERTATIONS

Aleksiev, Nikola. Starobŭlgarska knizhnina: Kiril i

Metodii, Episkop Konstantin, Chernorizets Kharabŭr i drugi. Sofia: 1948.

Andreev, Mikhail. Istoriia na Bŭlgarskata burzhoazna dŭrzhava i pravo (1878-1917). Sofia: 1975.

Angelov, Dimitŭr S. Istoriia bolgarskogo gosudarstva i prava. Translated from the Bulgarian by A.S. Mikhlina, V.M. Safronova, M.D. Mikhlinoi. Moscow: 1962.

Apanasewicz, Nellie M., and Rosen, Seymour M. Education in Bulgaria. Washington, D.C.: 1965.

Arnaudov, Mikhail. Bŭlgarski pisateli: Zhivot, tvorchestvo, idei. 6 vols. Sofia: 1929-1950.

──────. Liuben Karavelov: zhivot, delo, epokha. 1834-1879. Sofia: 1972.

──────. Tvortsi na Bŭlgarskoto vŭzrazhdane. Pŭrvi vŭzrozhdentsi. Sofia: 1969.

Atanasov, Petko. ed. Iubileina kniga na Rusenskata narodna mŭzhka gimnaziia, 1884-1934. Ruse: 1935.

Balabanov, Marko. Gavril Krŭstevich--naroden deets, knizhevnik, sŭdiia, upravitel. Sofia: 1914.

Balamezov, Stefan G. Ministrite--tekhnata roliia i tekhnata vlast' v parlamentarnata monarkhiia. Sofia: 1914.

──────. Sravnitelno i bŭlgarsko konstitutsionalno pravo. 2 vols. Sofia: 1936.

Berovski, Aleksandŭr N. Pŭrviiat rektor i pŭrvata bogoslovska shkola v Bŭlgariia. Sofia: 1939.

Beshkov, Liuben, Todorov, Petŭr, and Vurtuninska, Rada. Edin vek klasno uchilishte v Dobrich (Tolbukhin). Sofia: 1972.

Bobchev, Stefan. La Lutte du peuple bulgare pour une église nationale indépendante. Sofia: 1938.

————————. La Société bulgare sous la domination ottomane. Les tchorbadjis bulgare comme institution sociale et administrative. Sofia: 1935.

————————. Le Peuple bulgare et ses aspirations dans le passé et le present. Sofia: 1915.

————————. Quelques remarques sur le droit coutumier bulgare pendant l'époque de la domination ottomane. Belgrade: 1934.

————————. Titre et état des Hadjis bulgares au point de vue historiques et social. Sofia: 1936.

Bogdanov, Ivan. Bŭlgarska literatura v dati i kharakteristiki. Sofia: 1966.

————————. Iliia Blŭskov (1839-1913) naroden prosvetitel i pisatel. Sofia: 1940.

Boichev, T.N. Iubileina istoriia na 25 godishnina Bŭlgariia. Sofia: 1903.

Borshukov, Ivan. Istoriia na bŭlgarskata zhurnalistika, 1844-1877, 1878-1885. Sofia: 1965.

Bŭlgarska akademiia na naukite. Izsledvaniia v chest na Marin Drinov. Sofia: 1960.

Chakŭrov, Naiden. Istoriia na Bŭlgarskoto obrazovanie do Vŭzrazhdaneto, po leksiite. Sofia: 1948.

————————. Istoriia na Bŭlgarskoto obrazovanie. Chast pŭrva. Sofia: 1955.

————————. Istoriia na Bŭlgarskoto obrazovanie. Chast vtora. Sofia: 1957.

————————, and Atanasov, Zhecho. Istoriia na obrazovanieto i pedagogicheskata misŭl v Bŭlgariia. Sofia: 1962.

————————. Istoriia na pedagogiiata. Sofia: 1949.

————————. Khristomattiia po istoriia na bŭlgarskoto obrazovanie do poiava na Marksicheskata pedagogicheska misŭl u nas. Sofia: 1953.

_____. Ocherk po istoriia na bŭlgarskoto obrazovanie: pomagalo za pedagogicheskite uchilishta i uchitelskite instituti. Sofia: 1952.

_____. Uchilishtno zakonodatelstvo. Sofia: 1950.

Chilingirov, Stilian. Bŭlgarski chitalishta predi osvobozhdenieto; prinos kŭm istoriiata na bŭlgarskoto vŭzrazhdane. Sofia: 1930.

Clarke, James F. Bible Societies, American Missionaries and the National Revival of Bulgaria. New York: 1971.

Danchov, Nikola G., and Danchov, Ivan G. Bŭlgarska entsiklopediia. Sofia: 1956.

Dimitrov, Ilcho. Kniazŭt, konstitutsiiata, i narodŭt. Sofia: 1972.

Dimitrov, M., and Dinekov, P. eds. Khristo Botev: sbornik po sluchai 100 godini ot rozhdenieto mu. Sofia: 1949.

Dorosiev, Luka I. Nashite klasni, sredni i spetsialni uchilishta predi Osvobozhdenieto. Sofia: 1925.

_____. Neofit Rilski, patriarkh na bŭlgarskite knizhovnitsi. Sofia: 1931.

_____. Pŭrvi nashi uchilishta, uchiteli, i knizhovnitsi. Sofia: 1929.

_____. Uchebnoto delo v Koprivshtitsa predi Osvobozhdenieto. Sofia: 1925.

_____. Uchebnoto delo v Sofiia, 1878-1928gg. Sofia: 1928.

Duichev, Ivan. Il Cattolicesimo in Bulgaria nel sec. XVII. Vol. CXI-CXII. Orientalia Christiana Analecta. Rome: 1937.

Gandev, Khristo N. Faktori na Bŭlgarskoto vŭzrazhdanne. Sofia: 1943.

Ganev, Khristo. Prinos kŭm istoriiata na Bŭlgarskiia uchitelski s'iuz, 1895-1905. Sofia: 1905.

Gechev, Minko. Kiliinite uchilishta v Bŭlgariia: sŭzdavane i razprostranenie. Sofia: 1967.

Girginov, Aleksandur. Dŭrzhavnoto ustroistvo na Bŭlgariia. Sofia: 1921.

Iordanov, Veliko. Istoriia na narodnata biblioteka v Sofiia. Sofia: 1930.

———. L'Instruction publique en Bulgarie. Sofia: 1925.

Iubileen sbornik na Varnenskata dŭrzhavna mŭzhka gimnaziia "Ferdinand I" po sluchai 50 godishninata na gimnaziiata. 1879-1929. Varna: 1930.

Ivanov, Iordan. Bŭlgarski periodichen pechat ot vŭzrazhdane mu do dnes. Sofia: 1893.

Kaliiandzhiev, Tsani. Profesionalnoto obrazovanie u nas. Varna: 1925.

Karanovich, Milenko. "The Development of Education in Serbia, 1838-1858." Unpublished Ph.D. dissertation, University of Wisconsin in Madison: 1974.

Karolev, Racho. Istoriiata na Gabrovskoto uchilishte. Sofia: 1926.

Kasŭrov, Luka. Entsiklopedicheski rechnik. 6 vols. Plovdiv: 1899.

Kazamias, Andreas M. Education and the Quest for Modernity in Turkey. Chicago: 1966.

Khristov, Georgi. Svishtov v minaloto. Svishtov: 1927.

Khristov, Khristo. Bŭlgarskite obshtini prez vŭzrazhdaneto. Sofia: 1973.

———. Obrazovanieto na Bŭlgariia i politikata na zapadnite dŭrzhavi (1877-1878). Sofia: 1968.

Kiril, Bulgarian Patriarch. Bŭlgarskata ekzarkhiia v Odrinsko i Makedoniia sled Osvoboditelnata voina (1877-1878). Sofia: 1970.

_____. Katolicheskata propaganda sred Bŭlgarite prez vtorata polovina na XIX vek. 1859-1865. Sofia: 1962.

_____. Prinos kŭm Bŭlgarskiia tsŭrkoven vŭpros; dokumenti ot Avstriiskoto konsulstvo v Solun. Sofia: 1961.

_____. Sto godini ot uchrediavaneto na Bŭlgarskata Ekzarkhiia: sbornik statei. Sofia: 1971.

Krachunov, Krŭstiu. Iz Bŭlgarskata kulturna istoriia. Sofia: 1935.

_____. Marin Drinov, 1838-1906gg; zhivot i deinost. Sofia: 1938.

Krŭstev, Khristo, and Stefanov, Ivan. Iubileina kniga na pŭrva Sofiiska mŭzhka gimnaziia, 1879-1929. Sofia: 1929.

Kŭnchov, Vasil. Izbrani proizvedeniia. Sofia: 1970.

Laveleye, Emile de. La Peninsule des Balkans. 2 vols. Paris: 1888.

Markova, Zina. Bŭlgarskoto tsŭrkovno natsionalno dvizhenie do krimskata voina. Sofia: 1976.

McKay, Donald C. ed. Essays in the History of Modern Europe. New York: 1936.

Meininger, Thomas A. "The Formation of a Nationalist Bulgarian Intelligentsia, 1835-1878." Unpublished Ph.D. dissertation, University of Wisconsin in Madison, 1974.

Mikhov, N. Sofiia do osvobozhdenieto. Bibliografichesko-statisticheska skitsa. Sofia: 1942.

Milkova, Fani. Istoriia na bŭlgarskata dŭrzhava i pravo (izvori, isledvaniia, tezisii). Sofia: 1974.

Mojzes, Paul B. "A History of the Congregational and Methodist Churches in Bulgaria and Yugoslavia." Unpublished Ph.D. dissertation, Boston University: 1965.

Negentsov, Khristo, and Vazov, Ivan. Obrazovanieto v
    Iztochna Rumeliia, 1879-1885. Sofia: 1959.

Nikolov, Eniu, and Minkov, Tsvetan. Stroiteli na novo-
    bŭlgarskoto obrazovanie. Sofia: 1935.

Nikov, Petŭr. Bŭlgarskoto vŭzrazhdane v Varna i Varnen-
    sko. Mitropolit Ioakim i negovata korresponden-
    tsiia. Sofia: 1934.

──────. Vŭzrazhdane na Bŭlgarskiia narod, tsŭrkovno-
    natsionalni borbi i postizheniia. Sofia: 1934.

Noikov, Petŭr. Pogled vŭrkhu razvitieto na bŭlgarskoto
    obrazovanie do Paisiia. Sofia: 1925.

Obreshkov, Obreshko. Tezisi po istoriia na Bŭlgarskoto
    obrazovanie za II zadochen kurs na nachalnite
    uchiteli. Sofia: 1951.

Ovsianyi, N. Bolgariia i bolgary. St. Petersburg: 1900.

Paskaleva, Virzhiniia. Bŭlgarskata prez vŭzrazhdaneto;
    istoricheski ocherk. Sofia: 1964.

Penev, Boian. Istoriia na novata Bŭlgarska literatura.
    Sofia: 1933

Petrovich, Michael B. The Emergence of Russian Pan-
    slavism, 1856-1870. New York: 1956.

Prosenichkov, I. ed. Iubileina kniga na Rusenskata
    narodna mŭzhka gimnaziia "Kniaz Boris" po slu-
    chai 50 godishninata i. Ruse: 1934.

Radev, Simeon. Stroitelite na sŭvremenna Bŭlgariia.
    2 vols. Sofia: 1973.

Raichev, Raicho. Narodnata biblioteka v Sofiia. Sofia:
    1928.

Russell, William B. Schools in Bulgaria, with Special
    Reference to the Influence of the Agrarian Party
    on Elementary and Secondary Education. New York:
    1924.

Sekulov, B. Nashite pravitelstva i ministri ot Osvobozh-
    denieto do dnes. Sofia: 1911.

Shishmanov, Ivan D. Pŭrvoto bŭlgarsko tŭrgovsko uchilishte na D.E. Shishmanov v Svishtov. Sofia: 1903.

Shopov, Atanas. Bŭlgariia v tsŭrkovno otnoshenie. Plovdiv: 1889.

Snegarov, Ivan. Bŭlgarska tsŭrkovna istoriia. Sofia: 1947.

Sofia. University of. Almanakh na Sofiiskiia universitet Sveti Kliment Okhridski. Zhivotopisni svedeniia za prepodavateli, 1888-1939. Sofia: 1940.

Stanimirov, Stanimir. Istoriia na Bŭlgarskata Tsŭrkva. Sofia: 1925.

_____. Iz tsŭrkovnata istoriia na grad Lovech. Sofia: 1930.

Stoianov, Man'o. Bŭlgarska vŭzrozhdenska knizhnina: Analitichen repertoar na Bŭlgarskite knigi i periodichni izdaniiata, 1806-1878. 2 vols. Sofia: 1957-1959.

Stefan, Exarch of Bulgaria. Bŭlgarskata tsŭrkva. Sofia: 1932.

Stoianov, Man'o. Pŭrvite Bŭlgarski bukvari. Sofia: 1964.

Tabakov, Nikola, ed. Sbornik "Dobri P. Chintulov" (1822-1922) izdava iubileen komitet po sluchai stogodishninata ot rozhdenieto mu. Sliven: 1922.

Trifonov, Iurdan. Vasil Drumev, Kliment Branitski i Tŭrnovski. Sofia: 1926.

Tsonkov, Dimo. Razvitie na osnovnoto obrazovanie v Bŭlgariia ot 1878 do 1928 godina. Sofia: 1928.

Tsvetkova, Bistra. Izvŭnredni danŭtsi i dŭrzhavni povinnosti v Bŭlgarskite zemi pod turska vlast'. Sofia: 1958.

_____. Turski feodalen red i bŭlgarskiiat narod. Sofia: 1962.

USSR. Akademiia naukh. *Iz istoriia russko-bolgarskikh otnoshenii: sbornik statei.* Moscow: 1958.

_____. *Osvobozhdenie Bolgarii ot turetskogo iga: sbornik statei.* Moscow: 1953.

Umlenski, Ivan. ed. *Pŭrva gimnaziia "Neofit Rilski" Kiustendil. Osemdeset godini 1879-1959. Iubileen sbornik.* Kiustendil: 1959.

Vankov, Nikola Ivan, and Minev, Petŭr. *Razvoi na uchebnoto delo i uchilishtnoto zakonodatelstvo v Bŭlgariia.* Sofia: 1925.

Vasilev, Georgi pop. *Ucheben sŭvet i ucheben komitet.* Sofia: 1925.

Vladikin, Liubomir. *Istoriia na Tŭrnovskata konstitutsiia.* Sofia: 1936.

Vlaikov, Todor. *Prinos kŭm vupros na nashata obrazovatelna sistema.* Pleven: 1929.

Von Mach, Richard. *The Bulgarian Exarchate: Its History and the Extent of Its Authority in Turkey.* London: 1907.

Vŭrchov, Khristo B. *Konstitutsiiata na Bŭlgarskata pravoslavna tsŭrkva. Istoriia i razvoi na ekzarkhiiskiia ustav, 1871-1921.* Sofia: 1920.

Zhekov, Aleksandŭr N. *Svetlite figuri na Tŭrnovskite ierari.* Turnovo: 1921.

Zlatarski, V.D. *Iubileina kniga na V. Tŭrnovskata narodna gimnaziia "Sv. Kiril" po sluchai na 50 godishninata ot osnovavaneto i.* Tŭrnovo: 1933.

II. ARTICLES IN JOURNALS AND NEWSPAPERS

Améro, Justin. "Le Mouvement bulgare: ses causes et ses consequences." *Revue contemporaine*, XX (1861), 76-104.

Angelov, Dimitŭr. "Deloto na Konstantin Irechek." *Otechestven front*, July 24, 1955, p. 1.

_____. "Deloto na Prof. Marin Drinov." <u>Narodna prosveta,</u> XII (1956), 51-58.

_____. "K. Irechek i negovoto dialo." <u>Istoricheski pregled</u>, XI (1955), 100-112.

Atanasov, Zhecho G. "Marin Drinov--zasluzhil prosveten deets. Po povod petdesetgodishninata ot smŭrta mu." <u>Semeistvo i uchilishte</u>, VIII, 4 (1956), 20-22.

_____. "Marin Drinov--belezhit prosveten deets." <u>Narodna prosveta</u>, XIV, 12 (1958), 89-92.

_____. "Prosvetnata deinost na Marin Drinov prez vremennoto rusko upravlenie." <u>Godishnik na Sofiiskia universitet: filosofsko-istoricheski fakultet</u>, LI, 2 (1957), 61-77.

Baiadzhiev, Iliia V. "Uchebnoto delo v seloto Stelcha predi Osvobozhdenieto." <u>Narodna prosveta</u>, XVIII, 3 (1962), 89-93.

Balabanov, Marko D. "Todor S. Burmov." <u>Letopis na Bŭlgarskoto knizhovno druzhestvo</u>, VII (1907), 84-119.

Bobchev, Stefan C. "Metropolit Kliment (1841-1901)." <u>Bŭlgarska sbirka</u>, VIII (August, 1901), 1-16.

Boshniakov, D. "Bŭlgarskiiat dnevnik na Irechek. Bŭlgariia predi 50 godini, gledana prez ochilata na edin Evropeetz." <u>Sila</u>, November 4, 1930, pp. 3-4.

Bozhinov, Voain. "Solunskata gimnaziia "Kiril i Metodii" i obshtestveno-politicheskiia zhivot na bŭlgarskoto naselenie (1880-1913)." <u>Istoricheski pregled</u>, XXVII, 4 (1971), 87-95.

Bradinska, R.N. ""Vŭznikvaneto i razvitieto na devicheskite uchilishta prez epokata na Vŭzrazhdaneto kato faktor za probŭzhdaneto i vŭvlichaneto na zhenata i natsionalnoosvoboditelnoto dvizhenie." <u>Trudove na Vishiia ikonomicheski institut Karl Marks</u>, III (1962), 317-355.

Chakŭrov, Naiden. "Liuben Karavelov--viden predstavitel

na nashata revoliutsionna pedagocheska misŭl."
Narodna prosveta, XV, 3 (March, 1959), 75-84.

_____. "Marin Drinov i razvitieto na Bŭlgarskoto obrazovanie po sluchai 50 godini ot smŭrtta mu."
Uchilishtna praktika, VIII, 3 (1956), 161-173.

Chilingirov, Stilian. "Materialnoto i sotsialno plozhenie na Bŭlgarskiia uchitel predi Osvobozhdenieto." *Uchilishten pregled*, XXXVIIII (December, 1939), 1209-1225.

Datsov, S.Z. "Spas Vatsov (1856-1928)." *Letopis na Bŭlgarskata akademiia na naukite*, XI (1927-1928), 54-65.

Diakovich, A. "Pŭrviiat ofitsioz. K. Irechek kato bŭlgarski zhurnalist." *Vestnik na vestnitsite*, January 8, 1941, pp.1-3.

Dimitrov, M. "Bŭlgarskite chitalishta v Rumŭniia. Iz revoliutsionnoto minalo." *Chitalishte* (Sofia), II (1966), 7-8.

Dragova, Nadezhda. "Dobri Voinikov--vdŭkhnoven vŭzrozhdenski uchitel." *Narodna prosveta*, XIV, 5 (May, 1958), 90-100.

Dramaliev, K. "Doktor Konstantin Irechek prŭv organizator na uchebnoto delo u nas." *Narod*, April 14, 1948, p. 4.

Gandev, Khristo N. "Ruskoto okupatsionno upravlenie (1877-1879)." *Bŭlgarski misŭl*, XI (1936), 633-642.

Ganov, Banko. "Pedagogicheski idei v Paisievata 'Istoria slaviianobŭlgarska'." *Narodna prosveta*, XVIII, 10 (1962), 90-101.

Gechev, M.M. "Neofit Rilski--pŭrvi novobŭlgarski uchitel." *Narodna prosveta*, XII (January, 1956), 46-53.

_____. "Prosvetnoto delo na Konstantin Velichkov."
Narodna prosveta, XIII, 12 (1957), 49-55.

_____. "Sofroni Vrachanski--belezhit prosvetitel i knizhovnik." Narodna prosveta, SVI, 7 (January, 1960), 85-73.

Georgiev, Iordan pop. "Dokumenti po uchebnoto delo v Vratsa, Gradets, Elena, Gabrovo, Razgrad, Sofiia, Sliven, i Shumen." Uchilishten pregled, XII, 4 (1907), 370-397.

_____. "Selo Kelifarevo i manastirŭt mu Sv. Bogoroditsa." Periodichesko spisanie na Bŭlgarsko knizhovno druzhestvo, LXVII (1906), 427-448.

Georgiev, Liuben. "Dobri Chintulov naroden uchitel." Narodna prosveta, XII, 9 (1956), 60-64.

Georgov, Ivan A. "Nekolko dumi za nashite uchitelski sŭbori predi osvobozhdenieto." Uchilishten pregled, VI, 4 (1901), 302-305.

Giaurov, K. "Tsŭrkva i dŭrzhava." Dukhovna kultura, I, 13-14 (1922), 88-93.

Gospodinov, Iurdan S. "Stranitsi iz prosvetnoto minalo na Preslav, 1800-1878g." Uchilishten pregled, XXI (April, 1921), 228-244.

Gruev, I. "Vzaimnoto uchilishte v Koprivshtitsa prez 1837/38, 1838/39 uchebni godini." Periodichesko spisanie na Bŭlgarsko knizhovno druzhestvo, LII-LIII (1896), 688-695.

Haumant, Émile, "Les Origines de la lutte pour la Macédoine." Le Monde slave, X (October, 1926), 52-66.

Iordanov, Veliko. "Literaturno vŭzpitanie i obrazovanie v nashite uchilishte." Dukhovna kultura, I, 1-2 (1920), 63-66.

Ivanov, Boris D. "Isoricheski pogled vŭrkhu sistemata za podgotovka na nachalni uchiteli u nas." Narodna prosveta, XIII, 11 (November, 1957), 53-61.

Ivanov, Emanuil. "Ivan N. Giuzelev." Letopis na Bŭlgarsko knizhovno druzhestvo, XII (1915-1917), 156-160.

Ivanov, Konstantin. "Bolgradskata gimnaziia." Uchilishten pregled, XXXIV (March, 1935), 312-335.

Ivanovich, T. "Gramotnost na naselenieto v Bŭlgariia." Uchilishten pregled, I, 1 (1896), 27-66.

Karadzhov, S. "Georgi I. Kirkov." Letopis na Bŭlgarsko knizhovno druzhestvo, XII (1928-1929), 179-181.

Kosev, D. "Prosvetnoto dvizhenie v Bŭlgariia prez pŭrvata polovina na XIX vek." Uchilishten pregled, II, 2 (1897), 173-192.

Krachunov, Krŭstiu. "Marin Drinov i Tŭrnovskata konstitutsiia." Bŭlgarski misŭl, XI (October, 1938), 500-509.

──────. "Rusiia i bŭlgarskoto obrazovanie, 1856-1877." Uchilishten pregled, XXXIX (October, 1940), 1152-1164.

Krŭndzhalov, D. "Konstantin Irechek po sluchai 28 godini ot negovata smŭrt." Istoricheski pregled, II (1945-1946), 369-372.

Lekarskii, I.G. "Uchebnoto delo v osvobodena Sofiia, 1878 god." Izgrev, January 5, 1947, p.4.

Madzharov, M.I. "Bŭlgarskata tsŭrkva i svetskata vlast'." Dukhovna kultura, I, 5-6 (1921), 386-415.

Maslev, S. "Marin Drinov, 1838-1906. Po sluchai ot 120 godini ot rozhdenieto mu." Bibliotekar, III (1958), 20-24.

Miiatev, Petŭr. "Konstantin Irechek." Vecherni novini, January 9, 1954, p. 4.

──────. "Sto godini ot rozhdenieto na golemiia uchen K. Irechek (1854-1954)." Otechestven front, December 17, 1954, p. 2.

Milisavats, Zh. "Kul'turnoe sotrudnichestvo mezhdu iuzhnoslavianskimi narodami vo vtoroi polovine XIX i nachale XX v." Études balkaniques, IV (1966), 53-80.

Minev, Dimo. "Tsani Ginchev--naroden pisatel i uchitel." Narodna prosveta, XII, 11 (1956), 46-54.

Mosely, Philip B. "The Post-War Historiography of Modern Bulgaria." Journal of Modern History, IX (September, 1937), 348-366.

Mutafchiev, I. "Dukh i zaveti na vŭzrazhdaneto." Otets Paisii, VII (October, 1934), 198-200.

Nachov, N. "Raicho M. Karolev (1846-1928)." Letopis na Bŭlgarsko knizhovno druzhestvo, XI (1927-1928), 65-73.

―――――. "Tsarigrad kato kulturen tsentŭr na bŭlgarite do 1877 godina." Sbornik na Bŭlgarska akademiia na naukite, XIX (1925), 1-206.

Negentsov, Khristo. "Zavet za minaloto (osnovni idei v organizatsiiata na obrazovanieto predi Osvobozhdenieto)." Uchiltelski misŭl, VII, 1-2 (1925), 1-12, 65-72.

Nikolov, Iordan. "Poiava i razvitie na uchitelsko profs'iuzno dvizhenie." Narodna prosveta, XV, 7 (1959), 50-64.

Nitov, Ioto. "Konstantin Irechek po sluchai 100 godini ot rozhdenieto mu." Trud, December 17, 1954, p.2.

―――――. "Zaslugite na Dr. K. Irechek za nasheto prosvetno delo." Uchitelsko delo, July 25, 1954, p.4.

Pantazopoulos, N. "Community Laws and Customs of Western Macedonia under Ottoman Rule." Balkan Studies, II (1961), 1-22.

Parushev, Miroslav. "Niakovi novi biografichni danni za Dr. Petŭr Beron." Narodna prosveta, XV, 1 (1959), 91-92.

Pashev, G.S. "Uchitelski sŭbor v grad Shumen prez 1873 godina." Uchilishten pregled, XXI (May-June, 1922), 400-408.

Petrovich, Michael B. "The Russian Image in Renascence Bulgaria, 1760-1878." East European Quarterly, III (1967), 87-105.

"Petur Genchev, 1843-1905 g." Letopis na Bŭlgarsko knizhovno druzhestvo, VI (1905), 92-102.

Stamenov, Ivan. "Ideiata za trudovo vŭzpitanie i obuchenie sled Osvobozhdenieto." Narodna prosveta, XIV, 7 (1958), 88-98.

_____. "Za istoriia na Bŭlgarskata pedagogika." Narodna prosveta, XVI, 10 (1960), 78-91.

Stanimirov, Stanimir. "Nashite dukhovni uchilishta: iz istoriia na Tŭrnovskoto eparkhialno bogoslovsko uchilishte." Arkhiv na Ministerstvoto na Narodna Prosveta, I (1909), 81-121.

Stefanov, G. "Izvorski, uchitel i poet ot epokhata na vŭzrazhdaneto, 1815-1875. Prinos kŭm istoriiata na uchebnoto delo i poeziiata ni." Sbornik na Bŭlgarska akademiia na naukite, XXVIII (1935), 1-171.

Stoianov, Man'o. "Nachalo na protestanskata propaganda v Bŭlgariia." Izvestiia na Institut za istoriia pri Bŭlgarska akademiia na naukite, XIII-XIV (1964), 45-67.

_____. "Mladiiat Vasil Drumev." Prosveta, VII, 4 (1941), 420-427.

Tsviatkov, Andrei. "Marin Drinov, lichnost i delo. Po sluchai 40 godini ot smŭrtta mu." Uchilishten pregled, XLV, 3-4 (1946), 173-188.

Vankov, Nikola I. "Uchilishtnoto dvizhenie u nas i pedagogicheskata ni literatura prez tŭrsko vreme." Uchilishten pregled, V, 1-2 (1900), 1-24; IV, 11 (1900), 1362-1391.

Velev, S. "Marin S. Drinov kato prŭv urednik na uchebnoto i tsŭrkovnoto delo v osvobodena Bŭlgariia." Uchilishten pregled, XI (1906), 335.

Vlchek, Vatslav. "Konstantin Irechek po povod na 50 godishninata mu." Uchilishten pregled, IX, 7 (1904), 684-689; IX, 9 (1904), 920-934.

Zhechev, Nikolai. "Kŭm vŭprosa za nachaloto na profesionalnoto organizirane na Bŭlgarskoto uchitelstvo." Narodna prosveta, VI, 6 (1960), 86-90.

_____. "Uchitelskiiat sŭbor v Shumen 1873 g." Narodna prosveta, XVIII, 2 (1962), 77-89.

Zlatarski, Vasil D. "Deinostŭta na Dr. Konstantin Irechek v Bŭlgariia," Periodichesko spisanie na Bŭlgarsko knizhovno druzhestvo, LXVI (1905-1906), 1-50.

Zlatoustova, E. "Devicheskoto obrazovanie v Bŭlgariia predi osvobozhdenieto." Uchilishten pregled, XXIX, 9 (1930), 1404-1420.